Lonely Planet

386

Czech
PHRASEBOOK & DICTIONARY

Acknowledgments
Associate Publisher Mina Patria
Managing Editor Brigitte Ellemor
Editors Kate Mathews, Mardi O'Connor
Series Designer Mark Adams
Managing Layout Designer Chris Girdler
Layout Designer Carol Jackson
Production Support Larissa Frost, Jacqui Saunders
Language Writer Richard Nebeský

Thanks
Ben Handicott, James Hardy, Sandra Helou, Annelies Mertens, Wayne Murphy, Naomi Parker, Trent Paton, Piers Pickard, Branislava Vladisavljevic, Wendy Wright

Published by Lonely Planet Publications Pty Ltd
ABN 36 005 607 983

3rd Edition – March 2013
ISBN 978 1 74104 972 5
Text © Lonely Planet 2013
Cover Image Charles Bridge, Prague, Czech Republic. Frank Chmura/Alamy©

Printed in China 10 9 8 7 6 5 4 3 2 1

Contact lonelyplanet.com/contact

All rights reserved. No part of this publication may be reproduced, stored in a retrieval system or transmitted in any form by any means, electronic, mechanical, photocopying, recording or otherwise, except brief extracts for the purpose of review, without the written permission of the publisher. Lonely Planet and the Lonely Planet logo are trade marks of Lonely Planet and are registered in the U.S. Patent and Trademark Office and in other countries. Lonely Planet does not allow its name or logo to be appropriated by commercial establishments, such as retailers, restaurants or hotels. Please let us know of any misuses: www.lonelyplanet.com/ip

Although the authors and Lonely Planet try to make the information as accurate as possible, we accept no responsibility for any loss, injury or inconvenience sustained by anyone using this book.

Paper in this book is certified against the Forest Stewardship Council™ standards. FSC™ promotes environmentally responsible, socially beneficial and economically viable management of the world's forests.

This 3rd edition of Lonely Planet's *Czech phrasebook* is based on the previous edition by the Lonely Planet Language Products team and translator Richard Nebeský, who provided the translations and cultural advice.

Richard spent the first decade or so of his life in the bilingual environment of Czechoslovakia, where he also studied Russian in primary school. He moved to Australia, where French was added to his curriculum in high school, and he studied linguistics at Monash University. After graduating, extensive travels in many European and Asian countries as well as working in Austria, Switzerland and the USA broadened his linguistic horizons further. Richard has authored many European and Asian titles for Lonely Planet as well as the Czech chapter for the first editions of both the *Central Europe phrasebook* and *Eastern Europe phrasebooks*.

Richard would like to thank his wife Romana for fine-tuning phrases and proofing, his mother Jitka for tirelessly proofing the entire manuscript, Daniel Mourek for his assistance and Dr Pavel Sturza and his wife Stana for proofing the Health chapter.

Thanks also to the Lonely Planet Language Products team who produced the 2nd edition of the *Czech phrasebook* on which this one is based: Vanessa Battersby, Francesca Coles, Pablo Gastar, David Kemp, Karin Vidstrup Monk and Michael Ruff.

make the most of this phrasebook ...

Anyone can speak another language! It's all about confidence. Don't worry if you can't remember your school language lessons or if you've never learnt a language before. Even if you learn the very basics (on the inside front cover of this book), your travel experience will be the better for it. You have nothing to lose and everything to gain when the locals hear you making an effort.

finding things in this book

For easy navigation, this book is in sections. The Basics chapters are the ones you'll thumb through time and again. The Practical section covers basic travel situations like catching transport and finding a bed. The Social section gives you conversational phrases, pick-up lines, the ability to express opinions – so you can get to know people. Food has a section all of its own: gourmets and vegetarians are covered and local dishes feature. Safe Travel equips you with health and police phrases, just in case. Remember the colours of each section and you'll find everything easily; or use the comprehensive Index. Otherwise, check the two-way traveller's Dictionary for the word you need.

being understood

Throughout this book you'll see coloured phrases on each page. They're phonetic guides to help you pronounce the language. Start with them to get a feel for how the language sounds. The pronunciation chapter in Basics will explain more, but you can be confident that if you read the coloured phrase, you'll be understood. As you become familiar with the spoken language, move on to using the actual text in the language which will help you perfect your pronunciation.

communication tips

Body language, ways of doing things, sense of humour – all have a role to play in every culture. 'Local talk' boxes show you common ways of saying things, or everyday language to drop into conversation. 'Listen for ...' boxes supply the phrases you may hear. They start with the language (so a local can find the phrase they want and point it out to you) and then lead in to the phonetic guide and the English translation.

social 107

czech

Germany

Poland

Děčín
Teplice • Ústí nad Labem
Chomutov • Most
Liberec
Karlovy Vary • Kladno
Mladá Boleslav
Hradec Králové
Plzeň
⊗ Prague (Praha)
Pardubice

CZECH REPUBLIC

Karviná
Ostrava
Havířov
Český Těšín
Olomouc
Jablunkov
Jihlava
Prostějov
Frýdek-Místek
Přerov
Brno
Zlín

České Budějovice

Germany

Slovakia

Austria

▬ **official language**
For more details, see the **introduction**.

Denmark
Germany
Poland
Kaliningrad (Russia)
CZECH REPUBLIC
Slovakia
Austria
Hungary
Italy Slovenia

If the Czech language was a person, she could be excused for needing serious therapy. The Czech Republic may now be one of the most stable and well-off Eastern European countries, but over the centuries the land and the language have been regularly swallowed and regurgitated by their neighbours. Most recently, in 1993 the Velvet Divorce ended the patched-together affair that was Czechoslovakia, and allowed Czech to go its own way after being tied to Slovak for over 70 years.

Both Czech and Slovak belong to the western branch of the Slavic language family, pushed westward with the Slavic people by the onslaught of the Huns, Avars, Bulgars and Magyars in the 5th and 6th centuries. Czech is also related to Polish, though not as closely as to Slovak – adults in Slovakia and the Czech Republic can generally understand one another, although younger people who have not been exposed to much of the other language may have difficulty in communication.

at a glance ...

language name:
Czech

name in language:
Čeština chesh·tyi·nuh

language family:
Slavic

approximate number of speakers: 12 million

close relatives:
Polish, Slovak

donations to English:
dollar, howitzer, pistol, robot

The earliest written literature dates from the 13th century upswing in Czech political power, which continued for several centuries. In the 17th century, however, the Thirty Years War nearly caused literature in Czech to become extinct. Fortunately, the national revival of the late 18th century brought it to the forefront again, at least until the 20th century, when first Nazi and then Communist rule pressed it into a subordinate place once more.

introduction

9

Many English speakers flinch when they see written Czech – especially words like *prst* prst (finger) and *krk* krk (neck) with no apparent vowels, and the seemingly unpronounceable clusters of consonants in phrases like *čtrnáct dní* chtr·natst dnyee (fortnight). Don't despair! With a little practice and the coloured pronunciation guides in this book you'll be enjoying the buttery mouthfeel of Czech words in no time. Czech also has one big advantage in the pronunciation stakes – unlike English, each Czech letter is always pronounced exactly the same way, so once you've got the hang of the Czech alphabet you'll be able to read any word put before you with aplomb. Thank religious writer and martyr Jan Hus for this – he reformed the spelling system in the 15th and 16th centuries and introduced the *háček* ha·chek (ˇ) and the various other accents you'll see above Czech letters.

This book will give you all the practical phrases you need to explore the countryside, visit Golden Prague, and tour castles and mountains worthy of the Brothers Grimm (in fact, the 2005 movie of that name was filmed here). It also contains all the fun phrases you need to connect with local people and get a better understanding of the country and its culture. Local knowledge, new relationships and a sense of satisfaction are on the tip of your tongue. So don't just stand there – say something!

abbreviations used in this book

a	adjective	n	neuter (after Czech)
adv	adverb	n	noun (after English)
f	feminine	pl	plural
inf	informal	pol	polite
lit	literally	sg	singular
m	masculine	v	verb

BASICS > pronunciation

Most of the sounds in Czech are also found in English, and of the few that aren't, only one can be a little tricky to master – the infamous rzh (written ř). You can take comfort, however, from the fact that even some Czechs have difficulty with it! If you find it something of a struggle even after a bit of practice, don't worry – people will generally be able to understand you regardless (and they'll probably sympathise as well).

Czech letters always have the same pronunciation, so once you've mastered them you're ready to go. To make sure you're understood, always stress the first syllable of a word – this is indicated with italics in this book, so just follow the coloured pronunciation guides next to each phrase and you'll be fine.

Czech has a number of different regional dialects, as well as a formal variety (based on medieval Czech) that's used in books and the media. The pronunciation in this phrasebook is that of standard Czech as spoken in the Prague area in everyday communication. Using it you'll be understood by Czech speakers everywhere.

vowel sounds

Czech vowel sounds are similar to those found in the English words in the table on the following page. Just be aware that in the transliteration air only the vowel should be pronounced, (unlike in American English), not the r sound. You'll also notice that Czech has a number of vowel sound combinations (so-called diphthongs).

symbol	english equivalent	czech example	transliteration
a	father	*já*	ya
ai	aisle	*krajka*	*krai*·kuh
air	hair	*veliké*	*ve*·lee·kair
aw	law	*balcón*	*bal*·kawn
e	get	*pes*	pes
ee	bee	*prosím*	*pro*·seem
ey	hey	*dej*	dey
i	bit	*kolik*	*ko*·lik
o	hot	*noha*	*no*·huh
oh	oh	*koupit*	*koh*·pit
oo	moon	*ústa*	*oo*·stuh
oy	toy	*výstroj*	*vee*·stroy
ow	how	*autobus*	*ow*·to·bus
u	put	*muž*	muzh
uh	run	*nad*	nuhd

consonant sounds

The consonants in Czech are mostly the same as in English, with the exception of the kh sound (which is pronounced in the back of the throat as in the Scottish word *loch*), the r sound (which is rolled as it is in Spanish) and the rzh sound (a rolled r followed quickly by a zh sound as in the word 'leisure').

The sounds r, s and l can be used as quasi-vowels – hence the existence of those infamous Czech words that appear to have no vowels, like *krk* krk (neck), *osm* o·sm (eight) or *vlk* vlk (wolf). The r in the first word, for example, is pronounced like the 'r' in the American way of saying 'third'. If you find these clusters of consonants intimidating, just try putting a tiny uh sound between them.

Note also that some consonants are words in their own right – such as the prepositions *k* k (to), *s* s (with) or *v* v (in). They're usually joined with the following word in pronunciation.

symbol	english equivalent	czech example	transliteration
b	**big**	*bláto*	*bla·to*
ch	**cheer**	*odpočinek*	*ot·po·chi·nek*
d	**dive**	*nedávný*	*ne·dav·nee*
f	**fin**	*vyfotit*	*vi·fo·tit*
g	**gate**	*vegetarián*	*ve·ge·tuh·ri·an*
h	**hit**	*zahrady*	*zuh·hruh·di*
k	**skin**	*navěky*	*na·vye·ki*
kh	**loch**	*kuchyně*	*ku·khi·nye*
l	**loud**	*loni*	*lo·nyi*
m	**man**	*menší*	*men·shee*
n	**no**	*nízký*	*nyeez·kee*
p	**pause**	*dopis*	*do·pis*
r	**rolled, as in Spanish *rapido***	*rok*	*rok*
rzh	**rolled r followed by zh**	*řeka*	*rzhe·kuh*
s	**side**	*slovo*	*slo·vo*
sh	**shoe**	*pošta*	*posh·tuh*
t	**tell**	*fronta*	*fron·tuh*
ts	**lets**	*co*	*tso*
v	**van**	*otvor*	*ot·vor*
y	**yes**	*již*	*yizh*
z	**zero**	*zmiz*	*zmiz*
zh	**measure**	*už*	*uzh*
'	**a slight y sound**	*promiňte, déšť, teď*	*pro·min'·te, dairsht', ted'*

word stress

Word stress in Czech is easy – it's always on the first syllable of the word. Stress is marked with italics in the coloured pronunciation guides in this book as a reminder.

reading & writing

The Czech alphabet has 42 letters and is based on the Latin alphabet. The alphabet is entirely phonetic and letters are always pronounced the same. For spelling purposes (eg if you need to spell your name when booking a hotel room) we've included the pronunciation of each letter.

Czech has a long and a short version of each vowel – the long vowel always has an acute accent on it in the written language (eg é), and in the case of u, there are two letters for the long vowel, ú and ů. Note also that d, n and t, when followed in writing by ě, i or í, are pronounced with a slight 'y' sound after them – just like ď, ň and ť are always pronounced with that sound.

alphabet					
A a	uh	I i	ee	S s	es
Á á	a	Í í	*dloh*·hair ee	Š š	esh
B b	bair	J j	yair	T t	tair
C c	tsair	K k	ka	Ť ť	tyair
Č č	chair	L l	el	U u	u
D d	dair	M m	em	Ú ú	*dloh*·hair u
Ď ď	dyair	N n	en	Ů ů	u s *krohzh*·kem
E e	e	Ň ň	en'	V v	vair
É é	*dloh*·hair air	O o	o	W w	*dvo*·yi·tair vair
Ě ě	e s *hach*·kem	Ó ó	*dloh*·hair o	X x	iks
F f	ef	P p	pair	Y y	*ip*·si·lon
G g	gair	Q q	kair	Ý ý	*dloh*·hee *ip*·si·lon
H h	ha	R r	er	Z z	zet
Ch ch	cha	Ř ř	erzh	Ž ž	zhet

a–z phrasebuilder

contents

The list below shows the grammatical structures you can use to say what you want. Look under each function – given in alphabetical order – for information on how to build your own phrases. For example, to tell the taxi driver where your hotel is, look for **giving instructions** and you'll be directed to information on **case**, **demonstratives**, etc. A **glossary** of grammatical terms is included at the end of this chapter to help you. Abbreviations like **nom** and **acc** in the literal translations for each example refer to the case of the noun or pronoun – this is explained in the **glossary** and in **case**.

adjectives & adverbs

describing people/things

Adjectives come before the noun, and change their gender, number and case endings to agree with the nouns they describe. In the **dictionaries** and word lists in this phrasebook, adjectives are given in the masculine form and nominative case (see **case, gender** and **plurals**). The most common endings in the nominative case are -ý -ee for the masculine, -á -a for the feminine and -é -air for the neuter gender. These endings become -í -ee m, -é -air f and -á -a n in the plural.

wonderful liqueur   *báječný likér* m   *ba·yech·nee li·ker*
  (lit: wonderful liqueur)
wonderful vodka   *báječná vodka* f   *ba·yech·na vod·kuh*
  (lit: wonderful vodka)
wonderful beer   *báječné pivo* n   *ba·yech·nair pi·vo*
  (lit: wonderful beer)

Adverbs are formed by removing the nominative adjective ending (-ý or -í, both pronounced -ee) and replacing it with -o -o, -e -e or -ě -ye. Adverbs come after the verb, and they don't change to match the verb at all.

She cooks wonderfully.
  Ona vaří báječně.   onuh *vuh·*rzhee *ba·*yech·nye
  (lit: she cooks wonderfully)

articles

naming people/things

There are no equivalents for the words 'a' and 'the' in Czech – *pivo pi·*vo can mean both 'a beer' or 'the beer', depending on the context.

be

describing people/things • making statements

The verb *být* beet (be) changes to match the person and number of the subject. Below are the present tense forms of *být*. See also **negatives** and **verbs**.

be – present tense			
I	am	*jsem*	ysem
you sg inf	are	*jsi*	ysi
you sg pol	are	*jste*	yste
he/she/it	is	*je*	ye
we	are	*jsme*	ysme
you pl	are	*jste*	yste
they	are	*jsou*	ysoh

I'm a businessperson.
    Jsem obchodník. m&f   ysem *op*·khod·nyeek
    (lit: I-am businessperson)

I'm tired.
    Jsem unavený/á. m/f   ysem *u*·nuh·ve·nee/a
    (lit: I-am tired-m/f)

case

doing things • giving instructions • indicating location • naming people/things • possessing

Czech has a system of seven case endings (shown opposite), which are used to indicate the role of nouns, pronouns and adjectives in a sentence. The word lists, **menu decoder** and **dictionaries** in this phrasebook provide words in the nominative case – this will generally be understood, even when another case would normally be used within a sentence.

nominative **nom** – shows the subject of a sentence

The palace is beautiful.
Palác je krásný.   *puh*·lats ye *kras*·nee
(lit: palace-**nom** is beautiful)

accusative **acc** – shows the direct object of a sentence

Did you see the performance?
Viděli jste to představení?   *vi*·dye·li yste to *przheds*·tuh·ve·nyee
(lit: saw you-are-**pol** that performance-**acc**)

genitive **gen** – shows possession 'of'

Where's Franz Kafka's grave?
Kde je hrob Franze Kafky?   gde ye hrob *fruhn*·ze *kuhf*·ki
(lit: where is grave Franz-**gen** Kafka-**gen**)

dative **dat** – shows the indirect object of a sentence

I gave my passport to the policeman.
Dal/Dala jsem můj pas   duhl/*duh*·luh ysem mooy puhs
policajtovi. **m/f**   *po*·li·tsai·to·vi
(lit: gave-**m/f** I-am my passport policeman-**dat**)

locative **loc** – used with prepositions to show location

Does it stop in Prague?
Staví v Praze?   *sta*·vee f *pruh*·ze
(lit: stops in Prague-**loc**)

instrumental **inst** – shows how something is done

I came by train.
Přijel/Přijela jsem   *przhi*·yel/*przhi*·ye·la ysem
vlakem. **m/f**   *vluh*·kem
(lit: came-**m/f** I-am train-**inst**)

vocative **voc** – used to address someone

Hi Emil, what's new?
Ahoj Emile co je nového?   *uh*·hoy e·mi·le tso ye *no*·vair·ho
(lit: hi Emil-**voc** what is new)

The genitive case is also used with many prepositions (such as 'to', 'from' or 'at'). See also **prepositions**.

from May		
to June	*od kvetna*	od *kvyet*·nuh
	do cervna	do *cher*·vnuh
	(lit: from May-**gen** to June-**gen**)	

demonstratives

giving instructions · indicating location · naming people/things · pointing things out

Czech uses the same word for both 'this' and 'that'. This word changes in gender, number and case to agree with the noun it refers to. The different forms in the nominative and accusative case are shown below. See also **case**, **gender** and **plurals**.

this & that						
case	singular			plural		
	m	**f**	**n**	**m**	**f**	**n**
nom	*ten* ten	*ta* tuh	*to* to	*ti/ty* * ti/ti	*ty* ti	*ta* tuh
acc	*toho* to·ho	*tu* tu	*to* to	*ty* ti	*ty* ti	*ta* tuh

* animate/inanimate (for an explanation, see **gender**)

That's my seat.
> *To je moje místo.*   to ye *mo·ye mees·*to
> (lit: that-nom-n-sg is my-nom-n-sg seat-nom)

gender

naming people/things

Czech nouns have gender – masculine **m**, feminine **f** or neuter **n**. The masculine gender is further divided into 'animate' (anything living that can move) and 'inanimate' (anything not living or not able to move, like rocks or plants).

You need to learn the grammatical gender for each noun as you go, but you can often recognise it by the noun's ending – masculine nouns generally end in a consonant, feminine ones in *-a* -uh, *-e* -e or a 'soft' consonant (those with diacritical marks, such as *ť* or *š*), and neuter nouns in *-o* -o, *-e* -e or *-i* -i. You need to know gender to form adjectives and past tense verbs.

The nouns in this book's lists, **dictionaries** and **menu decoder** all have their gender marked.

castle	*hrad* m	hruhd
statue	*socha* f	*so*-khuh
city	*město* n	*myes*-to

See also **adjectives & adverbs**, **demonstratives** and **verbs**.

have

An easy way of expressing possession in Czech is to use the verb *mít* meet (have).

I have a lot of luggage.
Mám mnoho zavazadel.   mam *mno*-ho *zuh*-vuh-zuh-del
(lit: I-have much luggage-acc)

The present tense forms of 'have' are shown in the following table. See also **possessives**.

have – present tense			
I	have	*mám*	mam
you sg inf	have	*máš*	mash
you sg pol	have	*máte*	*ma*-te
he/she/it	has	*má*	ma
we	have	*máme*	*ma*-me
you pl	have	*máte*	*ma*-te
they	have	*mají*	*muh*-yee

a–z phrasebuilder

21

negatives

Making negatives in Czech is very simple – you just attach the prefix *ne-* ne- (no) to the verb:

I'm English.
   Jsem Angličan/   ysem *uhn*·gli·chuhn/
   Angličanka. m/f   *uhn*·gli·chuhn·kuh
   (lit: I-am English-m/f)

I'm not Czech.
   Nejsem Čech/Češka. m/f   *ney*·sem chekh/*chesh*·kuh
   (lit: no-I-am Czech-m/f)

See also **verbs**.

nouns

Czech nouns have many forms – various endings are used to show their role in the sentence. For more information, see **case**, **gender** and **plurals**.

personal pronouns

**doing things • making statements •
naming people/things • possessing**

Personal pronouns ('I', 'you', etc) aren't generally necessary in Czech, as the case endings make it clear what the role of each person or thing in a sentence is (eg whether it's a subject or an object). Their main use is for emphasis:

No, I had the goulash, you had the dumplings.
   Ne, já jsem měl/měla   ne ya ysem myel/*mye*·luh
   guláš a ty knedlíky. m/f   *gu*·lash uh ti *kne*·dlee·ki
   (lit: no I I-am had-m/f goulash-acc and you-inf dumplings-acc)

BASICS

22

The nominative and accusative cases of personal pronouns, used for the subject and the object of the sentence respectively, are shown in the following two tables. Czech has both an informal and a polite word for 'you' – basically, unless you know the person very well, use the polite form, *vy* vi and the second-person plural form of the verb. See the box **all about you** on page 172 for more information.

subject (nominative case) pronouns					
I	*já*	ya	we	*my*	mi
you sg inf	*ty*	ti	you pl	*vy*	vi
you sg pol	*vy*	vi			
he	*on*	on	they	*oni* m	o·nyi
she	*ona*	o·nuh		*ony* f	o·ni
it	*ono*	o·no		*ona* n	o·nuh

object (accusative case) pronouns					
me	*mne/mě*	m·ne/mye	us	*nás*	nas
you sg inf	*tebe/tě*	te·be/tye	you pl	*vás*	vas
you sg pol	*vás*	vas			
him	*jeho/ něho*	ye·ho/ nye·ho	them	*je/ně* m	ye/nye
her	*ji/ni*	yi/nyi		*je/ně* f	ye/nye
it	*je/ně*	ye/nye		*je/ně* n	ye/nye

Where there are two versions of the pronoun separated by a slash, the second version is for using with prepositions ('to him' etc).

See also **case**, **gender** and **plurals**.

plurals

Plurals are formed with a variety of word endings – the most common are *-y* -ee, *-a* -uh, *-e* -e and *-i* -i. If the singular word ends in a vowel, the vowel is replaced with the plural ending. If it ends in a consonant, just add the ending to form the plural.

singular			plural		
map	*mapa* f	*muh*·puh	maps	*mapy* f	*muh*·pi
bag	*zava-zadlo* n	*zuh*·vuh·zuhd·lo	bags	*zava-zadla* n	*zuh*·vuh·zuhd·luh
bed	*postel* f	*pos*·tel	beds	*postele* f	*pos*·te·le
thing	*věc* f	vyets	things	*věci* f	*vye*·tsi

possessives

As in English, possession can be shown in Czech by using the verb 'have' (see **have**) or by using words like 'my' and 'your'. The words for 'his' (*jeho* ye·ho), 'her' (*její* ye·yee) and 'their' (*jejich* ye·yikh) are always the same. The Czech versions of 'my', 'your' and 'our', however, change to match the case, number and gender of the noun they go with. Whether the form used is singular or plural depends on the number of the object (what's possessed), not the subject (who's possessing). The nominative case, which you'll hear and use most often, is listed in the tables opposite.

my friend
   můj/moje kamarád(ka) m/f   mooy/*mo*·ye *kuh*·muh·rad(·kuh)
   (lit: my-m/f friend-m/f)

my children
   moje děti n pl   *mo*·ye *dye*·tyi
   (lit: my-n-pl children)

possessive adjectives – singular	masculine		feminine		neuter	
my	*můj*	mooy	*moje*	*mo*·ye	*moje*	*mo*·ye
your sg inf	*tvůj*	tvooy	*tvoje*	*tvo*·ye	*tvoje*	*tvo*·ye
your sg pol	*váš*	vash	*vaše*	*vuh*·she	*vaše*	*vuh*·she
our	*náš*	nash	*naše*	*nuh*·she	*naše*	*nuh*·she
your pl	*váš*	vash	*vaše*	*vuh*·she	*vaše*	*vuh*·she

possessive adjectives – plural	masculine		feminine		neuter	
my	*moji*	*mo*·yi	*mé*	mair	*moje*	*mo*·ye
your sg inf	*tvoji*	*tvo*·yi	*tvé*	tvair	*tvoje*	*tvo*·ye
your sg pol	*vaši*	*vuh*·shi	*vaše*	*vuh*·she	*vaše*	*vuh*·she
our	*naši*	*nuh*·shi	*naše*	*nuh*·she	*naše*	*nuh*·she
your pl	*vaši*	*vuh*·shi	*vaše*	*vuh*·she	*vaše*	*vuh*·she

See also **case**, **gender** and **plurals**.

prepositions

**giving instructions · indicating location ·
pointing things out**

Prepositions are used to show relationships between words in
a sentence, just like in English. In Czech, where the meaning
is already clear from the case that's used, they may be left out
(see **case** for more information). Some useful ones are shown
on the next page.

prepositions					
about	*o*	o	in	*v*	v
at	*u*	u	on	*na*	nuh
from	*z*	z	to	*do*	do

questions

You can change a statement into a yes/no question in Czech by swapping the verb and the subject, as you would in English:

They're going to Brno.
   Oni/Ony jedou do Brna. **m/f**   *o·*nyi/*o·*ni *ye·*doh do *br·*nuh
   (lit: they-**m/f** go to Brno-**gen**)

Are they going to Brno?
   Jedou oni/ony do Brna? **m/f**   *ye·*doh *o·*nyi/*o·*ni do *br·*nuh
   (lit: go they-**m/f** to Brno-**gen**)

To get specific information, use a question word at the start of a sentence.

question words					
How?	*Jak?*	yuhk	Where?	*Kde?*	gde
What?	*Co?* **inf** *Prosím?* **pol**	tso *pro·*seem	Who?	*Kdo?*	gdo
When?	*Kdy?*	gdi	Why?	*Proč?*	proch

verbs

Czech has three tenses – past, present and future. Past and present tenses are formed by taking the infinitive (or 'dictionary form') of the verb, dropping the *-t* ending, and adding the appropriate tense ending.

present

The present tense endings used depend on the verb class. There are four classes: the verbs in the first class end in -at -uht or -át -at, the second in -ovat -o·vuht, -ít -eet or -ýt -eet, the third in -it -it, -et -et or -ět -yet, and the fourth includes all other endings. Here are the endings for the verb 'drink', pít peet.

pít (drink) – present tense			
I	drink	piju	pi·yu
you sg inf/pol	drink	piješ/pijete	pi·yesh/pi·ye·te
he/she/it	drinks	pije	pi·ye
we	drink	pijeme	pi·ye·me
you pl	drink	pijete	pi·ye·te
they	drink	pijí	pi·yee

I don't drink alcohol.

Nepiju alkohol.　　　　　　ne·pi·yu uhl·ko·hol
(lit: I-not-drink alcohol-acc)

past

To form the past tense, take the -t -t off the end of the infinitive, and replace it with an ending that matches the gender and number of who or what is performing the action (the subject):

dělat (do) – past tense							
m sg	-l	dělal	dye·luhl	m pl	-li	dělali	dye·luh·li
f sg	-la	dělala	dye·luh·luh	f pl	-ly	dělaly	dye·luh·li
n sg	-lo	dělalo	dye·luh·lo	n pl	-la	dělala	dye·luh·luh

Add the present tense form of *být* beet (be), unless the subject is 'he/she/it' or 'they', in which case *být* is omitted. See also **be**.

We did that last year.

Udělali jsme to minulý rok.　　u·dye·luh·li ysme to mi·nu·lee rok
(lit: did-m-pl we-are that-acc-n-sg last year)

He did it yesterday.
    Udělal to včera.   *u·dye·luhl to fche·ruh*
    (lit: he-did-m-sg that-acc-n-sg yesterday)

If you're female, of course, 'I/she did' is *udělala* u·dye·luh·luh.

future

Future tense is formed with the future tense of *být* beet (be), shown in the table below, followed by the infinitive of the verb.

be – future tense			
I	will be	**budu**	*bu·du*
you sg inf/pol	will be	**budeš/budete**	*bu·desh/bu·de·te*
he/she/it	will be	**bude**	*bu·de*
we	will be	**budeme**	*bu·de·me*
you pl	will be	**budete**	*bu·de·te*
they	will be	**budou**	*bu·doh*

Will you go out with me?
    Budeš se mnou chodit?   *bu·desh se mnoh kho·dyit*
    (lit: you-will-inf with me go-out)

word order

making statements

Word order in Czech is flexible, because the case endings and verb endings make it clear who's doing what to whom. However, the default order of a simple sentence is still subject–verb–object, as in English. If you change this order, it puts a strong emphasis on whatever comes first in the sentence.

It doesn't fit.
    Nepadne mi to.   *ne·puhd·ne mi to*
    (lit: not-fit me that-acc-n-sg)

glossary

accusative (case)	type of *case marking*, used to show the *direct object* of the sentence – 'Czechs celebrate **beer drinking** at numerous festivals'
adjective	a word that describes something – '**Czech brewing** traditions go back many centuries'
adverb	a word that explains how an action was done – 'with Czech beer, you can drink **freely** and not worry about ill effects'
article	the words 'a', 'an' and 'the'
case (marking)	word ending which tells us the role of a thing or person in the sentence
dative (case)	type of *case marking* which shows the *indirect object* – 'local breweries are important to **Czechs** as part of their national culture'
demonstrative	a word that means 'this' or 'that'
direct object	the thing or person in the sentence that has the action directed to it – 'Czech breweries use only **natural ingredients** for the fermentation process'
gender	classification of *nouns* into classes (masculine, feminine and neuter), requiring other words (eg *adjectives*) to belong to the same class
genitive (case)	type of *case marking* which shows ownership or possession – 'Czech beer is one of the **world's** finest'
indirect object	the person or thing in the sentence that is the recipient of the action – 'Czechs usually return beer bottles to **the seller** for a refund'

infinitive	the dictionary form of a *verb* – 'they say it's impossible to **get** a hangover from Czech beer'
instrumental (case)	type of *case marking* which shows how something is done – 'Czech beer is fermented by **a bottom method**'
locative (case)	type of *case marking* used to show where the *subject* is – 'there are no chemicals in **Czech beer**'
nominative (case)	type of *case marking* used for the *subject* of the sentence – '**Czech beer** is served at cellar temperature'
noun	a thing, person or idea – '**Czechs** have many **sayings** about **beer**'
number	whether a word is singular or plural – 'there are over 60 **breweries** in the Czech Republic'
personal pronoun	a word that means 'I', 'you', etc
possessive adjective	a word that means 'my', 'your', etc
preposition	a word like 'for' or 'before' in English
subject	the thing or person in the sentence that does the action – '**people** in the Czech Republic consume an ocean of beer every year'
tense	form of a *verb* that tells you whether the action is in the present, past or future – eg 'drink' (present), 'drank' (past), 'will drink' (future)
verb	the word that tells you what action happened – 'many beer-inspired competitions **are organised** in the Czech Republic '

language difficulties
jazykové problémy

Do you speak (English)?
 Mluvíte (anglicky)?   mlu·vee·te (*uhn*·glits·ki)

Does anyone speak (English)?
 Mluví tady někdo   mlu·vee tuh·di *nye*·gdo
 (anglicky)?   (*uhn*·glits·ki)

Do you understand?
 Rozumíte?   ro·zu·mee·te

Yes, I understand.
 Ano, rozumím.   *uh*·no ro·zu·meem

No, I don't understand.
 Ne, nerozumím.   ne *ne*·ro·zu·meem

I speak (English).
 Mluvím (anglicky).   mlu·veem (*uhn*·glits·ki)

I don't speak (Czech).
 Nemluvím (česky).   ne·mlu·veem (*ches*·ki)

I speak a little.
 Mluvím trochu.   mlu·veem *tro*·khu

I'd like to practise (Czech).
 Rád/Ráda bych si procvičil/   rad/*ra*·duh bikh si *prots*·vi·chil/
 procvičila (češtinu). **m/f**   *prots*·vi·chi·luh (*chesh*·tyi·nu)

Let's speak (Czech).
 Mluvme (česky).   *mluf*·me (*ches*·ki)

---

tongue torture

Czech is famous for its absence of vowels – many words lack them totally, and there's a well-known tongue twister composed entirely of consonants:

Strč prst skrz krk.   **Stick your finger**
 strch prst skrz krk   **through your neck.**

Pardon?
   Promiňte?   pro·min'·te

What does (knedlík) mean?
   Co znamená (knedlík)?   tso znuh·me·na (kned·leek)

How do you ...?	*Jak se ...?*	yuhk se ...
pronounce this	*toto vyslovuje*	toh·to vis·lo·vu·ye
write (krtek)	*píše (krtek)*	pee·she (kr·tek)

Could you	*Prosím,*	pro·seem
please ...?	*můžete ...?*	moo·zhe·te ...
repeat that	*to opakovat*	to o·puh·ko·vuht
speak more	*mluvit*	mlu·vit
slowly	*pomaleji*	po·muh·le·yi
write it down	*to napsat*	to nuhp·suht

---

false friends

There are a number of Czech words that look or sound very similar to English words, but have a completely different meaning. For example:

med n   med   **honey**
  not 'mad', which is *šílený* shee·le·nyee

mít   meet   **have**
  not 'meet', which is *potkat* pot·kuht

police f pl   po·li·tse   **shelves**
  not 'police', which is *policie* po·li·tsi·ye

pórek m   paw·rek   **leek**
  not 'pork', which is *vepřové* ve·przho·vair

svit   svit   **shine**
  not 'sweet', which is *sladký* sluhd·kee

trafika f   truh·fi·kuh   **tobacconist**
  not 'traffic', which is *doprava* do·pruh·vuh

cardinal numbers

základní číslovky

Czech numbers from 21 to 29, 31 to 39 and so on, have two forms – both are used in everyday speech.

0	nula	nu·luh
1	jeden/jedna/	ye·den/yed·na/
	jedno m/f/n	yed·no
2	dva m	dvuh
	dvě f&n	dvye
3	tři	trzhi
4	čtyři	chti·rzhi
5	pět	pyet
6	šest	shest
7	sedm	se·dm
8	osm	o·sm
9	devět	de·vyet
10	deset	de·set
11	jedenáct	ye·de·natst
12	dvanáct	dvuh·natst
13	třináct	trzhi·natst
14	čtrnáct	chtr·natst
15	patnáct	puht·natst
16	šestnáct	shest·natst
17	sedmnáct	se·dm·natst
18	osmnáct	o·sm·natst
19	devatenáct	de·vuh·te·natst
20	dvacet	dvuh·tset
21	dvacet jedna/	dvuh·tset yed·nuh/
	jednadvacet	yed·nuh·dvuh·tset
22	dvacet dva/	dvuh·tset dvuh/
	dvaadvacet	dvuh·uh·dvuh·tset

30	*třicet*	*trzhi·tset*
40	*čtyřicet*	*chti·rzhi·tset*
50	*padesát*	*puh·de·sat*
60	*šedesát*	*she·de·sat*
70	*sedmdesát*	*se·dm·de·sat*
80	*osmdesát*	*o·sm·de·sat*
90	*devadesát*	*de·vuh·de·sat*
100	*sto*	sto
200	*dvěstě*	*dvye·stye*
1000	*tisíc*	*tyi·seets*
1,000,000	*milión*	*mi·li·yawn*

as simple as one, two, three

Most numbers in Czech have just one form, regardless of the noun's gender, and are followed by the noun in the genitive case and in the plural:

devět jelenů **m pl**   *de·*vyet *ye·*le·noo   **nine deers**

There are only two exceptions to this rule. The number 'one' and numbers ending in 'one' are followed by the nominative singular form of a noun. The word 'one' has three forms, to agree with the gender of the noun that follows it (see the **phrasebuilder** for more on case, gender and number):

jeden stan **m sg**   *ye·*den stuhn   **one tent**
jedna hruška **f sg**   *yed·*nuh *hrush·*kuh   **one pear**
jedno auto **n sg**   *yed·*no *ow·*to   **one car**

The number 'two' also agrees with the gender of the following noun (it has one form for the masculine gender and another for both the feminine and neuter gender). The following noun is in the nominative or accusative plural form:

dva roky **m pl**   dvuh *ro·*ki   **two years**
dvě motorky **f pl**   dvye *mo·*tor·ki   **two motorcycles**
dvě vajíčka **n pl**   dvye *vuh·*yeech·kuh   **two eggs**

Of course, when counting in Czech, the forms used are simply *jeden, dva, tři ye·*den dvuh trzhi – 'one, two, three …'

ordinal numbers

Ordinal numbers are generally formed by adding the ending *-(t)ý* -(t)ee to cardinal numbers. The exceptions are shown below. They're abbreviated in writing as the numeral followed by a full stop (eg '1.' or '18.') and are used to write dates, just like in English – so '18th October' is written as *18. října*.

1st	první	prv·nyee
2nd	druhý	dru·hee
3rd	třetí	trzhe·tyee
4th	čtvrtý	chtvr·tee
5th	pátý	pa·tee
6th	šestý	shes·tee
7th	sedmý	sed·mee
8th	osmý	os·mee
9th	devátý	de·va·tee
10th	desátý	de·sa·tee

fractions & decimals

a quarter	čtvrtina	chtvr·tyi·nuh
a third	třetina	trzhe·tyi·nuh
a half	polovina	po·lo·vi·nuh
three-quarters	tříčtvrtina	trzhi·chtvr·tyi·nuh
all	všechno	fshe·khno
none	nic	nyits

Decimals are generally written as in English, except on price tags, where a comma is used instead of the full stop – eg 'eight crowns and fifty heller' is written as 8,50 Kč.

3.14	tři celé čtrnáct	trzhi tse·lair chtr·natst
4.2	čtyři celé dvě	chti·rzhi tse·lair dvye
5.1	pět celých jedna	pyet tse·leekh yed·nuh

useful amounts

How much/many?	Kolik?	ko·lik
Please give me ...	Prosím dejte mi ...	pro·seem dey·te mi ...
100 grams	deset deka	de·set de·kuh
a dozen	tucet	tu·tset
half a dozen	půl tuctu	pool tuts·tu
a kilo	kilo	ki·lo
half a kilo	půl kila	pool ki·luh
a bottle	láhev	la·hef
a jar	sklenici	skle·nyi·tsi
a packet	balíček	buh·lee·chek
a slice	plátek	pla·tek
a tin	plechovku	ple·khof·ku
a few	několik	nye·ko·lik
less	méně	mair·nye
(just) a little	trochu	tro·khu
a lot	hodně	hod·nye
many	mnoho	mno·ho
more	více	vee·tse
some	několik	nye·ko·lik

For more amounts, see self-catering, page 174.

a couple of things about pairs

In spoken Czech, the word *pár* par (pair) doesn't necessarily mean 'two' – rather, it's used in the sense of 'a few' or 'several'. For example, *pár dnů* par dnoo is 'a few days' (not strictly two days).

The word *párek* pa·rek (lit: little pair) is a diminutive of *pár* (diminutives are words used to express the 'smallness' of something or affection – eg 'doggy' in English). You might hear it in a phrase such as *To je hezký párek!* to ye *hez*·kee *pa*·rek, which means 'What a nice couple!'

BASICS

telling the time

Officially (eg in timetables and shop hours), Czechs use the 24-hour clock – so '2pm' is *14.00 hodin* (*čtrnáct hodin* chtr·natst ho·dyin). However, the 12-hour clock is still used in everyday speech. The Czech word for both 'hour' and 'o'clock' is *hodina* ho·dyi·nuh when used with 'one', *hodiny* ho·dyi·ni with 'two', 'three' and 'four' and *hodin* ho·dyin with higher numbers.

When it comes to shorter time segments, Czechs look ahead at the coming hour – 'quarter past ten' and 'half past ten' becomes 'quarter of eleven' (*čtvrt na jedenáct* chtvrt nuh ye·de·natst) and 'half eleven' (*půl jedenácté* pool ye·de·nats·tair).

What time is it?
   Kolik je hodin?   ko·lik ye *ho*·dyin

It's one o'clock.
   Je jedna hodina.   ye yed·nuh ho·dyi·nuh

It's (ten) o'clock.
   Je (deset) hodin.   ye (de·set) ho·dyin

Five past (ten).
   (Deset hodin) a pět minut.   (de·set ho·dyin) a pyet *mi*·nut
   (lit: ten hours and five minutes)

Quarter past ten.
   Čvrt na jedenáct.   chtvrt nuh ye·de·natst

Half past ten.
   Půl jedenácté.   pool ye·de·nats·tair

Quarter to (eleven).
Třičtvrtě na (jedenáct).   trzhi·chtvr·tye nuh (*ye*·de·natst)
(lit: three-quarters of eleven)

Twenty to (eleven).
Za pět minut třičtvrtě   zuh pyet *mi*·nut trzhi·chtvr·tye
na (jedenáct).   nuh (*ye*·de·natst)
(lit: in five minutes
three-quarters of eleven)

am (midnight–8am)	*ráno*	*ra*·no
am (8am–noon)	*dopoledne*	*do*·po·led·ne
pm (noon–7pm)	*odpoledne*	*ot*·po·led·ne
pm (7pm–midnight)	*večer*	*ve*·cher

At what time?	*V kolik hodin?*	f *ko*·lik *ho*·dyin
At (five).	*V (pět).*	f (pyet)
At (7.57pm).	*V (sedm padesát*	f (*se*·dm *puh*·de·sat
	sedm večer).	*se*·dm *ve*·cher)

the calendar

kalendář

days

Monday	*pondělí* n	*pon*·dye·lee
Tuesday	*úterý* n	*oo*·te·ree
Wednesday	*středa* f	*strzhe*·duh
Thursday	*čtvrtek* m	*chtvr*·tek
Friday	*pátek* m	*pa*·tek
Saturday	*sobota* f	*so*·bo·tuh
Sunday	*neděle* f	*ne*·dye·le

months

January	*leden* m	le·den
February	*únor* m	oo·nor
March	*březen* m	brzhe·zen
April	*duben* m	du·ben
May	*květen* m	kvye·ten
June	*červen* m	cher·ven
July	*červenec* m	cher·ve·nets
August	*srpen* m	sr·pen
September	*září* n	za·rzhee
October	*říjen* m	rzhee·yen
November	*listopad* m	li·sto·puht
December	*prosinec* m	pro·si·nets

the poetry of nature

Unlike most European languages, Czech doesn't use the Latin-based words to name months. The Czech names for months have Slavic roots dating from before the onset of Christianity and reflect the seasonal changes in the world of nature. Some of these poetic meanings are obvious, while others have been forgotten and can only be guessed.

January	*leden*	Month of Ice (from *led* led – 'ice', as it's the coldest month of the year)
May	*květen*	Month of Blooming Flowers (from *květ* kvyet – 'flower', as most flowers bloom in May)
August	*srpen*	Month of the Sickle (from *srp* srp – 'sickle', a tool used during harvest time to cut plants)
November	*listopad*	Month of Falling Leaves (from *list* list – 'leaf' and *padat* puh·duht – 'to fall')

time & dates

39

dates

When numerals are used for writing dates, they are followed by a full stop in Czech – eg '18th October' is written as *18. října.*

What date is it today?
    Kolikátého je dnes?   ko·li·ka·tair·ho ye dnes

It's (18 October).
    Je (osmnáctého října).   ye (o·sm·nats·tair·ho *rzheey*·nuh)

seasons

spring	*jaro* n	*yuh*·ro
summer	*léto* n	*lair*·to
autumn	*podzim* m	*pod*·zim
winter	*zima* f	*zi*·muh

present

přítomnost

now	*teď*	teď
today	*dnes*	dnes
tonight	*večer*	ve·cher
this	*dnes ...*	dnes ...
morning (early)	*ráno*	*ra*·no
morning (late)	*dopoledne*	*do*·po·led·ne
afternoon	*odpoledne*	*ot*·po·led·ne
this ...	*tento ...*	*ten*·to ...
week	*týden*	*tee*·den
month	*měsíc*	*mye*·seets
year	*rok*	rok

past

day before yesterday	předevčírem	przhe·def·chee·rem
(three days) ago	před (třemi dny)	przhet (trzhe·mi dni)
since (May)	od (května)	od (kvyet·nuh)
last night	včera v noci	fche·ruh v no·tsi
last week	minulý týden	mi·nu·lee tee·den
last month	minulý měsíc	mi·nu·lee mye·seets
last year	vloni	vlo·nyi
yesterday ...	včera ...	fche·ruh ...
morning (early)	ráno	ra·no
morning (late)	dopoledne	do·po·led·ne
afternoon	odpoledne	ot·po·led·ne
evening	večer	ve·cher

future

day after tomorrow	podelzítří	po·del·zeet·rzhe
in (six days)	za (šest dnů)	zuh (shest dnoo)
until (June)	do (června)	do (cher·vnuh)
next ...	příští ...	przheesh·tyee ...
week	týden	tee·den
month	měsíc	mye·seets
year	rok	rok
tomorrow ...	zítra ...	zee·truh ...
morning (early)	ráno	ra·no
morning (late)	dopoledne	do·po·led·ne
afternoon	odpoledne	ot·po·led·ne
evening	večer	ve·cher

time & dates

during the day

afternoon	*odpoledne* n	ot·po·led·ne
dawn	*svítání* n	svee·ta·nyee
day	*den* m	den
evening	*večer* m	ve·cher
midday/noon	*poledne* n	po·led·ne
midnight	*půlnoc* f	pool·nots
morning	*ráno* n	ra·no
night	*noc* f	nots
sunrise	*východ slunce* m	vee·khod slun·tse
sunset	*západ slunce* m	za·puhd slun·tse

festival fun

The most important festivals in the Czech Republic are the modern-day setting for some colourful local traditions:

The Burning of the Witches

Pálení Čarodějnic   pa·le·nyee chuh·ro·dyey·nyits

On 30 April, friends in towns gather to make big bonfires (*hranice* hruh·nyi·tse), and in the countryside the whole village has one big, communal bonfire. This end of winter celebration was originally a pagan ritual during which people cleaned their houses and then burned their brooms on top of the nearest hill to ward off evil spirits, especially witches (*čarodějnice* chuh·ro·dyey·nyi·tse).

The Devil and St Nicholas Day

Čert a Mikuláš   chert uh mi·ku·lash

Celebrated on the eve of 5 December (the day of St Nicholas, the patron saint of children, falls on the next day). Three people dress up as St Nicholas, the devil (*čert* chert) and an angel (*anděl* uhn·dyel) and visit children to see if they've been good during the year. They give the good children chocolate and fruit – the naughty children get coal or potatoes.

Since the Czech Republic has joined the European Union in 2004, the government is expecting to change its currency from the Czech crown (*Česká koruna* ches·ka ko·ru·nuh) to the euro (*euro* e·u·ro) by 2010.

How much is it?
Kolik to stojí?   ko·lik to sto·yee

Can you write down the price?
Můžete mi napsat cenu?   moo·zhe·te mi nuhp·suht tse·nu

Do I have to pay?
Mám zaplatit?   mam zuh·pluh·tyit

There's a mistake in the bill.
Na účtu je chyba.   nuh ooch·tu ye khi·buh

I'd like to …, please.	Chtěl/Chtěla bych …, prosím. m/f	khtyel/khtye·luh bikh … pro·seem
cash a cheque	proplatit šek	pro·pluh·tyit shek
change a travellers cheque	vyměnit cestovní šek	vi·mye·nyit tses·tov·nyee shek
change money	vyměnit peníze	vi·mye·nyit pe·nyee·ze
get a cash advance	zálohu v hotovosti	za·lo·hu v ho·to·vos·tyi
get change for this note	drobné za tuto bankovku	drob·nair zuh tu·to buhn·kof·ku
transfer money	převést peníze	przhe·vairst pe·nyee·ze
withdraw money	vybrat peníze	vi·bruht pe·nyee·ze

Where's …?	Kde je …?	gde ye …
an ATM	bankomat	buhn·ko·muht
a foreign exchange office	směnárna	smye·nar·nuh

What's the ...?	Jaký je ...?	yuh·kee ye ...
charge	poplatek	po·pluh·tek
exchange rate	devizový kurz	de·vi·zo·vee kurz

It's ...	Je to ...	ye to ...
free	bez poplatku	bez po·pluht·ku
(12) crowns	(dvanáct) korun	(dvuh·natst) ko·run
(5) euros	(pět) eur	(pyet) e·ur

Do you accept ...?	Může se platit ...?	moo·zhe se pluh·tyit ...
credit cards	kreditními kartami	kre·dit·nyee·mi kuhr·tuh·mi
debit cards	platebními kartami	pluh·teb·nyee·mi kuhr·tuh·mi
travellers cheques	cestovními šeky	tses·tov·nyee·mi she·ki

I'd like ..., please.	Chtěl/Chtěla bych ..., prosím. m/f	khtyel/khtye·luh bikh ... pro·seem
a receipt	účtenku	ooch·ten·ku
a refund	vrátit peníze	vra·tyit pe·nyee·ze
my change	mé drobné	mair drob·nair
to return this	vrátit toto	vra·tyit to·to

For more money-related phrases, see **banking**, page 91.

---

money talk

One of the most common slang words for 'money' in Czech is *prachy* pruh·khi (lit: dust). Slang words are also used for specific denominations:

kačka f (lit: ducky)	kuhch·kuh	one crown
bůra n (no literal meaning)	boo·ruh	five crowns
kilo n (lit: kilogram)	ki·lo	a hundred crowns
litr m (lit: litre)	li·tr	a thousand crowns

getting around

On public transport, most young people readily give up their seats for the elderly or disabled, and pregnant women. When entering a train compartment, it's customary to greet the other passengers with *dobrý den* dob·ree den (good day), and when leaving, to say *nashledanou* nuhs·khle·duh·noh (goodbye).

Which … goes to (České Budějovice)?	Který/á … jede do (Českých Budějovic)? m/f	kte·ree/a … ye·de do (ches·keekh bu·dye·yo·vits)
bus	autobus m	ow·to·bus
train	vlak m	vluhk
tram	tramvaj f	truhm·vai
trolleybus	trolejbus m	tro·ley·bus
Is this the … to (Mělník)?	Jede tento/tato … do (Mělníka)? m/f	ye·de ten·to/tuh·to … do (myel·nyee·kuh)
bus	autobus m	ow·to·bus
train	vlak m	vluhk
tram	tramvaj f	truhm·vai
trolleybus	trolejbus m	tro·ley·bus
When's the … (bus)?	V kolik jede … (autobus)?	f ko·lik ye·de … (ow·to·bus)
first	první	prv·nyee
last	poslední	po·sled·nyee
next	příští	przhee·shtyee

What time does the bus/train leave?

V kolik hodin odjíždí   f *ko*·lik *ho*·dyin *od*·yeezh·dyee
autobus/vlak?   *ow*·to·bus/vluhk

What time does the bus/train get to (Plzeň)?

V kolik hodin přijede   f *ko*·lik *ho*·dyin *przhi*·ye·de
autobus/vlak do (Plzně)?   *ow*·to·bus/vluhk do (*pl*·znye)

How long will it be delayed?

Jak dlouho bude   yuhk *dloh*·ho *bu*·de
mít zpoždění?   meet *zpozh*·dye·nyee

Is this seat available?

Je toto místo volné?   ye *to*·to *mees*·to *vol*·nair

That's my seat.

To je mé místo.   to ye mair *mees*·to

Please tell me when we get to (Přerov).

Prosím vás řekněte mi   *pro*·seem vas *rzhek*·nye·te mi
kdy budeme v (Přerově).   kdi *bu*·de·me f (*przhe*·ro·vye)

Please stop here.

Prosím vás zastavte.   *pro*·seem vas *zuhs*·tuhf·te

How long do we stop here?

Jak dlouho zde   yuhk *dloh*·ho zde
budeme stát?   *bu*·de·me stat

---

listen for ...

automat na	*ow*·to·muht nuh	**ticket machine**
lístky m	*leest*·ki	
cestovní	*tses*·tov·nyee	**travel agent**
kancelář f	*kuhn*·tse·larzh	
jízdní řád m	*yeezd*·nyee rzhad	**timetable**
nástupiště n	*na*·stu·pish·tye	**platform**
obsazeno	*op*·suh·ze·no	**full**
pokladna n	*po*·kluh·dnuh	**ticket window**
tamten	*tuhm*·ten	**that one**
tenhle	*ten*·hle	**this one**
zpoždění	*zpozh*·dye·nyee	**delayed**
zrušen	*zru*·shen	**cancelled**

tickets

Where do I buy a ticket?
Kde koupím jízdenku?   gde *koh*·peem *yeez*·den·ku

Do I need to book?
Potřebuji místenku?   pot·rzhe·bu·yi *mees*·ten·ku

A ... ticket to (Telč), please.	... do (Telče), prosim.	... do (tel·che) pro·seem
1st-class	Jízdenku první třídy	yeez·den·ku prv·nyee trzhee·di
2nd-class	Jízdenku druhé třídy	yeez·den·ku dru·hair trzhee·di
child's	Dětskou jízdenku	dyets·koh yeez·den·ku
one-way	Jednosměrnou jízdenku	yed·no·smyer·noh yeez·den·ku
return	Zpáteční jízdenku	zpa·tech·nyee yeez·den·ku
student	Studentskou jízdenku	stu·dents·koh yeez·den·ku

I'd like a/an ... seat.	Chtěl/Chtěla bych ... m/f	khtyel/khtye·luh bikh ...
aisle	místo v uličce	mees·to f u·lich·tse
nonsmoking	nekuřácké místo	ne·ku·rzhats·kair mees·to
smoking	kuřácké místo	ku·rzhats·kair mees·to
window	místo u okna	mees·to u ok·nuh

I'd like to ... my ticket, please.	Chtěl/Chtěla bych ... mojí jízdenku, prosím. m/f	khtyel/khtye·luh bikh ... mo·yee yeez·den·ku pro·seem
cancel	zrušit	zru·shit
change	změnit	zmye·nyit
collect	vyzvednout	vi·zved·noht
confirm	potvrdit	pot·vr·dyit

Is there (a) …? *Je tam …?* ye tuhm …
   air conditioning *klimatizace* kli·muh·ti·zuh·tse
   blanket *deka* de·kuh
   sick bag *sáček při* sa·chek przhi
   nevolnosti ne·vol·nos·tyi
   toilet *toaleta* to·uh·le·tuh

Can I get a couchette/sleeping berth?
   Mohu si koupit mo·hu si koh·pit
   lehátko/lůžko? le·hat·ko/loozh·ko

How much is it?
   Kolik to stojí? ko·lik to sto·yee

How long does the trip take?
   Jak dlouho trvá cesta? yuhk dloh·ho tr·va tses·tuh

Is it a direct route?
   Je to přímá cesta? ye to przhee·ma tses·tuh

What time should I check in?
   V kolik hodin se mám f ko·lik ho·dyin se mam
   dostavit k odbavení? do·stuh·vit k od·buh·ve·nyee

luggage

zavazadla

Where can I find *Kde mohu* gde mo·hu
a/the …? *najít …?* nuh·yeet …
   baggage claim *výdej* vee·dey
   zavazadel zuh·vuh·zuh·del
   left-luggage *úschovnu* oos·khov·nu
   office *zavazadel* zuh·vuh·zuh·del
   luggage locker *zavazadlová* zuh·vuh·zuhd·lo·va
   schránka skhran·kuh
   trolley *vozík* vo·zeek

Can I have some coins/tokens?
Můžete mi dát několik   *moo·zhe·te mi dat nye·ko·lik*
mincí/žetonů?   *min·tsee/zhe·to·noo*

My luggage	*Moje zavazadlo*	*mo·ye zuh·vuh·zuhd·lo*
has been …	*bylo …*	*bi·lo …*
damaged	*poškozeno*	*posh·ko·ze·no*
lost	*ztraceno*	*ztruh·tse·no*
stolen	*ukradeno*	*u·kruh·de·no*

backpack	*batoh* m	*buh·tawh*
bag	*taška* t	*tuhsh·kuh*
box	*krabice* f	*kruh·bi·tse*
rucksack	*ruksak* m	*ruk·suhk*
suit bag	*vak na oblek* m	*vuhk nuh o·blek*
suitcase	*kufr* m	*ku·fr*
toiletry bag	*necesér* m	*ne·tse·ser*

kabinové zavazadlo n	kuh·bi·no·vair zuh·vuh·zuhd·lo	**carry-on baggage**
nadměrné zavazadlo n	nuhd·myer·nair zuh·vuh·zuhd·lo	**excess baggage**
palubní vstupenka f	puh·lub·nyee vstu·pen·kuh	**boarding pass**
pas m	puhs	**passport**
přestup m	przhes·tup	**transfer**
tranzit m	tran·zit	**transit**
žeton m	zhe·ton	**token**

plane

letadlo

Where does flight (OK25) arrive?

Kam přiletí let (OK25)?	kuhm przhi·le·tyee let (aw·ka dvuh·tset pyet)

Where does flight (OK25) depart?

Kde odlítá let (OK25)?	gde od·lee·ta let (aw·ka dvuh·tset pyet)

Where's (the) ...?	Kde je ...?	gde ye ...
airport shuttle	letištní kyvadlová doprava	le·tyisht·nyee ki·vuhd·lo·va do·pruh·vuh
arrivals hall	příletová hala	przhee·le·to·va huh·luh
departures hall	odletová hala	od·le·to·va huh·luh
duty-free shop	prodejna bezcelního zboží	pro·dey·nuh bez·tsel·nyee·ho zbo·zhe
gate (8B)	východ k letadlu (8B)	vee·khod k le·tuhd·lu (o·sm bair)

bus & coach

Is this a bus stop?
Je toto autobusová
zastávka?

ye *to*·to *ow*·to·bu·so·va
zuh·staf·kuh

How often do buses come?
Jak často jezdí
autobusy?

yuhk *chuh*·sto yez·dyee
ow·to·bu·si

Does it stop at (Klatovy)?
Staví v (Klatovech)?

sta·vee v (*kluh*·to·vekh)

What's the next stop?
Která je příští
zastávka?

kte·ra ye *przheesh*·tyee
zuhs·taf·kuh

How many stops to (the market)?
Kolik je zastávek (na trh)?

ko·lik ye *zuhs*·ta·vek (nuh trh)

I'd like to get off at (Příbram).
Chtěl/Chtěla bych
vystoupit v (Příbrami). m/f

khtyel/*khtye*·luh bikh
vi·stoh·pit f (*przhee*·bruh·mi)

How much is it to (Brno)?
Kolik stojí jízdenka
do (Brna)?

ko·lik *sto*·yee *yeez*·den·kuh
do (*br*·nuh)

... bus	... autobus	... *ow*·to·bus
city	městský	*myest*·skee
intercity	meziměstský	*me*·zi·myest·skee
hotel	hotelový	*ho*·te·lo·vee
local	místní	*meest*·nyee

departure bay	nástupiště n	*nas*·tu·pish·tye
local bus	místní	*meest*·nyee
station	autobusové	*ow*·to·bu·so·vair
	nádraží n	*na*·dra·zhee
long distance	autobusové	*ow*·to·bu·so·vair
bus station	nádraží n	*na*·dra·zhee
timetable	tabule jízdního	*tuh*·bu·le yeezd·nyee·ho
display	řádu f	*rzha*·du

transport

51

bus & train station signs

Čekárna	che·kar·nuh	Waiting Room
Informace	in·for·muh·tse	Information
Jízdní řády	yeezd·nyee rzha·di	Timetables
Metro	me·tro	Underground
Mezinárodní	me·zi·na·rod·nyee	International
Místenkové	mees·ten·ko·vair	Reservations
pokladny	po·kluhd·ni	
Nádraží	na·dra·zhee	Station
Nástupiště	nas·tu·pish·tye	Platform
Nouzový východ	noh·zo·vee vee·khod	Emergency Exit
Odjezdy	od·yez·di	Departures
Pokladna	po·kluhd·nuh	Ticket Office
Příjezdy	przhee·yez·di	Arrivals
Úschovna	oos·khov·nuh	Left-luggage
zavazadel	zuh·vuh·zuh·del	Office
Vchod	vkhod	Entrance
Vnitrostraní	vnyi·tros·truh·nyee	Domestic
Vstup Zakázán	vstup zuh·ka·zan	No Entry
Zákaz	za·kuhz	No Smoking
Kouření	koh·rzhe·nyee	

train & metro

What's the next station?
Která je příští stanice?   kte·ra ye przheesh·tyee stuh·nyi·tse

Does it stop at (Cheb)?
Zastaví to v (Chebu)?   zuhs·tuh·vee to f (khe·bu)

Do I need to change?
Musím přestupovat?   mu·seem przhes·tu·po·vuht

Which carriage is for (Domažlice)?
Který vagon jede   kte·ree vuh·gon ye·de
do (Domažlic)?   do (do·muh·zhlits)

Which carriage is (for) …?	*Který vagon má …?*	kte·ree *vuh*·gon ma …
1st class	*první třídu*	*prv*·nyee *trzhee*·du
dining	*jídelní část*	*yee*·del·nyee chast
smoking	*kuřácké místa*	*ku*·rzhats·kair *mees*·tuh
Is it (a/an)…?	*Je to …?*	ye to …
EuroCity	*EC*	*e*·tsair
express	*rychlík*	*rikh*·leek
fast train	*spěšný vlak*	*spyesh*·nee vluhk
InterCity	*IC*	*i*·tsair
local train	*osobní vlak*	*o*·sob·nyee vluhk
SuperCity	*SC*	*es*·tsair

taxi

taxík

I'd like a taxi …	*Potřebuji taxíka …*	po·*trzhe*·bu·yi *tuhk*·see·kuh …
at (9am)	*v (devět hodin dopoledne)*	f (*de*·vyet ho·dyin *do*·po·led·ne)
now	*teď*	teď
tomorrow	*zítra*	*zee*·truh

Where's the taxi rank?
Kde je taxi stanoviště? gde ye *tuhk*·si *stuh*·no·vish·tye

Is this taxi available?
Je tento taxík volný? ye *ten*·to *tuhk*·seek *vol*·nee

Please take me to (this address).
Prosím odvezte mě na (tuto adresu). pro·*seem od*·ves·te mye na (*tu*·to *uh*·dre·su)

Please put the meter on.
Prosím zapněte taxametr.
pro·seem zuhp·nye·te tuhk·suh·me·tr

How much is it to …?
Kolik stojí jízdenka do …?
ko·lik sto·yee yeez·den·kuh do …

How much is the flag fall/hiring charge?
Kolik je nástupní sazba?
ko·lik ye nas·tup·nyee suhz·buh

Please …	*Prosím …*	pro·seem …
come back at (10 o'clock)	*přijeďte zpět v (deset hodin)*	przhi·yed'·te spyet f (de·set ho·dyin)
slow down	*zpomalte*	spo·muhl·te
stop here	*zastavte zde*	zuhs·tuhf·te zde
wait here	*počkejte zde*	poch·key·te zde

For other useful phrases, see **directions**, page 63 and **money**, page 43.

car & motorbike

auto & motorka

car & motorbike hire

I'd like to hire a/an …	*Chtěl/Chtěla bych si půjčit …* m/f	khtyel/khtye·luh bikh si pooy·chit …
4WD	*auto s náhonem na čtyři kola*	ow·to s na·ho·nem nuh chti·rzhi ko·luh
automatic	*auto s automatickou převodovkou*	ow·to s ow·to·muh·tits·koh przhe·vo·dof·koh
car	*auto*	ow·to
manual	*auto s manuální převodovkou*	ow·to s muh·nu·al·nyee przhe·vo·dof·koh
motorbike	*motorku*	mo·tor·ku

with …   *s …*   *s …*
  air conditioning   *klimatizací*   *kli·muh·ti·zuh·tsee*
  a driver   *řidičem*   *rzhi·dyi·chem*

How much for daily/weekly hire?
Kolik stojí půjčení   *ko·lik sto·yee pooy·che·nyee*
na den/týden?   *nuh den/tee·den*

Does that include insurance?
Je v tom započítané   *ye f tom zuh·po·chee·tuh·nair*
pojištění?   *po·yish·tye·nyee*

Does that include mileage?
Jsou v tom započítané   *ysoh f tom zuh·po·chee·tuh·nair*
najeté kilometry?   *nuh·ye·tair ki·lo·me·tri*

Do you have a guide to the road rules (in English)?
Máte příručku   *ma·te przhee·ruch·ku*
dopravních předpisů   *do·pruhv·nyeekh przhed·pi·soo*
(v angličtině)?   *(f uhn·glich·tyi·nye)*

Do you have a road map?
Máte automapu?   *ma·te ow·to·muh·pu*

road signs

Jednosměrný	*yed·nos·myer·nee*	**One Way**
provoz	*pro·voz*	
Objížďka	*ob·yeezhd'·kuh*	**Detour**
Průjezd	*proo·yezd*	**No Through**
zakázán	*zuh·ka·zan*	**Traffic Allowed**
Úsek měření	*oo·sek mye·rzhe·nyee*	**Speed Detection**
rychlosti	*rikh·los·tyi*	**Sector**
Vjezd	*vyezd*	**Entrance**
Východ	*vee·khod*	**Exit**
Zákaz	*za·kuhz*	**No Parking**
parkování	*puhr·ko·va·nyee*	
Zákaz vjezdu	*za·kuhz vyez·du*	**No Entry**

transport

55

on the road

What's the speed limit?
Jaká je povolená rychlost?   yuh·ka ye po·vo·le·na rikh·lost

Is this the road to (Cheb)?
Vede tato silnice do   ve·de tuh·to sil·ni·tse do
(Chebu)?   (khe·bu)

Where's a petrol station?
Kde je benzinová pumpa?   gde ye ben·zi·no·va pum·puh

Can you check the ...?	*Můžete zkontrolovat ...?*	moo·zhe·te zkon·tro·lo·vuht ...
oil	*olej*	o·ley
tyre pressure	*tlak vzduchu*	tluhk vzdu·khu
	v pneumatikách	f pne·u·muh·ti·kakh
water	*vodu*	vo·du

How long can I park here?
Jak dlouho zde mohu   yuhk dloh·ho zde mo·hu
parkovat?   puhr·ko·vuht

Can I park here?
Mohu zde parkovat?   mo·hu zde puhr·ko·vuht

Do I have to pay?
Musím platit?   mu·seem pluh·tyit

Can I have a receipt for my fine payment?
Můžete mi dát   moo·zhe·te mi dat
potvrzení za   pot·vr·ze·nyey zuh
zaplacenou pokutu?   zuh·pluh·tse·noh po·ku·tu

listen for ...

bez poplatku	bez po·pluht·ku	**free**
dálniční	dal·nyich·nyee	
známka f	znam·kuh	**motorway pass**
parkovací	puhr·ko·vuh·tsee	**parking meter**
automat m	ow·to·muht	
řidičský	rzhi·dyich·skee	**drivers licence**
průkaz m	proo·kuhz	

Addresses in Czech are written in a different way from English. The number of the house or apartment block is written after the street name, not before. Although each apartment has a number, these are rarely used. Instead, a person's name is written next to the bell at the main entrance and on the main door to the apartment.

Aleš Nový	name
Žižkova 24	street & number
903 20 Palcátov 2	postcode & suburb
Tábor	town
Česká republika	country

As shown above, Czechs don't use the words 'street' (*ulice* u·li·tse), 'lane' (*ulička* u·lich·kuh) or 'avenue' (*třída* trzhee·duh), after the actual name in addresses and on maps, but they do use the words *náměstí* na·myes·tyee (square) and *nábřeží* na·brzhe·zhee (quay):

Karlovo náměstí	Charles Square
Dvořákovo nábřeží	Dvořák Quay

problems

I need a mechanic.
  Potřebuji mechanika.   pot·rzhe·bu·yi me·khuh·ni·kuh

I've had an accident.
  Stala se mi dopravní   stuh·luh se mi do·pruhv·nyee
  nehoda.   ne·ho·duh

The car has broken down (at Třebíč).
  Porouchalo se mi auto   po·roh·khuh·lo se mi ow·to
  (v Třebíči).   (f trzhe·bee·chi)

The motorbike has broken down (at Třebíč).
  Porouchala se mi   po·roh·khuh·luh se mi
  motorka (v Třebíči).   mo·tor·kuh (f trzhe·bee·chi)

The car/motorbike won't start.
Auto/Motorka nechce   *ow·*to/*mo·*tor·kuh *nekh·*tse
nastartovat.   *nuhs·*tuhr·to·vuht

I have a flat tyre.
Mám defekt.   mam *de·*fekt

I've lost my car keys.
Ztratil/Ztratila jsem   *ztruh·*tyil/*ztruh·*tyi·luh ysem
své klíče od auta. **m/f**   svair *klee·*che od *ow·*tuh

I've locked the keys inside.
Zamknul/Zamknula jsem   *zuhm·*knul/*zuhm·*knu·luh ysem
si uvnitř klíče. **m/f**   si *uv·*nyi·trzh *klee·*che

I've run out of petrol.
Došel mi benzin.   *do·*shel mi *ben·*zin

Can you fix it (today)?
Můžete to opravit (dnes)?   *moo·*zhe·te to o·pruh·vit (dnes)

How long will it take?
Jak dlouho to bude trvat?   yuhk *dloh·*ho to *bu·*de *tr·*vuht

pe
benzir
ben·

windscreen
přední sklo **n**
*przhed·*nyee sklo

batt
bate
buh·te·

eng
moto
me·

tyre
pneumatika **f**
*pne·*u·muh·ti·kuh

headl
reflekt
re·fle

PRACTICAL

bicycle

kolo

I'd like to … a bicycle.	Chtěl/Chtěla bych si … kolo. m/f	khtyel/*khtye*·luh bikh si … *ko*·lo
buy	koupit	koh·pit
hire	půjčit	pooy·chit

I'd like a … bike.	Chtěl/Chtěla bych … kolo. m/f	khtyel/*khtye*·luh bikh … *ko*·lo
mountain	horské	hors·kair
racing	závodní	za·vod·nyee
second-hand	použité	po·u·zhi·tair

How much is it per …?	Kolik to stojí na …?	ko·lik to sto·yee nuh …
hour	hodinu	ho·dyi·nu
day	den	den

Do I need a helmet?
Potřebuji helmu?   pot·rzhe·bu·yi *hel*·mu

Are there bicycle paths?
Jsou tam cyklistické trasy?   ysoh tuhm *tsi*·klis·tits·kair *truh*·si

Is there a bicycle-path map?
Existuje mapa   ek·sis·tu·ye *muh*·puh
cyklistické trasy?   *tsi*·klis·tits·kair *truh*·si

I have a puncture.
Mám defekt.   mam *de*·fekt

I'd like my bicycle repaired.
Potřebuji opravit kolo.   pot·rzhe·bu·yi o·pruh·vit *ko*·lo

---

lonely letters

The single consonants in our coloured pronunciation guides haven't been pushed out of an overcrowded Czech word by mistake. They're Czech versions of some common prepositions (eg 'with', 'in') and are usually joined in pronunciation with the following word. You'll see v or f for the sound of the letter v, k for k and s or z for the letters s and z. For more on prepositions, see the **phrasebuilder**, page 25.

transport

59

Finding those strange Czech letters a bit intimidating? Maybe the consonants aren't rolling easily off your tongue? If you're having trouble and the locals don't understand you, the best solution is to practice your pronunciation.

Start with some of the most useful words for a traveller – common placenames. Here's a list of placenames you'll probably need while making your way around the Czech Republic – in particular, remember to say *Praha* pruh·huh, not 'Prague', when admiring the Golden City!

Brno	br·no	**Brno**
Cheb	tsheb	**Cheb**
České	ches·kair	**České**
Budějovice	bu·dye·yo·vi·tse	**Budějovice**
Český Krumlov	ches·kee krum·lof	**Český Krumlov**
Český Těšín	ches·kee tye·sheen	**Český Těšín**
Děčín	dye·cheen	**Děčín**
Domažlice	do·muh·zhli·tse	**Domažlice**
Havířov	huh·vee·rzhov	**Havířov**
Hradec Králové	hruh·dets kra·lo·vair	**Hradec Králové**
Karlovy Vary	kuhr·lo·vi vuh·ri	**Karlovy Vary**
Karlštejn	kuh·rl·shteyn	**Karlštejn**
Kutná Hora	kut·na ho·ruh	**Kutná Hora**
Mělník	myel·neek	**Mělník**
Olomouc	o·lo·mohts	**Olomouc**
Plzeň	pl·zen'	**Plzeň**
Praha	pruh·huh	**Prague**
Přerov	przhe·rov	**Přerov**
Rožnov Pod	rozh·nov pod	**Rožnov Pod**
Radhoštěm	ruhd·hosh·tyem	**Radhoštěm**
Třebíč	trzhe·beech	**Třebíč**
Telč	telch	**Telč**

border crossing

hraniční přechod

I'm here ...	Jsem zde ...	ysem zde ...
in transit	v tranzitu	f truhn·zi·tu
on business	na služební cestě	nuh slu·zheb·nyee tses·tye
on holiday	na dovolené	nuh do·vo·le·nair

I'm here for ...	Jsem zde na ...	ysem zde nuh ...
(10) days	(deset) dní	(de·set) dnyee
(three) weeks	(tři) týdny	(trzhi) teed·ni
(two) months	(dva) měsíce	(dvuh) mye·see·tse

I'm going to (Valtice).
Jedu do (Valtic).   ye·du do (vuhl·tyits)

I'm staying at the (Hotel Špalíček).
Jsem ubytovaný/á   ysem u·bi·to·vuh·nee/a
v (Hotelu Špalíček). **m/f**   v (ho·te·lu shpuh·lee·chek)

The children are on this passport.
Děti jsou zapsané   dye·tyi ysoh zuhp·suh·nair
v tomto pasu.   f tom·to puh·su

listen for ...

pas **m**	puhs	passport
rodina **f**	ro·dyi·nuh	family
sám/sama **m/f**	sam/suh·ma	alone
skupina **f**	sku·pi·nuh	group
vízum **n**	vee·zum	visa

at customs

I have nothing to declare.
Nemám nic k proclení.   ne·mam nyits k *prots*·le·nyee

I have something to declare.
Mám něco k proclení.   mam *nye*·tso k *prots*·le·nyee

Do I have to declare this?
Musím to nahlásit   mu·seem to *nuh*·hla·sit
k proclení?   k *prots*·le·nyee

I didn't know I had to declare it.
Nevěděl/Nevěděla   ne·vye·dyel/ne·vye·dye·luh
jsem že to musím   ysem zhe to *mu*·seem
nahlásit k proclení. m/f   *nuh*·hla·sit k *prots*·le·nyee

That's mine.
To je moje.   to ye *mo*·ye

That's not mine.
To není moje.   to ne·nyee *mo*·ye

Do I need an export permit?
Potřebuji vývozní   pot·rzhe·bu·yi *vee*·voz·nyee
povolení?   *po*·vo·le·nyee

I have an export permit.
Mám vývozní povolení.   mam *vee*·voz·nyee *po*·vo·le·nyee

I have a Tax-Free shopping voucher.
Mám poukázku   mam *poh*·kaz·ku
nepodléhající dani.   ne·pod·lair·huh·yee·tsee *duh*·nyi

For phrases on payments and receipts, see **money**, page 43.

signs		
Celnice	*tsel*·ni·tse	**Customs**
Duty-Free	*dyu*·ti free	**Duty-Free**
Karanténa	*kuh*·ruhn·tair·nuh	**Quarantine**
Passová kontrola	*puh*·so·va *kon*·tro·luh	**Passport Control**

PRACTICAL

62

directions
pokyny na cestu

Where's the (market)?
Kde je (trh)? — gde ye (trh)

What's the address?
Jaká je adresa? — yuh·ka ye uh·dre·suh

Can you show me (on the map)?
Můžete mi to ukázat (na mapě)? — moo·zhe·te mi to u·ka·zuht (nuh muh·pye)

How far is it?
Jak je to daleko? — yuhk ye to duh·le·ko

How do I get there?
Jak se tam dostanu? — yuhk se tuhm dos·tuh·nu

It's ...	Je to ...	ye to ...
behind ...	za ...	zuh ...
far	daleko	duh·le·ko
here	zde	zde
in front of ...	před ...	przhed ...
near	blízko	bleez·ko
next to ...	vedle ...	ved·le ...
on the corner	na rohu	nuh ro·hu
opposite ...	naproti ...	nuh·pro·tyi ...
straight ahead	přímo	przhee·mo
there	tam	tuhm

Turn ...	Odbočte ...	od·boch·te ...
at the corner	za roh	zuh rawh
at the traffic lights	u semaforu	u se·muh·fo·ru
left	do leva	do le·vuh
right	do prava	do pruh·vuh

directions

63

north	*sever* m	se·ver
south	*jih* m	yih
east	*východ* m	vee·khod
west	*západ* m	za·puhd
by bus	*autobusem*	ow·to·bu·sem
by taxi	*taxikem*	tuhk·si·kem
by train	*vlakem*	vluh·kem
on foot	*pěšky*	pyesh·ki
What … is this?	*Jak se jmenuje …?*	yuhk se yme·nu·ye …
square	*toto náměstí*	to·to na·myes·tyee
street	*tato ulice*	tuh·to u·li·tse
village	*tato vesnice*	tuh·to ves·nyi·tse
avenue	*třída* f	trzhee·duh
quay	*nábřeží* n	nab·rzhe·zhee
square	*náměstí* n	na·myes·tyee
street	*ulice* f	u·li·tse

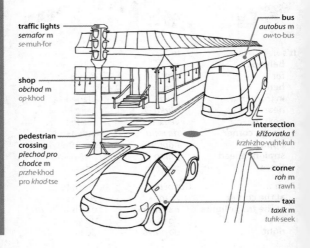

traffic lights
semafor m
se·muh·for

shop
obchod m
op·khod

**pedestrian
crossing**
*přechod pro
chodce* m
przhe·khod
pro khod·tse

bus
autobus m
ow·to·bus

intersection
křižovatka f
krzhi·zho·vuht·kuh

corner
roh m
rawh

taxi
taxík m
tuhk·seek

finding accommodation

The 'international' terms *hostel* hos·tel (youth hostel) and *auto-kemp* ow·to·kemp (camping ground) are used in addition to the more complicated Czech phrases for these accommodation options given in the list below. The German phrase *Zimmer frei* (rooms available) is often found on signs for private accommodation around the country, for the attention of many German-speaking visitors.

Where's (a) ...?	*Kde je ...?*	gde ye ...
camping ground	*tábořiště*	ta·bo·rzhish·tye
guesthouse	*penzion*	pen·zi·on
hotel	*hotel*	ho·tel
some private accommodation	*privát*	pri·vat
student hostel	*studentská*	stu·dents·ka
	noclehárna	nots·le·har·nuh
youth hostel	*mládežnická*	mla·dezh·nyits·ka
	ubytovna	u·bi·tov·nuh
Can you recommend somewhere ...?	*Můžete mi doporučit něco ...?*	moo·zhe·te mi do·po·ru·chit nye·tso ...
cheap	*levného*	lev·nair·ho
clean	*čistého*	chis·tair·ho
good	*dobrého*	dob·rair·ho
luxurious	*luxusního*	luk·sus·nyee·ho
nearby	*nejbližšího*	ney·blizh·shee·ho
romantic	*romantického*	ro·muhn·tits·kair·ho
safe for women travellers	*bezpečného pro cestovatelky*	bez·pech·nair·ho pro tses·to·vuh·tel·ki

I want something near the …	Potřebuji něco blízko …	pot·rzhe·bu·yi nye·tso bleez·ko …
city centre	středu města	strzhe·du myes·tuh
shops	obchodů	op·kho·doo
train station	železničního nádraží	zhe·lez·nych·nyee·ho na·druh·zhee

What's the address?

Jaká je adresa? yuh·ka ye uh·dre·suh

For responses, see **directions**, page 63.

local talk		
dive	pelech m	pe·lekh
rat-infested	zavšivenej	zuhv·shi·ve·ney
top spot	nóbl hotel m	naw·bl ho·tel

booking ahead & checking in

rezervace & ubytování

I'd like to book a room, please.

Chtěl/Chtěla bych
rezervovat pokoj, prosím. m/f

khtyel/*khtye*·luh bikh
re·zer·vo·vuht po·koy pro·seem

I have a reservation.

Mám rezervaci. mam re·zer·vuh·tsi

My name's …

Mé jméno je … mair ymair·no ye …

For (three) nights/weeks.

Na (tři) noci/týdny. nuh (trzhi) no·tsi/teed·ni

From (2 July) to (6 July).

Od (druhého července)
do (šestého července).

od (dru·hair·ho cher·ven·tse)
do (shes·tair·ho cher·ven·tse)

Do you have a double room?

Máte pokoj s manželskou
postelí?

ma·te po·koy s muhn·zhels·koh
pos·te·lee

Kolik nocí?	*ko·lik no·*tsee	**How many nights?**
doklad totožnosti m	*dok·*luhd *to·*tozh·nos·tyi	**identification**
obsazeno	*op·*suh·ze·no	**full**
pas m	puhs	**passport**

Do you have a ... room?	*Máte ... pokoj?*	*ma·*te ... *po·*koy
single	*jednolůžkový*	*yed·*no·loozh·ko·vee
twin	*dvoulůžkový*	*dvoh·*loozh·ko·vee
How much is it per ...?	*Kolik to stojí ...?*	*ko·*lik to *sto·*yee ...
night	*na noc*	nuh nots
person	*za osobu*	zuh *o·*so·bu
week	*na týden*	nuh *tee·*den

Can I see it?
Mohu se na něj podívat?   *mo·*hu se na nyey *po·*dyee·vuht

I'll take it.
Vezmu ho.   *vez·*mu ho

Do I need to pay upfront?
Musím zaplatit dopředu?   *mu·*seem zuh·pluh·tyit *dop·*rzhe·du

Can I pay by ...?	*Mohu zaplatit ...?*	*mo·*hu zuh·pluh·tyit ...
credit card	*kreditní kartou*	*kre·*dit·nye *kuhr·*toh
travellers cheque	*cestovním šekem*	*tses·*tov·nyeem *she·*kem

For other methods of payment, see **money**, page 43, and **banking**, page 91.

accommodation

67

Koupelna	*koh·pel·nuh*	**Bathroom**
Kuchyň	*ku·khin'*	**Kitchen**
Obsazeno	*ob·suh·ze·no*	**No Vacancy**
Prádlo	*prad·lo*	**Laundry**
Recepce	*re·tsep·tse*	**Reception**
Snídaně	*snyee·duh·nye*	**Breakfast**
Volné pokoje	*vol·nair po·ko·ye*	**Vacancy**
WC	*vair·tsair*	**Toilet**
Dámy/Ženy	*da·mi/zhe·ni*	**Women**
Páni/Muži	*pa·ni/mu·zhi*	**Men**

requests & queries

Is breakfast included?
Je to včetně snídaně? — ye to *fchet·*nye *snyee·*duh·nye

When is breakfast served?
V kolik se podává snídaně? — f *ko·*lik se *po·*da·va *snyee·*duh·nye

Where is breakfast served?
Kde se podává snídaně? — gde se *po·*da·va *snyee·*duh·nye

Is there hot water all day?
Teče teplá voda po celý den? — *te·*che *tep·*la *vo·*duh po *tse·*lee den

Please wake me at (seven).
Prosím probuďte mě v (sedm). — *pro·*seem *pro·*buď'·te mye f (*se·*dm)

Can I use the …?	*Mohu použít …?*	*mo·*hu *po·*u·zheet …
kitchen	*kuchyň*	*ku·*khin'
laundry	*prádelnu*	*pra·*del·nu
telephone	*telefon*	*te·*le·fon

Do you have a/an …?	Máte …?	*ma*·te …
elevator	*výtah*	*vee*·tah
laundry service	*prádelní službu*	*pra*·del·nyee *sluzh*·bu
message board	*tabuly na vzkazy*	*tuh*·bu·li nuh *fskuh*·zi
safe	*trezor*	*tre*·zor
swimming pool	*bazén*	*buh*·zairn

Could I have …, please?	Můžete mi dát …, prosím?	*moo*·zhe·te mi dat … *pro*·seem
a receipt	*stvrzenku*	*stvr*·zen·ku
my key	*můj klíč*	mooy kleech

Do you arrange tours here?
Organizujete zde zájezdy? or·guh·ni·zu·ye·te zde *za*·yez·di

Do you change money here?
Měníte zde peníze? *mye*·nyee·te zde *pe*·nyee·ze

Is there a message for me?
Je tam pro mě vzkaz? ye tuhm pro mye fskuhz

Can I leave a message for someone?
Mohu nechat pro někoho vzkaz? *mo*·hu *ne*·khuht pro *nye*·ko·ho fskuhz

I'm locked out of my room.
Zabouchl/Zabouchla jsem si dveře. m/f zuh·boh·khl/*zuh*·boh·khluh ysem si *dve*·rzhe

listen for …		
klíč m	kleech	**key**
recepce f	*re*·tsep·tse	**reception**

accommodation

69

complaints

It's too …	Je moc …	ye mots …
bright	*světlý*	*svyet·lee*
cold	*studený*	*stu·de·nee*
dark	*tmavý*	*tmuh·vee*
expensive	*drahý*	*druh·hee*
noisy	*hlučný*	*hluch·nee*
small	*malý*	*muh·lee*

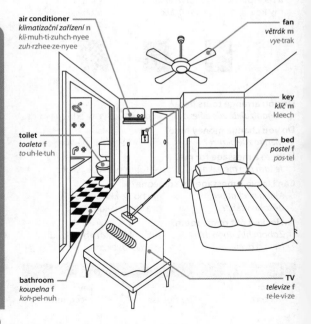

air conditioner
klimatizační zařízení n
kli·muh·ti·zuhch·nyee
zuh·rzhee·ze·nyee

toilet
toaleta f
to·uh·le·tuh

bathroom
koupelna f
koh·pel·nuh

fan
větrák m
vye·trak

key
klíč m
kleech

bed
postel f
pos·tel

TV
televize f
te·le·vi·ze

The ... doesn't work.   *... nefunguje.*   *... ne·fun·gu·ye*

air conditioner	*Klimatizace*	*kli·muh·ti·zuh·tse*
fan	*Větrák*	*vye·trak*
heater	*Ohřívač*	*o·hrzhee·vuhch*
toilet	*Toaleta*	*to·uh·le·tuh*

Can I get another (blanket)?
Mohu dostat další   *mo·hu dos·tuht duhl·shee*
(deku)?   *(de·ku)*

This (pillow) isn't clean.
Tento (polštář) není čistý.   *ten·to (pol·shtarzh) ne·nyi chis·tee*

There's no hot water.
Neteče teplá voda.   *ne·te·che tep·la vo·duh*

---

a knock at the door ...

Who is it?	*Kdo je to?*	*gdo ye to*
Just a moment.	*Počkejte chvíli.*	*poch·key·te khvee·li*
Come in.	*Vstupte.*	*vstup·te*
Come back later, please.	*Vraťte se později, prosím.*	*vruht'·te se poz·dye·yi pro·seem*

---

checking out

odchod z hotelu

What time is checkout?
V kolik hodin máme   *f ko·lik ho·dyin ma·me*
vyklidit pokoj?   *vi·kli·dyit po·koy*

Can I have a late checkout?
Můžem vyklidit pokoj   *moo·zhem vi·kli·dyit po·koy*
později?   *poz·dye·yi*

Can you call a taxi for me (for 11 o'clock)?
Můžete mi zavolat   *moo·zhe·te mi zuh·vo·luht*
taxika (na jedenáctou   *tuhk·si·kuh (nuh ye·de·nats·toh*
hodinu)?   *ho·dyi·nu)*

I'm leaving now.
Teď odjíždím.   teď *od*·yeezh·dyeem

Can I leave my bags here?
Mohu si zde nechat   *mo*·hu si zde *ne*·khuht
zavazadla?   zuh·vuh·zuhd·luh

There's a mistake in the bill.
Na účtu je chyba.   nuh *ooch*·tu ye *khi*·buh

I had a great stay, thanks.
Měl/Měla jsem   myel/*mye*·luh ysem
báječný pobyt. **m/f**   ba·yech·nee po·bit

Could I have	Můžete mi	moo·zhe·te mi
my ..., please?	vratit ..., prosím?	vra·tyit ... pro·seem
deposit	zálohu	za·lo·hu
passport	pas	puhs
valuables	cennosti	tse·nos·tyi

I'll be back ...	Vrátím se ...	vra·tyeem se ...
in (three) days	za (tři) dny	zuh (trzhi) dni
on (Tuesday)	v (úterý)	f (oo·te·ree)

camping

táboření

Who do I ask to stay here?
Koho se mám zde zeptat   *ko*·ho se mam zde *zep*·tuht
na ubytování?   nuh *u*·bi·to·va·nyee

Can I ...?	Mohu ...?	mo·hu ...
camp here	zde stanovat	zde *stuh*·no·vuht
park next to	parkovat	*puhr*·ko·vuht
my tent	vedle mého	*ved*·le *mair*·ho
	stanu	*stuh*·nu

How much is it per ...?	Kolik to stojí ...?	ko·lik to sto·yee ...
caravan	za karavan	zuh kuh·ruh·vuhn
person	na osobu	nuh o·so·bu
tent	za stan	zuh stuhn
vehicle	za vůz	zuh vooz

Do you have ...?	Máte ...?	ma·te ...
a laundry	prádelnu	pra·del·nu
a site	místo na	mees·to nuh
	stanování	stuh·no·va·nyee
electricity	elektrický proud	e·lek·trits·kee prohd
shower	sprchové	spr·kho·vair
facilities	zařízení	zuh·rzhee·ze·nyee
tents for hire	stany na	stuh·ni nuh
	pronajmutí	pro·nai·mu·tyee

Is it coin-operated?
Je to automat na mince?   ye to ow·to·muht nuh min·tse

Is the water drinkable?
Je ta voda pitná?   ye tuh vo·duh pit·na

Could I borrow ...?
Mohu si půjčit ...?   mo·hu si pooy·chit ...

renting

Do you have a/an ... for rent?	Pronajímáte ...?	pro·na·yee·ma·te ...
cabin	chatu	khuh·tu
house	dům	doom
room	pokoj	po·koy
villa	vilu	vi·lu

I'm here about the (apartment) for rent.
Přišel/Přišla jsem   przhi·shel/przhi·shluh ysem
ohledně pronájmu   o·hled·nye pro·nai·mu
(bytu). m/f   (bi·tu)

Is there a bond?	Platí se záloha?	pluh·tyee se za·lo·huh
Are bills extra?	Jsou účty zvlášť?	ysoh ooch·ti zvlasht'
furnished	zařízený	zuh·rzhee·ze·nee
partly	částečně	chas·tech·nye
furnished	zařízený	zuh·rzhee·ze·nee
unfurnished	nezařízený	ne·zuh·rzhee·ze·nee

staying with locals

Czechs are traditionally polite and conservative people. You'll be expected to use the formal 'you' form (vy vi) when addressing your hosts, unless you're told otherwise. As hosts, Czechs are very generous and will ply you with food and drink – it's polite to consume a lot to show them that you really enjoy it.

Can I stay at your place?
  Mohu u vás zůstat?   mo·hu u vas zoos·tuht

Is there anything I can do to help?
  Mohu s něčím pomoci?   mo·hu s nye·cheem po·mo·tsi

I have my own …	Mám …	mam …
mattress	svoji matraci	svo·yi muh·truh·tsi
sleeping bag	svuj spací	svuy spuh·tsee
	pytel	pi·tel
Can I …?	Mohu …?	mo·hu …
bring anything	přinést něco	przhi·nairst nye·tso
for the meal	k jídlu	k yeed·lu
do the dishes	umýt nádobí	u·meet na·do·bee
set/clear the	prostřít/	prost·rzheet/
table	uklidit stůl	u·kli·dyit stool
take out the	vynést odpadky	vi·nairst ot·puht·ki
rubbish		

Thanks for your hospitality.
  Děkuji za pohoštění.   dye·ku·yi zuh po·hosh·tye·nyee

To compliment your hosts' cooking, see **eating out**, page 166.

looking for ...

Are shops open on (Czechoslovakian Foundation Day)?
Jsou obchody otevřené na (Den vzniku Československa)?
ysoh op·kho·di o·tev·rzhe·nair na (den vznyi·ku ches·ko·slo·vens·kuh)

What hours are the shops open?
Jaká je otvírací doba obchodů?
yuh·ka ye ot·vee·ruh·tsee do·buh ob·kho·doo

Where can I buy (a padlock)?
Kde si mohu koupit (zámek)?
gde si mo·hu koh·pit (za·mek)

Where's a ...?	*Kde je ...?*	gde ye ...
convenience store	*večerka*	ve·cher·kuh
grocery store	*konzum*	kon·zum
department store	*obchodní dům*	op·khod·nyee doom
market	*tržnice*	trzh·nyi·tse
shopping centre	*nákupní centrum*	na·kup·nyee tsen·trum
souvenir shop	*obchod se suvenýry*	op·khod se su·ve·nee·ri
supermarket	*samoobsluha*	suh·mo·op·slu·huh

For more items and shopping locations, see the **dictionary**.

making a purchase

I'm just looking.
    Jenom se dívám.   *ye·*nom se dyee·vam

I'd like to buy (an adaptor plug).
    Chtěl/Chtěla bych koupit   khtyel/*khtye·*la bikh *koh·*pit
    (adaptér do zásuvky). **m/f**   (*uh·*duhp·ter do *za·*suf·ki)

How much is it?
    Kolik to stojí?   *ko·*lik to *sto·*yee

Can you write down the price?
    Můžete mi napsat cenu?   moo·zhe·te mi *nuhp·*suht *tse·*nu

Do you have any others?
    Máte ještě jiné?   ma·te yesh·tye yi·nair

Can I look at it?
    Mohu se na to podívat?   mo·hu se nuh to po·dyee·vuht

Is this (240) volts?
    Má to (dvěstě čtyřicet)   ma to (dvye·stye chti·rzhi·tset)
    voltů?   vol·too

Do you accept …?	*Mohu platit …?*	mo·hu pluh·tyit …
credit cards	*kreditními*	kre·dit·nyee·mi
	kartami	kuhr·tuh·mi
debit cards	*platebními*	pluh·teb·nyee·mi
	kartami	kuhr·tuh·mi
travellers	*cestovními*	tses·tov·nyee·mi
cheques	*šeky*	she·ki
Could I have	*Můžete mi dát*	moo·zhe·te mi dat
a …, please?	*…, prosím?*	… pro·seem
bag	*tašku*	tuhsh·ku
receipt	*účet*	oo·chet

I don't need a bag, thanks.
Nepotřebuji tašku,
děkuji.
ne·pot·rzhe·bu·yi *tuhsh*·ku
dye·ku·yi

Could I have it wrapped?
Můžete mi to zabalit?
moo·zhe·te mi to *zuh*·buh·lit

Could I get a Tax-Free shopping voucher?
Mohu dostat Tax Free
poukázku?
mo·hu dos·tuht *taks*·free
poh·kaz·ku

Does it have a guarantee?
Je na to záruka?
ye nuh to *za*·ru·kuh

Can I have it sent abroad?
Můžete mi to poslat
do zahraničí?
moo·zhe·te mi to *pos*·luht
do *zuh*·hruh·nyi·chee

Can you order it for me?
Můžete to pro mě
objednat?
moo·zhe·te to pro mye
ob·yed·nuht

Can I pick it up later?
Mohu si to vyzvednout
později?
mo·hu si to *viz*·ved·noht
poz·dye·yi

The quality isn't good.
Není to kvalitní.
ne·nyi to *kvuh*·lit·nyee

It's faulty.
Je to vadné.
ye to *vuhd*·nair

I'd like …,
please.
  a refund
  my change
  to return this
Chtěl/Chtěla bych
…, prosím. **m/f**
  vrátit peníze
  mé drobné
  toto vrátit
khtyel/*khtye*·la bikh
… *pro*·seem
  vra·tyit pe·nyee·ze
  mair *drob*·nair
  to·to *vra*·tyit

local talk

bargain	*výhodná cena* **f**	vee·hod·na *tse*·nuh
rip-off	*zloděna* **f**	zlo·dyey·nuh
sale	*výprodej* **f**	vee·pro·dey
specials	*slevy* **f pl**	sle·vi

bargaining

That's too expensive.
To je moc drahé.　　　　　　to ye mots *druh*·hair

Can you lower the price?
Můžete mi snížit cenu?　　　moo·zhe·te mi snyee·zhit tse·nu

Do you have something cheaper?
Máte něco levnějšího?　　　ma·te nye·tso lev·nyey·shee·ho

What's your final price?
Jaká je vaše konečná　　　yuh·ka ye vuh·she ko·nech·na
cena?　　　　　　　　　　tse·nuh

I'll give you (200 crowns).
Dám vám (dvěstě korun).　　dam vam (dvye·stye ko·run)

books & reading

Is there an	*Je tam … s*	ye tuhm … s
(English)-	*(anglickýma)*	(*uhn*·glits·kee·muh)
language …?	*knihama?*	*knyi*·huh·muh
bookshop	*knihkupectví*	*knyih*·ku·pets·tvee
section	*sekce*	*sek*·tse
Do you have …?	*Máte …?*	*ma*·te …
a book by	*knihu od*	*knyi*·hu od
(Milan	*(Milana*	(*mi*·luh·nuh
Kundera)	*Kundery)*	*kun*·de·ri)
an entertainment	*přehled*	*przhe*·hled
guide	*kulturních*	*kul*·tur·nyeekh
	pořadů	*po*·rzhuh·doo

I'd like a ...	Chtěl/Chtěla bych ... m/f	khtyel/khtye·luh bikh ...
dictionary	slovník	slov·nyeek
newspaper	noviny	no·vi·ni
(in English)	(v angličtině)	(f uhn·glich·tyi·nye)
notepad	blok	blok

Can you recommend a book for me?
Můžete mi doporučit knihu?
moo·zhe·te mi do·po·ru·chit knyi·hu

Do you have Lonely Planet guidebooks?
Máte Lonely Planet průvodce?
ma·te loh·ne·li pluh·net proo·vod·tse

listen for ...

Mohu vám pomoci? mo·hu vam po·mo·tsi	**Can I help you?**
Přejete si ještě něco? przhe·ye·te si yesh·tye nye·tso	**Anything else?**
Ne, nemáme žádné. ne ne·ma·me zhad·nair	**No, we don't have any.**

clothes

oblečení

My size is ...	Mám ... velikost.	mam ... ve·li·kost
small	malou	muh·loh
medium	střední	strzhed·nyee
large	velikou	ve·li·koh

My size is (40).
Mám číslo (čtyřicet).
mam chee·slo (chti·rzhi·tset)

Can I try it on?
Mohu si to zkusit?
mo·hu si to sku·sit

It doesn't fit.
Nepadne mi to.
ne·puhd·ne mi to

hairdressing

I'd like (a) ...	Chtěl/Chtěla bych ... m/f	khtyel/khtye·luh bikh ...
colour	odbarvit	od·buhr·vit
foils/streaks	melírovat	me·lee·ro·vuht
haircut	ostříhat	ost·rzhee·huht
	vlasy	vluh·si
my beard	zastřihnout	zuhst·rzhih·noht
trimmed	plnovous	pl·no·vohs
my hair washed/	umýt/usušit	u·meet/u·su·shit
dried	vlasy	vluh·si
shave	oholit	o·ho·lit
trim	kaskádový	kuhs·ka·do·vee
	sestřih	sest·rzhih

Don't cut it too short.
Nestříhejte mi to
příliš na krátko.
nest·rzhee·hey·te mi to
przhee·lish nuh krat·ko

Please use a new blade.
Můžete prosím
použít novou žiletku.
moo·zhe·te pro·seem
po·u·zheet no·voh zhi·let·ku

Shave it all off!
Oholte vše!
o·hol·te vshe

I don't like this!
Nelíbí se mi to!
ne·lee·bee se mi to

I love it!
Je to úžasné!
ye to oo·zhuhs·nair

I should never have let you near me!
Nikdy jsem se neměl/
neměla nechat zde
ostříhat! m/f
nyik·di ysem se ne·myel/
ne·mye·luh ne·khuht zde
ost·rzhee·huht

music & DVD

I'd like a ...	Chtěl/Chtěla bych ... m/f	khtyel/khtye·luh bikh ...
blank tape	*prázdnou pásku*	prazd·noh pas·ku
CD	*CD*	tsair·dairch·ko
DVD	*DVD*	dee·vee·deech·ko
video	*video*	vi·de·o

I'm looking for something by (Kabát).
Hledám něco od (Kabátu).   hle·dam nye·tso od (kuh·ba·tu)

What's their best recording?
Jakou mají nejlepší   yuh·koh muh·yee ney·lep·shee
nahrávku?   nuh·hraf·ku

Will this work on any DVD player?
Bude to hrát na   bu·de to hrat nuh
jakýmkoliv DVD   yuh·keem·ko·liv dee·vee·dee
přehrávači?   przhe·hra·vuh·chi

Is this for a (PAL/NTSC) system?
Má to (PAL/NTSC)   ma to (puhl/en·tair·es·tsair)
systém?   sis·tairm

video & photography

I need a/an ...	Potřebuji ...	pot·rzhe·bu·yi ...
film for this camera.	*film pro tento fotoaparát.*	film pro ten·to fo·to·uh·puh·rat
APS	*APS*	a·pair·es
B&W	*černobílý*	cher·no·bee·lee
colour	*barevný*	buh·rev·nee
slide	*diapozitivní*	di·uh·po·zi·tiv·nye
(200) speed	*film s citlivostí (dvěstě)*	film s tsit·li·vos·tye (dvye·stye)

Can you …?	Můžete …?	moo·zhe·te …
develop digital photos	*vyvolat digitální fotografie*	*vi·vo·luht di·gi·tal·nyee fo·to·gruh·fi·ye*
develop this film	*vyvolat tento film*	*vi·vo·luht ten·to film*
load my film	*vložit můj film*	*vlo·zhit mooy film*
recharge the battery for my digital camera	*nabít baterii do mého digitálního fotoaparátu*	*nuh·beet buh·te·ri·i do mair·ho di·gi·tal·nyee·ho fo·to·uh·puh·ra·tu*
transfer photos from my camera to CD	*uložit fotografie z mého fotoaparátu na CD*	*u·lo·zhit fo·to·gruh·fi·ye z mair·ho fo·to·uh·puh·ra·tu nuh tsair·dairch·ko*

Do you have (a) … for this camera?	Máte … do tohoto fotoaparátu?	ma·te … do to·ho·to fo·to·uh·puh·ra·tu
batteries	*baterie*	*buh·te·ri·ye*
flash	*blesk*	blesk
flash bulb	*žárovku na blesk*	*zha·rof·ku nuh blesk*
(zoom) lens	*(zoomový) objektiv*	*(zoo·mo·vee) ob·yek·tif*
light meter	*expozimetr*	*eks·po·zi·me·tr*
memory cards	*paměťovou kartu*	*puh·mye·tyo·voh kuhr·tu*

… camera	… fotoaparát m	… fo·to·uh·puh·rat
digital	*digitální*	*di·gi·tal·nyee*
disposable	*jednorázový*	*yed·no·ra·zo·vee*
underwater	*podvodní*	*pod·vod·nyee*

I need a cable to connect my camera to a computer.

Potřebuji kabel na	*pot·rzhe·bu·yi kuh·bel nuh*
připojení fotoaparátu	*przhi·po·ye·nyee fo·to·uh·puh·ra·tu*
k počítači.	*k po·chee·tuh·chi*

I need a cable to recharge this battery.

Potřebuji kabel na	*pot·rzhe·bu·yi kuh·bel nuh*
nabití této baterie.	*nuh·bi·tyee tair·to buh·te·ri·ye*

I need a video cassette for this camera.

Potřebuji videokazetu	*pot·rzhe·bu·yi vi·de·o·kuh·ze·tu*
pro tuto kameru.	*pro tu·to kuh·me·ru*

souvenirs

antiques	*starožitnictví* n pl	*stuh·ro·zhit·nyits·tvee*
classical music CDs	*CD s klasickou hudbou* n pl	*tsair·dairch·ka s kluh·sits·koh hud·boh*
crystal	*křišťál* m	*krzhish·tyal*
decorated Easter eggs	*zdobená velikonoční vajíčka* f pl	*zdo·be·na ve·li·ko·noch·nyee vuh·yeech·kuh*
folk decorated ceramics	*malovaná lidová keramika* f	*muh·lo·vuh·na li·do·va ke·ruh·mi·kuh*
folk wooden tools	*dřevěné nástroje lidových řemesel* n pl	*drzhe·vye·nair na·stro·ye li·do·veekh rzhe·me·sel*
garnets	*granáty* m pl	*gruh·na·ti*
glassware	*sklo* n	*sklo*
lace	*krajka* f	*krai·kuh*
'onion' porcelain	*cibulový porcelán* m	*tsi·bu·lo·vee por·tse·lan*
puppets	*loutky* f pl	*loht·ki*
second-hand books	*antikvární knihy* f pl	*uhn·tik·var·nyee knyi·hi*
wooden toys	*dřevěné hračky* f pl	*drzhe·vye·nair hruhch·ki*

When will it be ready?
Kdy to bude hotové? gdi to bu·de ho·to·vair

How much is it?
Kolik to stojí? ko·lik to sto·yee

I need a passport photo taken.
Potřebuji fotografii pot·rzhe·bu·yi fo·to·gruh·fi·i
na pas. nuh puhs

I'm not happy with these photos.
Nejsem spokojený/á ney·sem spo·ko·ye·nee/a
s těmito fotkami. m/f s tye·mi·to fot·kuh·mi

I don't want to pay the full price.
Nechci platit plnou cenu. nekh·tsi pluh·tyit pl·noh tse·nu

repairs

opravy

Can I have my … repaired here?	*Můžete zde opravit … ?*	moo·zhe·te zde o·pruh·vit …
backpack	*můj batoh*	mooy buh·tawh
bag	*moji tašku*	mo·yi tuhsh·ku
(video)camera	*moji (video) kameru*	mo·yi (vi·de·o) kuh·me·ru
(sun)glasses	*mé (slunečné) brýle*	mair (slu·nech·nair) bree·le
rucksack	*můj ruksak*	mooy ruk·suhk
shoes	*mé boty*	mair bo·ti

When will it be repaired?
Kdy to bude opravené? gdi to bu·de o·pruh·ve·nair

who's talking?

Masculine and feminine markers (m and f) in our phrases always refer to the subject of a sentence – in the phrase *Chtěl/Chtěla bych …* m/f khtyel/khtye·luh bikh … (I'd like …) the m/f refers to the gender of the speaker.

the internet

internet

Where's the local Internet café?
Kde je místní — gde ye *meest*·nyee
internetová kavárna? — in·ter·ne·to·va *kuh*·var·nuh

Do you have public Internet access here?
Máte zde přístup na — *ma*·te zde *przhee*·stup nuh
internet pro veřejnost? — in·ter·net pro *ve*·rzhey·nost

I'd like to ...	*Chtěl/Chtěla bych ...* **m/f**	khtyel/*khtye*·luh bikh ...
burn a CD	*vypálit CD*	*vi*·pa·lit *tsair*·dairch·ko
check my email	*zkontrolovat můj email*	*skon*·tro·lo·vuht mooy *ee*·meyl
download my photos	*přesunout si mé fotografie*	*przhe*·su·noht si mair *fo*·to·gruh·fi·e
get Internet access	*přístup na internet*	*przhees*·tup nuh in·ter·net
use a printer	*použít tiskárnu*	*po*·u·zheet *tyis*·kar·nu
use a scanner	*použít skener*	*po*·u·zheet *ske*·ner
Do you have ...?	*Máte ...?*	*ma*·te ...
Macs	*Mackintoshe*	*muh*·kin·to·she
PCs	*osobní počítače*	*o*·sob·nyee *po*·chee·tuh·che
a Zip drive	*ZIP mechaniku*	zip *me*·khuh·ni·ku

Can I connect my ... to this computer?	Mohu si připojit ... k tomuto počítači?	mo·hu si przhi·po·yit ... k to·mu·to po·chee·tuh·chi
camera	fotoaparát	fo·to·uh·puh·rat
media player	multimediální přehrávač	mul·ti·me·di·al·nyee przhe·hra·vuhch
portable hard drive	přenosný pevný disk	przhe·nos·nee pev·nee disk
USB drive	USB paměť	u·es·bair puh·myet'

How much per ...?	Kolik to stojí ...?	ko·lik to sto·yee ...
hour	na hodinu	nuh ho·dyi·nu
(five) minutes	na (pět) minut	nuh (pyet) mi·nut
page	za stránku	zuh stran·ku

How do I log on?
Jak se přihlásím?   yuhk se przhi·hla·sim

Please change it to the (English)-language setting.
Prosím vás změňte nastavení na (angličtinu).   pro·seem vas zmyen'·te nuh·stuh·ve·nyee nuh (uhn·glich·tyi·nu)

It's crashed.
Zhroutil se.   zhroh·tyil se

I've finished.
Skončil/Skončila jsem. m/f   skon·chil/skon·chi·luh ysem

phone code

In Czech, phone numbers are usually read in pairs – eg '246 576 821' is read as *dvacet čtyři, šedesát pět, sedmdesát šest, osmdesát dva, jedna* dvuh·tset chti·rzhi she·de·sat pyet se·dm·de·sat shest o·sm·de·sat dvuh yed·nuh (twenty-four, sixty-five, seventy-six, eighty-two, one).

mobile/cell phone

I'd like a …	Chtěl/Chtěla bych … m/f	ktyel/khtye·luh bikh …
charger for my phone	nabíječku pro můj mobil	nuh·bee·yech·ku pro mooy mo·bil
mobile/cell phone for hire	si půjčit mobil	si pooy·chit mo·bil
prepaid mobile/ cell phone	předplacenou mobil sadu	przhed·pluh·tse·noh mo·bil suh·du
SIM card for your network	SIM kartu pro vaší síť	sim kuhr·tu pro vuh·shee seet'

What are the rates?
Jaké jsou tarify?   yuh·kair ysoh tuh·ri·fi

(Seven crowns) per minute.
(Sedm korun) za jednu minutu.   (se·dm ko·run) zuh yed·nu mi·nu·tu

phone

What's your phone number?
Jaké je vaše telefonní číslo?   yuh·kair ye vuh·she te·le·fo·nyee chees·lo

Where's the nearest public phone?
Kde je nejbližší veřejný telefon?   gde ye ney·blizh·shee ve·rzhey·nee te·le·fon

Can I look at a phone book?
Mohu se podívat do telefonního seznamu?   mo·hu se po·dyee·vuht do te·le·fo·nyee·ho sez·nuh·mu

Can I have some coins/tokens?
Mohu dostat nějaké mince/žetony?   mo·hu dos·tuht nye·yuh·kair min·tse/zhe·to·ni

I want to …	Chtěl/Chtěla bych … m/f	ktyel/khtye·luh bikh …
buy a phonecard	koupit telefonní kartu	koh·pit te·le·fo·nyee kuhr·tu
call (Singapore)	telefonovat do (Singapůru)	te·le·fo·no·vuht do (sin·guh·poo·ru)
make a (local) call	si zavolat (místně)	si zuh·vo·luht (meest·nye)
reverse the charges	telefonovat na účet volaného	te·le·fo·no·vuht na oo·chet vo·luh·nair·ho
speak for (three) minutes	mluvit (tři) minuty	mlu·vit (trzhi) mi·nu·ti

How much does … cost?	Kolik stojí …?	ko·lik sto·yee …
a (three)-minute call	(tří) minutový hovor	(trzhee) mi·nu·to·vee ho·vor
each extra minute	každá další minuta	kuzh·da duhl·shee mi·nu·tuh

What's the country code for (New Zealand)?
Jaké je národní směrové číslo (Nového Zélandu)?

yuh·kair ye na·rod·nyee smye·ro·vair chees·lo (no·vair·ho zair·luhn·du)

The number is …
Číslo je …

chees·lo ye …

It's engaged.
Je obsazeno.

ye op·suh·ze·no

I've been cut off.
Byl/Byla jsem přerušen/ přerušena. m/f

bil/bi·luh ysem przhe·ru·shen/ przhe·ru·she·nuh

The connection's bad.
Spojení je špatné.

spo·ye·nyee ye shpuht·nair

Hello.
Haló. huh·law

Can I speak to (Mr Novák)?
Mohu mluvit s mo·hu mlu·vit s
(panem Novákem)? (puh·nem no·va·kem)

It's …
To je … to ye …

My number is …
Mé telefonní číslo je … mair te·le·fo·nyee chees·lo ye …

I don't have a contact number.
Nemám telefonní číslo. ne·mam te·le·fo·nyee chees·lo

I'll call back later.
Zavolám později. zuh·vo·lam poz·dye·yi

What time should I call?
V kolik hodin mám zavolat? f ko·lik ho·dyin mam zuh·vo·luht

Can I leave a message?
Mohu nechat vzkaz? mo·hu ne·khuht vskuhz

Please tell him/her I called. (said by a man)
Prosím sdělte jemu/jí pro·seem sdyel·te ye·mu/yee
že jsem telefonoval. zhe ysem te·le·fo·no·vuhl

Please tell him/her I called. (said by a woman)
Prosím sdělte jemu/jí pro·seem sdyel·te ye·mu/yee
že jsem telefonovala. zhe ysem te·le·fo·no·vuh·luh

For telephone numbers, see **numbers & amounts**, page 33.

---

listen for …

Kdo volá?
  gdo vo·la **Who's calling?**

S kým chcete mluvit?
  s keem khtse·te mlu·vit **Who do you want to speak to?**

Špatné číslo.
  shpuht·nair chees·lo **Wrong number.**

On/Ona tady není.
  on/o·nuh tuh·di ne·nyee **He/She isn't here.**

post office

I want to send a …	Chci poslat …	khtsi·*po*·sluht …
letter	*dopis*	*do*·pis
parcel	*balík*	*buh*·leek
postcard	*pohled*	*po*·hled
I want to buy a/an …	*Chci koupit …*	khtsi *koh*·pit …
aerogram	*aerogram*	*uh*·e·ro·gruhm
envelope	*obálku*	*o*·bal·ku
stamp	*známku*	*znam*·ku
customs declaration	*celní prohláška* f	*tsel*·nyee *pro*·hlash·kuh
mailbox	*poštovní schránka* f	*posh*·tov·nyee *skhran*·kuh
PO box	*poštovní přihrádka* f	*posh*·tov·nyee *przhi*·hrad·kuh
postcode	*poštovní směrovací číslo* n	*posh*·tov·nyee *smye*·ro·vuh·tsee *chees*·lo

Please send it by air/surface mail to (Australia).
Prosím vás pošlete to   *pro*·seem vas *po*·shle·te to
letecky/obyčejnou   *le*·tets·ki/o·bi·chey·noh
poštou do (Austrálie).   *posh*·toh do (*ow*·stra·li·ye)

Where's the poste restante section?
Kde je poste restante?   gde ye *pos*·te *res*·tuhn·te

---

snail mail

by … mail	… *poštou*	… *posh*·toh
express	*expresní*	*eks*·pres·nyee
registered	*doporučenou*	*do*·po·ru·che·noh
sea	*lodní*	*lod*·nyee
surface	*obyčejnou*	*o*·bi·chey·noh
by airmail	*leteckou poštou*	*le*·tets·koh *posh*·toh

What times/days is the bank open?

| Jaké jsou úřední | yuh·kair ysoh oo·rzhed·nyee |
| hodiny/dny? | ho·dyi·ni/dni |

Where can I …?	Kde mohu …?	gde mo·hu …
I'd like to …	Chtěl/Chtěla	kthyel/khtye·luh
	bych … **m/f**	bikh …
cash a cheque	proměnit šek	pro·mye·nyit shek
change a	proměnit	pro·mye·nyit
travellers	cestovní šek	tses·tov·nyee shek
cheque		
change money	vyměnit	vi·mye·nyit
	peníze	pe·nyee·ze
get a cash	zálohu v	za·lo·hu v
advance	hotovosti	ho·to·vos·tyi
get change	drobné za	drob·nair zuh
for this note	tuto bankovku	tu·to buhn·kof·ku
transfer money	převést	przhe·vairst
	peníze	pe·nyee·ze
withdraw money	vybrat peníze	vi·bruht pe·nyee·ze

What's the …?	Jaký je …?	yuh·kee ye …
charge for that	poplatek za to	po·pluh·tek zuh to
exchange rate	devizový kurz	de·vi·zo·vee kurz

Where's …?	Kde je …?	gde ye …
an ATM	bankomat	buhn·ko·muht
a foreign	směnárna	smye·nar·nuh
exchange office		

The ATM took my card.
　Bankomat mi　　　　　　*buhn*·ko·muht mi
　nevrátil kartu.　　　　　*ne*·vra·tyil *kuhr*·tu

I've forgotten my PIN.
　Zapomněl/Zapomněla　*zuh*·pom·nyel/*zuh*·pom·nye·luh
　jsem svůj PIN. **m/f**　ysem svooy pin

Can I use my credit card to withdraw money?
　Mohu si vybrat peníze　*mo*·hu si *vi*·bruht pe·*nyee*·ze
　z mé kreditní karty?　s mair *kre*·dit·nyee *kuhr*·ti

Has my money arrived yet?
　Přišly už moje peníze?　*przhi*·shli uzh *mo*·ye pe·*nyee*·ze

How long will it take to arrive?
　Jak dlouho bude trvat　yuhk *dloh*·ho *bu*·de *tr*·vuht
　než přijdou?　　　　　nezh *przhiy*·doh

---

listen for ...

občanský	*ob*·chuhn·skee	**identification**
průkaz **m**	*proo*·kuhz	
pas **m**	puhs	**passport**

Máme problém.
　ma·me *prob*·lairm　　　　　**There's a problem.**

Nezbývají vám finanční prostředky.
　nez·bee·vuh·yee vam　　　　**You have no funds left.**
　fi·*nuhn*·chnyee *prost*·rzhed·ki

Nemůžeme to udělat.
　ne·*moo*·zhe·me to *u*·dye·luht　**We can't do that.**

Podepište se zde.
　po·de·pish·te se zde　　　　　**Sign here.**

PRACTICAL

For other useful phrases, see **money**, page 43.

92

I'd like a/an ...   *Chtěl/Chtěla*   khtyel/*khtye*·luh
                        bych ... m/f   bikh ...

  audio set   *audio guide*   *ow*·di·o gaid
  catalogue   *katalog*   *kuh*·tuh·log
  guide   *průvodce*   *proo*·vod·tse
  (in English)   *(v angličtině)*   (f *uhn*·glich·tyi·nye)
  (local) map   *mapu (okolí)*   *ma*·pu (*o*·ko·lee)

Do you have   *Máte informace*   *ma*·te *in*·for·muh·tse
information   *o ... pamětihod-*   o ... *puh*·mye·ti·hod·
on ... sights? *nostech?*   nos·tekh
  cultural   *kulturních*   *kul*·tur·nyeekh
  historical   *historických*   *his*·to·rits·keekh
  religious   *náboženských*   *na*·bo·zhens·keekh

I'd like to see ...
  Chtěl/Chtěla bych   khtyel/*khtye*·luh bikh
  vidět ... m/f   *vi*·dyet ...

What's that?
  Co je to?   tso ye to

Who built it?
  Kdo to nechal postavit?   kdo to *ne*·khuhl *pos*·tuh·vit

Who made it?
  Kdo to stvořil?   kdo to *stvo*·rzhil

How old is it?
  Jak je to staré?   yuhk ye to *stuh*·rair

Could you take a photo of me/us?
    Můžete mě/nás vyfotit?   *moo·zhe·te mye/nas vi·fo·tyit*

Can I take a photo of this?
    Mohu toto fotografovat?   *mo·hu to·to fo·to·gruh·fo·vuht*

Can I take a photo of you?
    Mohu si vás vyfotit?   *mo·hu si vas vi·fo·tyit*

I'll send you the photo.
    Pošlu vám fotografii.   *posh·lu vam fo·to·gruh·fi·i*

getting in

navštěvování

What time does it open/close?
    V kolik hodin otevírají/   *f ko·lik ho·dyin o·te·vee·ruh·yee/*
    zavírají?   *zuh·vee·ruh·yee*

What's the admission charge?
    Kolik stojí vstupné?   *ko·lik sto·yee vstup·nair*

Is there a discount for ...?	*Máte slevu pro ...?*	*ma·te sle·vu pro ...*
children	*děti*	*dye·tyi*
families	*rodiny*	*ro·dyi·ni*
groups	*skupiny*	*sku·pi·ni*
older people	*starší lidi*	*stuhr·shee li·dyi*
pensioners	*důchodce*	*doo·khod·tse*
students	*studenty*	*stu·den·ti*

tours

okružní jízdy

Can you recommend a sightseeing tour?
    Můžete mi doporučit   *moo·zhe·te mi do·po·ru·chit*
    okružní jízdu po   *o·kruzh·nyee yeez·du po*
    pamětihodnostech?   *puh·mye·tyi·hod·nos·tekh*

When's the next ...?	Kdy je příští ...?	gdi ye przheesh·tyee ...
boat trip	projížďka	pro·yeezhd'·kuh
	lodí	lo·dyee
day trip	celodenní	tse·lo·de·nyee
	výlet	vee·let
(sightseeing) tour	okružní jízda (po pamětihodnostech)	o·kruzh·nyee yeez·duh (po puh·mye·tyi·hod·nos·tekh)
Is ... included?	Je zahrnuto/a ...? n/f	ye zuh·hr·nu·to/uh ...
accommodation	ubytování n	u·bi·to·va·nyee
admission	vstupné n	fstup·nair
food	strava f	struh·vuh
transport	doprava f	do·pruh·vuh

The guide will pay.
Průvodce zaplatí.
proo·vod·tse zuh·pluh·tyee

The guide has paid.
Průvodce zaplatil.
proo·vod·tse zuh·pluh·tyil

How long is the tour?
Jak dlouho bude trvat tento zájezd?
yuhk dloh·ho bu·de tr·vuht ten·to za·yezd

What time should we be back?
V kolik hodin se máme vrátit?
f ko·lik ho·dyin se ma·me vra·tyit

I'm with them.
Jsem s nimi.
ysem s nyi·mi

I've lost my group.
Ztratil/Ztratila jsem se mojí skupině. m/f
struh·tyil/struh·tyi·luh ysem se mo·yee sku·pi·nye

Informace	*in*·for·muh·tse	**Information**
Otevřeno	*o*·tev·rzhe·no	**Open**
Studené	*stu*·de·nair	**Cold**
Teplé	*tep*·lair	**Hot**
Toalety/WC	to·uh·*le*·ti/*vair*·tsair	**Toilet**
Dámy/Ženy	*da*·mi/*zhe*·ni	**Women**
Páni/Muži	*pa*·ni/*mu*·zhi	**Men**
Vjezd	vyezd	**Entrance**
Východ	*vee*·khod	**Exit**
Zákazáno	*za*·kuh·za·no	**Prohibited**
Zákaz kouření	*za*·kuhz koh·rzhe·nyee	**No Smoking**
Zákaz fotografování	*za*·kuhz fo·to·gruh·fo·va·nyee	**No Photography**
Zavřeno	*zuh*·vrzhe·no	**Closed**

doing business

obchodování

I'm attending a ...	Jsem účastníkem ...	ysem oo·chuhst·nyee·kem ...
conference	konference	kon·fe·ren·tse
course	kursu	kur·su
meeting	schůze	skhoo·ze
trade fair	veletrhu	ve·le·tr·hu
I'm with ...	Jsem ...	ysem ...
my colleague	s kolegou	s ko·le·goh
my colleagues	s kolegi	s ko·le·gi
(Papírny Vetřní)	z (Papírny Vetřní)	z (puh·peer·ni vetrzh·nyee)
the others	s ostatními	s os·tuht·nyee·mi

I'm alone.
Jsem sám/sama. m/f   ysem sam/*suh*·muh

I have an appointment with ...
Mám schůzku s ...   mam skhooz·ku s ...

I'm staying at the (Hotel u Medvídků), room (205).
Jsem ubytovaný/á v (Hotelu u Medvídků), pokoj (dvěstě pět). m/f
ysem u·bi·to·vuh·nee/a v (ho·te·lu u med·veed·koo) po·koy (dvyes·tye pyet)

I'm here for (two) days/weeks.
Jsem zde na (dva) dny/týdny.
ysem zde nuh (dvuh) dni/teed·ni

Can I please have your business card?
Můžete mě prosím dát vaší vizitku?
moo·zhe·te mye pro·seem dat vuh·shee vi·zit·ku

Here's my business card.
Tady je má visitka.   tuh·di ye ma vi·sit·kuh

Here's my ...	Zde je moje ...	zde ye mo·ye ...
What's your ...?	Jaké/Jaká je vaše ...? n/f	yuh·kair/yuh·ka ye vuh·she ...
(email) address	(email) adresa f	(ee·meyl) uh·dre·suh
mobile/cell number	číslo mobilu n	chees·lo mo·bi·lu
fax number	faxové číslo n	fuhk·so·vair chees·lo
phone number	telefonní číslo n	te·le·fo·nyee chees·lo
work number	číslo do kanceláře n	chees·lo do kuhn·tse·la·rzhe
Where's the ...?	Kde je ...?	gde ye ...
business centre	kongresový sál	kon·gre·so·vee sal
conference	konference	kon·fe·ren·tse
meeting	schůze	skhoo·ze
I need ...	Potřebuji ...	pot·rzhe·bu·yi ...
a computer	počítač	po·chee·tuhch
an Internet connection	připojení na internet	przhi·po·ye·nyee nuh in·ter·net
an interpreter who speaks (English)	(anglicko) mluvícího tlumočníka	(uhn·glits·ko) mlu·vee·tsee·ho tlu·moch·nyee·kuh
more business cards	více vizitek	vee·tse vi·zi·tek
space to set up	místo pro své věci	mees·to pro svair vye·tsi
to send a fax	poslat fax	po·sluht fuhks

That went very well.
To vyšlo výborně.   to vish·lo vee·bor·nye

Thank you for your time.
Děkuji za vaší pozornost.   dye·ku·yi zuh vuh·shee po·zor·nost

Shall we go for a drink/meal?
Půjdem na skleničku/jídlo?   pooy·dem nuh skle·nyich·ku/yeed·lo

looking for a job

Where are jobs advertised?
> *Kde jsou inzerce*
> *zaměstnání?*

gde ysoh in·zer·tse
zuh·myest·na·nyee

I'm enquiring about the position advertised.
> *Můžete mi dát*
> *informace o*
> *vámi inzerované práci?*

moo·zhe·te mi dat
in·for·muh·tse o
va·mi in·ze·ro·va·nair pra·tsi

I'm looking for ... work.	*Hledám ....*	*hle·dam ...*
bar	práci v baru	pra·tsi f buh·ru
casual	příležitostnou práci	przhee·le·zhi·tost·noh pra·tsi
English-teaching	práci učitele angličtiny	pra·tsi u·chi·te·le uhn·glich·tyi·ni
fruit-picking	práci ve sběru ovoce	pra·tsi ve sbye·ru o·vo·tse
full-time	práci na plný úvazek	pra·tsi nuh pl·nee oo·vuh·zek
labouring	práci jako pomocný dělník	pra·tsi yuh·ko po·mots·nee dyel·nyeek
office	kancelářskou práci	kuhn·tse·larzh·skoh pra·tsi
part-time	práci na zkrácený úvazek	pra·tsi nuh zkra·tse·nee oo·vuh·zek
waitering	práci jako číšník	pra·tsi yuh·ko cheesh·nyeek

Do I need (a) …?	Potřebuji …?	pot·rzhe·bu·yi …
contract	smlouvu	smloh·vu
experience	praxi	pruh·ksi
insurance	pojištění	po·yish·tye·nyee
work permit	pracovní	pruh·tsov·nyee
	povolení	po·vo·le·nyee

I've had experience.
Měl/Měla jsem praxi. m/f   myel/*mye*·luh ysem *pruh*·ksi

What's the wage?
Jaká je mzda?   yuh·ka ye mzduh

Here are my bank account details.
Zde jsou podrobnosti	zde ysoh po·drob·nos·tyi
mého bankovního účtu.	*mair*·ho *buhn*·kov·nyee·ho *ooch*·tu

Here's my …	Zde je …	zde ye …
CV	můj životopis	mooy zhi·vo·to·pis
visa	mé vísum	mair vee·sum
work permit	mé pracovní	mair pruh·tsov·nyee
	povolení	po·vo·le·nyee

I can start …	Mohu nastoupit …	mo·hu nuh·stoh·pit …
at (eight) o'clock	v (osm) hodin	f (o·sm) ho·dyin
today	dnes	dnes
tomorrow	zítra	zee·truh
next week	příští týden	przheesh·tyee tee·den

What time do I …?	V kolik hodin …?	f ko·lik ho·dyin …
start	začínám	zuh·chee·nam
have a break	mám přestávku	mam przhes·taf·ku
finish	končím	kon·cheem

senior & disabled travellers
senioři & tělesně postižení cestovatelé

I have a disability.
Jsem tělesně — ysem *tye*·les·nye
postižený/á. m/f — *pos*·tyi·zhe·nee/a

I need assistance.
Potřebuji pomoc. — *pot*·rze·bu·yi *po*·mots

I'm deaf.
Jsem hluchý/á. m/f — ysem *hlu*·khee/a

I have a hearing aid.
Mám naslouchátko. — mam *nuh*·sloh·khat·ko

My companion's blind.
Muj druh je slepý. m — muy drooh ye *sle*·pee
Moje družka je slepá. f — *mo*·ye *druzh*·kuh ye *sle*·pa

What services do you have for people with a disability?
Jaké služby poskytujete — *yuh*·kair *sluzh*·bi *pos*·ki·tu·ye·te
tělesně postiženým? — *tye*·les·nye *pos*·tyi·zhe·neem

Are guide dogs permitted?
Je vstup slepeckým — ye fstup *sle*·pets·keem
psům povolen? — psoom *po*·vo·len

Are there disabled parking spaces?
Jsou tam parkovací — ysoh tuhm *puhr*·ko·vuh·tsee
místa pro invalidy? — *mees*·tuh pro *in*·vuh·li·di

Is there wheelchair access?
Je tam přístup pro — ye tuhm *przhees*·tup pro
invalidní vozík? — *in*·vuh·lid·nyee *vo*·zeek

How wide is the entrance?
Jak široký je vchod? — yuhk *shi*·ro·kee ye fkhod

How many steps are there?
Kolik je zde schodů? — *ko*·lik ye zde *skho*·doo

Is there an elevator?
Je tam výtah? — ye tuhm *vee*·tah

Are there disabled toilets?

Jsou tam toalety pro　　ysoh tuhm *to*·uh·le·ti pro
tělesně postižené?　　*tye*·les·nye *pos*·tyi·zhe·nair

Are there rails in the bathroom?

Jsou v koupelně madla?　　ysoh v *koh*·pel·nye *muhd*·luh

Is there somewhere I can sit down?

Je někde místo na　　ye *nyek*·de *mees*·to nuh
sezení?　　se·ze·nyee

Could you help me cross the street safely?

Můžete mě bezpečně　　moo·zhe·te mye *bez*·pech·nye
převést přes ulici?　　*przhe*·vairst przhes u·li·tsi

Could you call me a disabled taxi?

Můžete mi zavolat　　moo·zhe·te mi *zuh*·vo·luht
taxi pro tělesně　　*tuhk*·si pro *tye*·les·nye
postižené?　　*pos*·tyi·zhe·nair

guide dog	*slepecký pes* m	*sle*·pets·kee pes
older person	*senior* m	se·nyi·or
person with	*člověk s*	*chlo*·vyek s
a disability	*tělesným*	*tye*·les·neem
	postiženým m	*pos*·tyi·zhe·neem
ramp	*rampa* f	*ruhm*·puh
walking frame	*chodítko* n	*kho*·dyeet·ko
walking stick	*hůl* f	hool
wheelchair	*invalidní vozík* m	*in*·vuh·lid·nyee *vo*·zeek

---

every day is a holiday

Czechs have a tradition of celebrating 'name days' (*svátek sva*·tek). They aren't birthdays (*narozeniny nuh*·ro·ze·nyi·ni), but celebrations for all people bearing the same name. Each day of the year has a name of a saint attached to it. The name day is an opportunity for friends and family to get together and celebrate, without having to deal with their age. The appropriate greeting is:

Happy name day!

Všechno nejlepší　　vshekh·no *ney*·lep·shee
k svátku!　　k svat·ku

PRACTICAL

travelling with children

cestování s dětmi

Is there a crèche?	*Jsou zde jesle?*	ysoh zde *yes*·le
Is there a ...?	*Máte ...?*	*ma*·te ...
baby change room	*zde přebalovací místnost pro děti*	zde *przhe*·buh·lo·vuh·tsee *meest*·nost pro *dye*·tyi
child-minding service	*zde službu pro hlídání dětí*	zde *sluzh*·bu pro *hlee*·da·nyee *dye*·tyee
children's menu	*dětský jídelníček*	*dyets*·kee *yee*·del·nyee·chek
child's portion	*dětské porce*	*dyets*·kair *por*·tse
discount for children	*slevy pro děti*	*sle*·vi pro *dye*·tyi
family ticket	*rodinné vstupné*	*ro*·dyi·nair *vstup*·nair
I need a/an ...	*Potřebuji ...*	*pot*·rzhe·bu·yi ...
baby seat	*auto sedačku*	*ow*·to *se*·duch·ku
(English-speaking) babysitter	*(anglicko mluvící) chůvu*	(*uhn*·glits·ko *mlu*·vee·tsee) *khoo*·vu
booster seat	*podsedák*	*pod*·se·dak
highchair	*dětskou stoličku*	*dyet*·skoh *sto*·lich·ku
plastic bag	*igelitovou tašku*	*i*·ge·li·to·voh *tuhsh*·ku
plastic sheet	*igelitové prostěradlo*	*i*·ge·li·to·vair *pros*·tye·ruhd·lo
potty	*nočník*	*noch*·nyeek
pram	*kočárek*	*ko*·cha·rek
sick bag	*sáček při nevolnosti*	*sa*·chek przhi *ne*·vol·nos·tyi

Do you sell ...?	Prodáváte ...?	pro-da-va-te ...
baby wipes	dětské utěrky	dyets-kair u-tyer-ki
disposable nappies/diapers	jednorázové pleny	yed-no-ra-zo-vair ple-ni
painkillers for infants	prášky proti bolesti u kojenců	prash-ki pro-tyi bo-les-tyi u ko-yen-tsoo
tissues	kosmetické kapesníky	kos-me-tits-kair kuh-pes-nyee-ki

Where's the nearest ...?	Kde je nejbližší ...?	gde ye ney-blizh-shee ...
drinking fountain	fontánka s pitnou vodou	fon-tan-kuh s pit-noh vo-doh
park	park	puhrk
playground	hřiště	hrzhish-tye
swimming pool	bazén	buh-zairn
tap	kohoutek	ko-hoh-tek
theme park	zábavný park	za-buhv-nee puhrk
toyshop	hračkářství	hruhch-karzh-stvee

Are there any good places to take children around here?

Jsou v okolí nějaká zajímavá místa pro děti?

ysoh f o-ko-lee nye-yuh-ka zuh-yee-muh-va mees-tuh pro dye-tyi

Are children allowed?

Je povolen vstup dětem?

ye po-vo-len vstup dye-tem

Is there space for a pram?

Je tam místo pro kočárek?

ye tuhm mees-to pro ko-cha-rek

Where can I change a nappy/diaper?

Kde mohu vyměnit plenu?

gde mo-hu vi-mye-nyit ple-nu

Do you mind if I breast-feed here?

Nebude vám vadit, když nakojím své dítě?

ne-bu-de vam vuh-dyit gdizh nuh-ko-yeem svair dyee-tye

Could I have some paper and pencils, please?

Můžete mi dát papír a tužky, prosím?

moo-zhe-te mi dat puh-peer uh tuzh-ki pro-seem

Is this suitable for (six)-year-old children?
   Je to vhodné pro   ye to *vhod*·nair pro
   (šesti)leté děti?   (*shes*·tyi·)*le*·tair *dye*·ti

Do you know a dentist/doctor who is good with children?
   Znáte zubaře/lékaře   *zna*·te zu·buh·rzhe/*lair*·kuh·rzhe
   který to umí s dětmi?   *kte*·ree to u·mee s *dyet*·mi

If your child is sick, see **health**, page 191.

talking with children

In this section, phrases are in the informal *ty* ti (you) form only.
See the box **all about you** on page 172 for more details.

What's your name?
   Jak se jmenuješ?   yuhk se *yme*·nu·yesh

How old are you?
   Kolik je ti let?   *ko*·lik ye tyi let

When's your birthday?
   Kdy máš narozeniny?   gdi mash *nuh*·ro·ze·nyi·ni

Do you go to school/kindergarten?
   Chodíš do školy/školky?   *kho*·dyeesh do *shko*·li/*shkol*·ki

What grade are you in?
   Do jaké třídy chodíš?   do *yuh*·kair *trzhee*·di *kho*·dyeesh

Do you like ...?	*Máš rád/*	mash rad/
	ráda ...? m/f	*ra*·duh ...
school	*školu*	*shko*·lu
sport	*sport*	sport
your teacher	*svého učitele* m	*svair*·ho u·chi·te·le
	svojí učitelku f	*svo*·yee u·chi·tel·ku

talking about children

When's the baby due?
Kdy očekáváte porod? — gdi o·che·ka·va·te po·rod

What are you going to call the baby?
Jaké jméno dáte miminku? — yuh·kair ymair·no da·te mi·min·ku

Is this your first child?
Je to vaše první dítě? — ye to vuh·she prv·nyee dyee·tye

How many children do you have?
Kolik máte dětí? — ko·lik ma·te dye·tyee

Is it a boy or a girl?
Je to kluk nebo holka? — ye to kluk ne·bo hol·kuh

How old is he/she?
Jak je starý/á? — yuhk ye stuh·ree/a

Does he/she go to school?
Chodí do školy? — kho·dyee do shko·li

What's his/her name?
Jaké je jeho/její jméno? — yuh·kair ye ye·ho/ye·yee ymair·no

What a beautiful child!
To je krásné dítě! — to ye kras·nair dyee·tye

He/She looks like you.
On/Ona se vám podobá. — on/o·nuh se vam po·do·ba

a guest appearance

If you're invited to someone's home for dinner, bring some flowers for the hostess, a bottle of wine for the host and chocolates for the children. Remember to give an odd number of flowers, as even numbers are placed on graves and are regarded as an insult if given to a living person. Take off the wrapping paper before you present the flowers.

When entering someone's home, take off your shoes or ask *Mám si zout boty?* mam si zoht bo·ti (Should I take off my shoes?). The hosts will normally offer a pair of slippers.

basics

základy

Yes.	Ano.	uh·no
No.	Ne.	ne
Please.	Prosím.	pro·seem
Thank you (very much).	(Mnohokrát) Děkuji.	(mno·ho·krat) dye·ku·yi
You're welcome.	Prosím.	pro·seem
Excuse me. (attention/apology)	Promiňte.	pro·min'·te
Excuse me. (to get past)	Pardon.	puhr·don
Sorry.	Promiňte.	pro·min'·te

it's a yes

Even though it sounds much like the English 'no', remember that the Czech word *ano* uh·no is actually the affirmative – 'yes'. Don't be confused either if you hear people saying *jo* yo or *no* no while nodding in agreement – these are the more informal versions of *ano* (like the English 'yeah').

greetings & goodbyes

pozdravy & loučení

In the Czech Republic, it's very common for people – whether friends or strangers, male or female – to shake hands when they meet. Family members and friends give each other a kiss on the cheek, and sometimes they might also embrace. At social events, a man may kiss a woman's hand after being introduced.

Hello.	*Ahoj.*	*uh*·hoy
Hi.	*Čau.*	chow
Good afternoon.	*Dobré odpoledne.*	*dob*·rair ot·po·led·ne
Good day.	*Dobrý den.*	*dob*·ree den
Good evening.	*Dobrý večer.*	*dob*·ree *ve*·cher
Good morning.	*Dobré ráno.*	*dob*·rair *ra*·no

How are you?
  Jak se máte?   yuhk se *ma*·te
Fine. And you?
  Dobře. A vy?   *dob*·rzhe a vi
What's your name?
  Jak se jmenujete?   yuhk se *yme*·nu·ye·te
My name is …
  Jmenuji se …   *yme*·nu·yi se …
I'd like to introduce you to (Zdeněk).
  Mohu vás představit   *mo*·hu vas *przhed*·stuh·vit
  (Zdeňkovi).   *(zden'*·ko·vi)

I'm pleased to meet you.
  Těší mě.   *tye*·shee mye

This is my ...	To je můj/ moje ... m/f	to ye mooy/ mo·ye ...
colleague	kolega m	ko·le·guh
	kolegyně f	ko·le·gi·nye
daughter	dcera f	dtse·ruh
friend	přítel m	przhee·tel
	přítelkyně f	przhee·tel·ki·nye
husband	manžel m	muhn·zhel
partner (intimate)	partner m	puhrt·ner
	partnerka f	puhrt·ner·kuh
son	syn m	sin
wife	manželka f	muhn·zhel·kuh

See you later.	Na viděnou.	nuh vi·dye·noh
Bye.	Ahoj/Čau.	uh·hoy/chow
Goodbye.	Na shledanou.	nuh·skhle·duh·noh
Good night.	Dobrou noc.	do·broh nots
Bon voyage!	Šťastnou cestu!	shtyuhst·noh tses·tu

addressing people

The following titles can be used with surnames or on their own:

Mr	pan	puhn
Mrs	paní	puh·nyee
Miss	slečna	slech·nuh

a few words between friends

There are several informal terms of address among friends. The most common one is *kamarád(ka)* kuh·muh·rad(·kuh) m/f (friend), which is often shortened to *kámoš* ka·mosh. The words *brácho* bra·kho (a variation of *bratr* bruh·tr – brother) and *chlape* khluh·pe (man) are used between male friends, just like the English 'mate' or 'buddy'. *Vole* vo·le (lit: ox) is another affectionate term used between both male and female friends, but it can also be used as an insult.

making conversation

What a beautiful day!
To je krásný den! — to ye *kras*·nee den

Nice/Awful weather, isn't it?
Neni krásně/ošklivo? — *ne*·nyi *kras*·nye/*osh*·kli·vo

What's happening?
Co se děje? — tso se *dye*·ye

Do you live here?
Bydlíte zde? — *bid*·lee·te zde

Where are you going?
Kam jdete? — kuhm *yde*·te

What are you doing?
Co děláte? — tso *dye*·la·te

in conversation

It's polite to maintain eye contact during a conversation. It's not polite, however, to interrupt someone speaking, keep your hands in your pockets, scratch yourself, blow your nose or smack your tongue!

Do you like it here?
Líbí se vám zde? — *lee*·bee se vam zde

I love it here.
Je to zde výborné. — ye to zde *vee*·bor·nair

What are your interests?
Jaké máte zájmy? — *yuh*·kair *ma*·te *zai*·mi

What's this called?
Jak se to jmenuje? — yuhk se to *yme*·nu·ye

That's (beautiful), isn't it!
To je (krásné), že! — to ye (*kras*·nair) zhe

Can I take a photo of this?
Mohu si toto vyfotit? — *mo*·hu si *to*·to *vi*·fo·tyit

Can I take a photo of you?
Mohu si vás vyfotit?   *mo*·hu si vas *vi*·fo·tyit

Can you take a photo of me/us?
Můžete mě/nás vyfotit?   *moo*·zhe·te mye/nas *vi*·fo·tyit

I'll send you the photo.
Pošlu vám fotku.   *posh*·lu vam *fot*·ku

How long are you here for?
Na jak dlouho jste zde?   nuh yuhk *dloh*·ho yste zde

I'm here for (four) weeks/days.
Jsem zde na (čtyři)   ysem zde nuh (*chti*·rzhi)
týdny/dny.   *teed*·ni/dni

Are you here on holiday?
Jste zde na dovolené?   yste zde nuh *do*·vo·le·nair

I'm here …	*Jsem zde …*	ysem zde …
for a holiday	*na dovolené*	nuh *do*·vo·le·nair
on business	*služebně*	*slu*·zheb·nye
to study	*na studiích*	nuh *stu*·di·eekh

local talk

Hey!	*Hej!*	hey
Great!	*Skvělý!*	*skvye*·lee
Sure.	*Jistě.*	*yis*·tye
Maybe.	*Možná.*	*mozh*·na
No way!	*V žádném*	v *zhad*·nairm
	případě!	*przhee*·puh·dye
Just a minute.	*Moment.*	*mo*·ment
Just joking.	*Jen žertuji.*	yen *zher*·tu·yi
It's OK.	*To je v pořádku.*	to ye v *po*·rzhad·ku
It's not worth it.	*Nestojí to za to.*	*nes*·to·yee to zuh to
Excellent!	*Výborný!*	*vee*·bor·nee
Superb!	*Super!*	*su*·per
No problem.	*Není problém.*	*ne*·ni *prob*·lairm

meeting people

nationalities

Where are you from?
Odkud jste?   ot·kud yste

I'm from …	*Jsem z …*	ysem s …
Australia	*Austrálie*	ow·stra·li·ye
Canada	*Kanady*	kuh·nuh·di
England	*Anglie*	uhn·gli·ye
USA	*Ameriky*	uh·meh·ri·ki

age

How old …?	*Kolik …?*	ko·lik …
are you	*je vám let*	ye vam let
is your	*let je vaší*	let ye vuh·shee
daughter	*dceři*	dtse·rzhi
is your son	*let je vašemu*	let ye vuh·she·mu
	synovi	si·no·vi

I'm … years old.
Je mi … let.   ye mi … let

He's … years old.
Je mu … let.   ye mu … let

She's … years old.
Jí je … let.   yee ye … let

Too old!
Moc starý!   mots stuh·ree

I'm younger than I look.
Jsem mladší než   ysem mluhd·shee nezh
vypadám.   vi·puh·dam

occupations & studies

What's your occupation?
Jaké je vaše povolání? — yuh·kair ye *vuh*·she po·vo·la·nye

I work in administration.
Jsem zaměstnaný/á — ysem *zuh*·myest·nuh·nee·a
v administrativě. m/f — v *uhd*·mi·ni·struh·ti·vye

I work in health.
Jsem zaměstnaný/á — ysem *zuh*·myest·nuh·nee·a
ve zdravotnictví. m/f — ve *zdruh*·vot·nyits·tvee

I work in sales and marketing.
Jsem zaměstnaný/á v — ysem *zuh*·myest·nuh·nee·a v
obchodu a marketingu. m/f — *op*·kho·du uh *muhr*·ke·tin·gu

I'm a/an ...	*Jsem ...*	ysem ...
artist	*umělec* m	*u*·mye·lets
	umělkyně f	*u*·myel·ki·nye
businessperson	*obchodník* m&f	*op*·khod·nyeek
farmer	*zemědělec* m	*ze*·mye·dye·lets
	zemědělkyně f	*ze*·mye·dyel·ki·nye
labourer	*dělník* m	*dyel*·nyeek
	dělnice f	*dyel*·nyi·tse
office worker	*úředník* m	*oo*·rzhed·nyeek
	úřednice f	*oo*·rzhed·nyi·tse
scientist	*vědec* m	*vye*·dets
	vědkyně f	*vyed*·ki·nye
student	*student* m	*stu*·dent
	studentka f	*stu*·dent·kuh

I'm ...	*Jsem ...*	ysem ...
retired	*v důchodu*	v *doo*·kho·du
self-employed	*samostatně*	*suh*·mo·stuht·nye
	výdělečně	*vee*·dye·lech·nye
	činný	*chi*·nee
unemployed	*nezaměst-*	*ne*·zuh·myest·
	naný/á m/f	nuh·nee·a

What are you studying?
Co studujete? tso stu·du·ye·te

I'm studying …	*Studuji …*	stu·du·yi …
Czech	*češtinu*	chesh·tyi·nu
humanities	*humanitní*	hu·muh·nit·nyee
	vědy	vye·di
science	*vědu*	vye·du

family

Do you have a …?	*Máte …?*	ma·te …
I (don't) have a …	*(Ne)Mám ….*	(ne·)mam …
brother	*bratra*	bruh·truh
daughter	*dceru*	dtse·ru
husband	*manžela*	muhn·zhe·luh
partner	*partnera* m	puhrt·ne·ruh
(intimate)	*partnerku* f	puhrt·ner·ku
sister	*sestru*	ses·tru
son	*syna*	si·nuh
wife	*manželku*	muhn·zhel·ku

Are you married?
Jste ženatý/vdaná? m/f yste zhe·nuh·tee/fduh·na

I'm married.
Jsem ženatý/vdaná. m/f ysem zhe·nuh·tee/fduh·na

I'm single.
Jsem svobodný/á. m/f ysem svo·bod·nee/a

I live with someone.
Žiju s někým jiným. zhi·yu s nye·keem yi·neem

I'm separated.
Žiju odděleně od zhi·yu od·dye·le·nye od
manželky/manžela. m/f mun·zhel·ki/muhn·zhe·luh

The family is very important to Czechs. When talking with friends and family members, they like to use diminutives (words that express the 'smallness' of something – like the word 'doggy' in English) to show affection. In Czech, diminutives are usually formed by adding the following endings to nouns: *-ek* -ek m, *-ka* -kuh f and *-ko* -ko n. In the examples below, diminutives are given after the 'neutral' kinship terms.

brother	*bratr/bratříček* m	*bruh*·tr/*bruht*·rzhee·chek
daughter	*dcera/dceruška* f	*dtse*·ruh/*dtse*·rush·kuh
grandfather	*děda/dědeček* m	*dye*·duh/*dye*·de·chek
grandmother	*babi/babička* f	*buh*·bee/*buh*·bich·kuh
sister	*sestra/sestřička* f	*ses*·truh/*sest*·rzhich·kuh
son	*syn/synáček* m	sin/*si*·na·chek

Teenage siblings also call each other *ségro* sair·gro (sister) and *brácho* bra·kho (brother). Furthermore, you might hear elderly people addressing boys as *chlapče* khluhp·che (boy) and girls as *děvče* dyev·che (girl).

farewells

Tomorrow is my last day here.
Zítra jsem tady naposled.   zee·truh ysem *tuh*·di *nuh*·po·sled

If you come to (Scotland), you can stay with me.
Až přijedete do (Skotska),   uhzh *przhi*·ye·de·te do (*skots*·kuh)
můžete zůstat u mě.   moo·zhe·te *zoos*·tuht u mye

It's been great meeting you.
Bylo skvělé že jsem se   bi·lo *skvye*·lair zhe ysem se
s vámi setkal/setkala. m/f   s *va*·mi *set*·kuhl/*set*·kuh·luh

Keep in touch!
Ozvěte se!   oz·vye·te se

What's your (email) address?
Jakou máte (email)   *yuh*·koh *ma*·te (*ee*·meyl)
adresu?   uh·dre·su

What's your phone number?
Jaké máte telefonní   *yuh*·kair *ma*·te te·le·fo·nyee
číslo?   chees·lo

Here's my ...	*Tady je moje ...*	*tuh*·di ye *mo*·ye ...
(email)	*(email)*	(*ee*·meyl)
address	*adresa*	uh·dre·suh
phone	*telefonní*	te·le·fo·nyee
number	*číslo*	chees·lo

well-wishing

Bless you!	*Na zdraví!*	nuh *zdruh*·vee
Congratulations!	*Blahopřeji!*	*bluh*·hop·rzhe·yi
Good luck!	*Mnoho štěstí!*	*mno*·ho *shtyes*·tyee

Happy birthday!
Všechno nejlepší k   *vshekh*·no *ney*·lep·shee k
narozeninám!   nuh·ro·ze·*nyi*·nam

Happy name day!
Všechno nejlepší   *vshekh*·no *ney*·lep·shee
k svátku!   k *svat*·ku

Happy Easter!
Veselé Velikonoce!   ve·se·lair ve·li·ko·no·tse

Happy New Year!
Šťastný Nový rok!   *shtyuhst*·nee *no*·vee rok

Merry Christmas!
Veselé Vánoce!   ve·se·lair va·no·tse

common interests

What do you do in your spare time?

Jak trávíte svůj volný čas?	yuhk *tra*·vee·te svooy *vol*·nee chuhs	

Do you like …?	*Máte rád/ráda …?* m/f	*ma*·te rad/*ra*·duh …
I like …	*Mám rád/ráda …* m/f	mam rad/*ra*·duh …
I don't like …	*Nemám rád/ráda …* m/f	ne·mam rad/*ra*·duh …
art	*umění*	u·mye·nyee
cooking	*vaření*	vuh·rzhe·nyee
dancing	*tancování*	tuhn·tso·va·nyee
drawing	*kreslení*	kre·sle·nyee
films	*filmy*	*fil*·mi
hiking	*turistiku*	tu·ris·ti·ku
mushrooming	*sbírání hub*	sbee·ra·nyee hub
music	*hudbu*	*hud*·bu
painting	*malování*	muh·lo·va·nyee
painting	*malování*	muh·lo·va·nyee
Easter eggs	*kraslic*	*kruhs*·lits
photography	*fotografii*	fo·to·gruh·fi·i
reading	*čtení*	chte·nyee
socialising	*chození do společnosti*	kho·ze·nyee do spo·lech·nos·tyi
sport	*sport*	sport
surfing the Internet	*brouzdání po internetu*	*brohz*·da·nyee po in·ter·ne·tu
travelling	*cestování*	tses·to·va·nyee
watching TV	*dívání se na televizi*	*dyee*·va·nyee se nuh te·le·vi·zi

For types of sport, see **sport**, page 145, and the **dictionary**.

hudba

Do you …?

dance	*Tancujete?*	tuhn·tsu·ye·te
go to concerts	*Chodíte na koncerty?*	kho·dyee·te nuh kon·tser·ti
listen to music	*Posloucháte hudbu?*	po·sloh·kha·te hud·bu
play an instrument	*Hrajete na hudební nástroj?*	hruh·ye·te nuh hu·deb·nyee nas·troy
sing	*Zpíváte?*	spee·va·te

Which … do you like?	*Líbí se vám …?*	lee·bee se vam …
bands	*skupiny*	sku·pi·ni
music	*hudba*	hud·buh
performers	*umělci* m	u·myel·tsi
	umělkyně f	u·myel·ki·nye
singers	*zpěváci* m	spye·va·tsi
	zpěvačky f	spye·vuhch·ki

… music	*… hudba*	… hud·buh
classical	*klasická*	kluh·sits·ka
electronic	*elektronická*	e·lek·tro·nits·ka
folk	*lidová*	li·do·va
pop	*populární*	po·pu·lar·nyee
rock	*rocková*	ro·ko·va
traditional	*tradiční*	truh·dyich·nyee

Planning to go to a concert? See **tickets**, page 47, and **going out**, page 129.

cinema & theatre

I feel like going to a/an ...	Chtěl/Chtěla bych vidět ... m/f	khtyel/khtye·luh bikh vi·dyet ...
Did you like the ...?	Máte rád/ráda ...? m/f	ma·te rad/ra·duh ...
ballet	balet	buh·let
film	film	film
opera	operu	o·pe·ru
play	hru	hru
puppet show	loutkové představení	loht·ko·vair przhed·stuh·ve·nyee

What's showing at the cinema/theatre tonight?

Co dávají v kině/ divadle dnes večer?

tso da·vuh·yee f ki·nye/ dyi·vuhd·le dnes ve·cher

Is it in (English)?

Je to v (angličtině)?

ye to f (uhn·glich·tyi·nye)

Does it have (English) subtitles?

Je to s (anglickými) titulky?

ye to s (uhn·glits·kee·mi) ti·tul·ki

Is this seat available?

Je toto místo volné?

ye to·to mees·to vol·nair

Do you have tickets for ...?

Máte lístky na ...?

ma·te leest·ki nuh ...

Are there any extra tickets?

Máte více lístků?

ma·te vee·tse leest·koo

I'd like the cheap tickets.

Chtěl/Chtěla bych levné lístky. m/f

khtyel/khtye·luh bikh lev·nair leest·ki

I'd like the best tickets.

Chtěl/Chtěla bych nejlepší lístky. m/f

khtyel/khtye·luh bikh ney·lep·shee leest·ki

Is there a matinee show?

Hraje se odpolední představení?

hruh·ye se od·po·led·nyee przhed·stuh·ve·nyee

interests

119

Have you seen (Želary)?
Viděli jste (Želary)?   *vi*·dye·li yste (*zhe*·luh·ri)

Who's in it?
Kdo v tom hraje?   gdo f tom *hruh*·ye

It stars (Aňa Gaislerová).
V hlavní roli hraje   v *hluhv*·nyee *ro*·li *hruh*·ye
(Aňa Gaislerová).   (*uh*·nyuh *gais*·le·ro·va)

I thought it was …	*Myslel/Myslela jsem že to bylo …* m/f	*mis*·lel/*mis*·le·luh ysem zhe to *bi*·lo …
excellent	*vynikající*	*vi*·nyi·kuh·yee·tsee
long	*dlouhé*	*dloh*·hair
OK	*fajn*	fain

I (don't) like …	*(Ne)Mám rád/ráda …* m/f	*(ne*·)mam rad/*ra*·duh …
action movies	*akční filmy*	*uhk*·chnyee *fil*·mi
animated films	*animované filmy*	*uh*·ni·mo·vuh·nair *fil*·mi
(Czech) cinema	*(českou) kinematografii*	(*ches*·koh) *ki*·ne·muh·to·gruh·fi·yi
comedies	*komedie*	*ko*·me·di·ye
documentaries	*dokumentární filmy*	*do*·ku·men·tar·nyee *fil*·mi
drama	*činohru*	*chi*·no·hru
horror movies	*horory*	*ho*·ro·ri
short films	*krátké filmy*	*krat*·kair *fil*·mi
thrillers	*napínavé příběhy*	*nuh*·pee·nuh·vair *przhee*·bye·hi
war movies	*válečné filmy*	*va*·lech·nair *fil*·mi

---

turn on the black lights

A popular art form in the Czech Republic is the black-light theatre (*černé divadlo cher*·nair *dyi*·vuhd·lo) – a mixture of mime, drama and puppetry. Objects, puppets and live actors in fluorescent costumes are illuminated by ultraviolet lights, with the stage completely black in order to eliminate distractions.

feelings

pocity

Are you …?	Jste …?	yste …
I'm/I'm not …	Jsem/Nejsem …	ysem/ney·sem …
annoyed	mrzutý/á m/f	mr·zu·tee/a
disappointed	zklamaný/á m/f	skluh·muh·nee/a
happy	šťastný/á m/f	shtyuhst·nee/a
hungry	hladový/á m/f	hluh·do·vee/a
sad	smutný/á m/f	smut·nee/a
surprised	překvapený/á m/f	przhek·vuh·pe·nee/a
thirsty	žíznivý/á m/f	zheez·nyi·vee/a
tired	unavený/á m/f	u·nuh·ve·nee/a
well	zdravý/á m/f	zdruh·vee/a
worried	znepokojený/á m/f	zne·po·ko·ye·nee/a

gender issues

In Czech, gender differences affect not only the form of nouns and pronouns, but also the endings of adjectives and verbs. The most frequent endings, which tell you whether an adjective is in the masculine or feminine form, are -ý -ee and -á -a respectively. To show that you need to substitute one letter for another, we've used a slash – eg smutný/á m/f smut·nee/a (sad). On the other hand, in some verb tenses the masculine form normally ends in -l -l or another consonant, and the ending -a -uh is added for the feminine form. In this case, we've spelled out both forms of the verb in full.

I'd like to practise Czech.

Rád/Ráda bych si	rad/ra·duh bikh si
procvičil/procvičila	prots·vi·chil/prots·vi·chi·luh
češtinu. m/f	chesh·tyi·nu

not at all	vůbec ne	*voo*·bets ne
I don't care at all.		
Mně na tom vůbec nezáleží.		mnye nuh tom *voo*·bets ne·za·le·zhee

a little	trochu	*tro*·khu
I'm a little sad.		
Jsem trochu smutný/á. **m/f**		ysem *tro*·khu smut·nee/a

very	velmi	*vel*·mi
I feel very lucky.		
Cítím se velmi šťastně.		*tsee*·tyeem se *vel*·mi shtyuhst·nye

extremely	nesmírně	ne·smeer·nye
I'm extremely sorry.		
Je mi to nesmírně líto.		ye mi to ne·smeer·nye *lee*·to

Are you cold?	*Je vám zima?*	ye vam *zi*·muh
I'm cold.	*Je mi zima.*	ye mi *zi*·muh
I'm not cold.	*Neni mi zima.*	ne·nyi mi *zi*·muh
Are you hot?	*Je vám horko?*	ye vam *hor*·ko
I'm hot.	*Je mi horko.*	ye mi *hor*·ko
I'm not hot.	*Neni mi horko.*	ne·nyi mi *hor*·ko
Are you in a hurry?	*Spěcháte?*	*spye*·kha·te
I'm in a hurry.	*Spěchám.*	*spye*·kham
I'm not in a hurry.	*Nespěchám.*	nes·pye·kham

If you're not feeling well, see **health**, page 191.

SOCIAL

opinions

Czechs love to discuss politics and sport. Though they're generally very polite and peaceful, Czechs can get quite animated in political discussions. They're also passionately proud of Czech sporting heroes who have achieved victories at world level.

Did you like it?
   Líbilo se vám to?   *lee*·bi·lo se vam to

What do you think of it?
   Co si o tom myslíte?   tso si o tom *mis*·lee·te

I thought	*Myslel/Myslela jsem*	*mis*·lel/*mis*·le·luh ysem
it was …	*si že to bylo …* **m/f**	si zhe to *bi*·lo …
It's …	*Je to …*	ye to …
awful	*hrozné*	*hroz*·nair
beautiful	*krásné*	*kras*·nair
boring	*nudné*	*nud*·nair
great	*nezapome-*	*ne*·zuh·po·me·
	nutelné	nu·tel·nair
interesting	*zajímavé*	*zuh*·yee·muh·vair
OK	*fajn*	fain
strange	*divné*	*dyiv*·nair
(too) expensive	*(moc) drahé*	(mots) *druh*·hair

hot topics

Some topics are best avoided, as they could arouse nationalistic reactions from many Czechs. You might be surprised to encounter racist attitudes towards the Roma (*Romové ro*·mo·vair), although these are generally not displayed openly and mostly appear to be just a reflection of what people have heard since childhood. The dislike of Russians (*Rusů ru*·soo) and Germans is a result of their communist legacy and the Nazi occupation respectively. A particularly touchy subject is the post-war expulsion of the Sudeten Germans (*Sudetští Němci su*·det·shtyee *nyem*·tsi) – a German minority that lived in the former Czechoslovakia.

politics & social issues

Who do you vote for?
Koho volíte?   ko·ho vo·lee·te

I support the (green) party.
Podporuji (zelenou)   pod·po·ru·yi (ze·le·noh)
stranu.   struh·nu

I'm a member	*Jsem členem*	ysem *chle*·nem
of the ... party.	*... strany.*	*... struh*·ni
communist	*komunistické*	ko·mu·nis·tits·kair
conservative	*konzervativní*	kon·zer·vuh·tiv·nyee
democratic	*demokratické*	de·mo·kruh·tits·kair
green	*zelené*	ze·le·nair
liberal	*liberální*	li·be·ral·nyee
social	*sociálně*	so·tsi·al·nye
democratic	*demokratické*	de·mo·kruh·tits·kair
socialist	*socialistické*	so·tsi·uh·lis·tits·kair

---

party talk

These are the main political parties in the Czech Republic:

Česká strana sociálně demokratická
 ches·ka *struh*·nuh   Czech Social
 so·tsi·al·nye de·mo·kruh·tits·ka   Democratic Party

Komunistická strana Čech a Moravy
 ko·mu·nis·tits·ka *struh*·nuh   Czech and Moravian
 chekh uh *mo*·ruh·vi   Communist Party

Křesťansko demokratická unie – Česká strana lidová
 krzhes·tyan·sko   Christian
 de·mo·kruh·tits·ka u·ni·ye –   Democratic Union –
 ches·ka *struh*·nuh li·do·va   Czech People's Party

Občanská demokratická strana
 ob·chuhn·ska de·mo·kruh·tits·ka   Civic Democratic
 struh·nuh   Party

SOCIAL

Did you hear about ...?
Slyšeli jste o ...?   sli·she·li yste o ...

Do you agree with it?
Souhlasíte s tím?   soh·hluh·see·te s tyeem

I agree/I don't agree with ...
Souhlasím/   soh·hluh·seem/
Nesouhlasím s ...   ne·soh·hluh·seem s ...

How do people feel about ...?
Co si lidé myslí o ...?   tso si li·dair mis·lee o ...

How can we protest against ...?
Jak můžeme   yuhk moo·zhe·me
protestovat proti ...?   pro·tes·to·vuht pro·tyi ...

How can we support ...?
Jak můžeme   yuhk moo·zhe·me
podpořit ...?   pot·po·rzhit ...

abortion	*potrat* m	po·truht
animal rights	*práva zvířat* f pl	pra·vuh zvee·rzhuht
communism	*komunismus* m	ko·mu·nis·mus
corruption	*korupce* f	ko·rup·tse
crime	*kriminalita* f	kri·mi·nuh·li·tuh
discrimination	*diskriminace* f	dis·kri·mi·nuh·tse
drugs	*drogy* f pl	dro·gi
the economy	*ekonomie* f	e·ko·no·mi·ye
education	*vzdělání* n	vzdye·la·nyee
the environment	*životní*	zhi·vot·nyee
	prostředí n	prost·rzhe·dyee
equal opportunity	*rovnoprávnost* f	rov·no·prav·nost
European Union	*Evropská unie* f	e·vrop·ska u·ni·ye
euthanasia	*euthanasie* f	eu·tuh·nuh·si·ye
globalisation	*globalizace* f	glo·buh·li·zuh·tse
human rights	*lidská práva* f pl	lid·ska pra·vuh
immigration	*imigrace* f	i·mi·gruh·tse
inequality	*nerovnoprávnost* f	ne·rov·no·prav·nost
nationalism	*nacionalismus* m	nuh·tsi·o·nuh·lis·mus
party politics	*stranická*	struh·nyits·ka
	politika f	po·li·ti·kuh

poverty	chudoba f	khu·do·buh
privatisation	privatizace f	pri·vuh·ti·zuh·tse
racism	rasismus m	ruh·sis·mus
sexism	sexismus m	sek·sis·mus
social welfare	sociální	so·tsi·al·nyee
	péče f	pair·che
terrorism	terorismus m	te·ro·ris·mus
unemployment	nezaměstnanost f	ne·zuh·myest·nuh·nost
the war in ...	válka v ... f	val·kuh v ...
Is there help	Jaké pomoci	yuh·kair po·mo·tsi
for (the) ...?	se dostává ...?	se dos·ta·va ...
aged	starým lidém	stuh·reem li·dem
beggars	žebrákům	zhe·bra·koom
disabled	invalidům	in·vuh·li·doom
homeless	bezdomovcům	bez·do·mof·tsoom
street kids	bezprizorním	bez·pri·zor·nyeem
	dětem	dye·tem

check your czech

The word 'Czech', in its one and only English form, can be
used for a number of different notions, together with another
word which clarifies what's meant. These various concepts
are covered by separate words in the Czech language itself:

the Czech language	čeština f	chesh·tyi·nuh
a Czech woman	Češka f	chesh·kuh
a Czech man	Čech m	chekh
the Czech Republic	Česká	ches·ka
	republika f	re·pu·bli·kuh
Czech (adjective)	český m	ches·kee
	česká f	ches·ka
	české n	ches·kair

SOCIAL

the environment

Is there a … problem here?
Je zde problém s …?   ye zde *pro*·blairm s …
What should be done about …?
Co se má dělat s …?   tso se ma *dye*·luht s …

acid rain	*kyselý déšť* m	*ki*·se·lee dairsht'
alternative	*alternativní*	*uhl*·ter·nuh·tiv·nyee
energy sources	*energetické*	*e*·ner·ge·tits·kair
	zdroje m pl	*zdro*·ye
animal rights	*práva zvířat* f pl	*pra*·vuh zvee·rzhuht
conservation	*ochrana*	*okh*·ruh·nuh
	přírody f	*przhee*·ro·di
deforestation	*odlesňování* n	*od*·les·nyo·va·nyee
drought	*období sucha* n	*ob*·do·bee *su*·khuh
ecosystem	*ekosystém* m	*e*·ko·sis·tairm
endangered	*ohrožené*	*o*·hro·zhe·nair
species	*druhy* m pl	*dru*·hi
the environment	*životní*	*zhi*·vot·nyee
	prostředí n	*prost*·rzhe·dyee
genetically	*geneticky*	*ge*·ne·tits·ki
modified food	*modifikované*	*mo*·di·fi·ko·vuh·nair
	potraviny f pl	*po*·truh·vi·ni
hunting	*lov* m	lof
hydroelectricity	*hydroelektřina* f	*hi*·dro·e·lek·trzhi·nuh
irrigation	*zavlažování* n	*zuh*·vluh·zho·va·nyee
nuclear energy	*jaderná energie* f	*yuh*·der·na *e*·ner·gi·e
ozone layer	*ozónová vrstva* f	*o*·zaw·no·va *vrst*·vuh
pesticides	*pesticidy* m pl	*pes*·ti·tsi·di
pollution	*znečištění*	*zne*·chis·tye·nyee
	životního	*zhi*·vot·nyee·ho
	prostředí n	*prost*·rzhe·dyee
recycling	*recyklace* f	*re*·tsi·kluh·tse
toxic waste	*toxický odpad* m	*tok*·sits·kee *od*·puhd
water supply	*zásobování*	*za*·so·bo·va·nyee
	vodou n	*vo*·doh

127

Is this a	*Je tento …*	ye *ten*·to …
protected …?	*chráněný?*	*khra*·nye·nee
forest	*les*	les
park	*park*	puhrk
species	*druh*	drukh

popular wisdom

Here are some of the Czech views on life, courtesy of local sayings …

In the middle of nowhere.
Místo kde lišky dávají   *mees*·to gde *lish*·ki *duh*·va·yee
dobrou noc.   *do*·broh nots
(lit: place where foxes say good night)

Look before you leap.
Ráno moudřejší   *ra*·no *mohd*·rzhey·shee
večera.   ve·che·ruh
(lit: morning wiser than evening)

Out of the frying pan into the fire.
Dostat se z bláta do   *dos*·tuht se z *bla*·tuh do
louže.   *loh*·zhe
(lit: out of the mud into the puddle)

To have a chip on the shoulder.
Mít máslo na hlavě.   meet *mas*·lo nuh *hluh*·vye
(lit: to have butter on the head)

It's all Greek to him.
Je to pro něj španělská   ye to pro nyey *shpuh*·nyel·ska
vesnice.   *ves*·ni·tse
(lit: it's a Spanish village to him)

It's as old as the hills.
To je starý jak Praha.   to ye *stuh*·ree yuhk *pruh*·huh
(lit: it's as old as Prague)

Beer makes beautiful bodies.
Pivo dělá hezká těla.   pi·vo *dye*·la *hez*·ka *tye*·luh

In this chapter, phrases are in the informal *ty* ti (you) form. If you're not sure what this means, see the box **all about you** on page 172 for more details.

where to go

kam jít

What's there to do in the evenings?
Kam se dá večer jít?   kuhm se da *ve*·cher yeet

What's on …?	*Kde se … můžeme pobavit?*	gde se … *moo*·zhe·me *po*·buh·vit
locally	*v okolí*	f o·ko·lee
today	*dnes*	dnes
tonight	*večer*	*ve*·cher
this weekend	*tento víkend*	*ten*·to vee·kend

Where can I find …?	*Kde mohu najít …?*	gde *mo*·hu *nuh*·yeet …
cafés	*kavárny*	*kuh*·var·ni
clubs	*kluby*	*klu*·bi
gay/lesbian venues	*homosexuální/ lesbický zábavné podniky*	*ho*·mo·sek·su·al·nyee/ *les*·bits·kee *za*·buhv·nair *pod*·ni·ki
places to eat	*stravovací místa*	*struh*·vo·vuh·tsee *mees*·tuh
pubs	*hospody*	*hos*·po·di

Is there a local ... guide?	Existuje ...?	ek·sis·tu·ye ...
entertainment	přehled kulturních programů	przhe·hled kul·tur·nyeekh pro·gruh·moo
film	program kin	pro·gruhm kin
gay/lesbian entertainment	přehled kulturních programů pro homosexuály/ lesbičky	przhe·hled kul·tur·nyeekh pro·gruh·moo pro ho·mo·sek·su·a·li/ les·bich·ki
music	přehled hudebních programů	przhe·hled hu·deb·nyeekh pro·gruh·moo
I feel like going to a ...	Rád/Ráda bych šel/šla ... m/f	rad/ra·duh bikh shel/shluh ...
ballet	na balet	nuh buh·let
bar	do baru	do buh·ru
café	do kavárny	do kuh·var·ni
concert	na koncert	nuh kon·tsert
film	do kina	do ki·nuh
karaoke bar	do karaoke baru	do kuh·ruh·o·ke buh·ru
nightclub	do večerního klubu	do ve·cher·nyee·ho klu·bu
party	na mejdan/ večírek	nuh mey·duhn/ ve·chee·rek
performance	na představení	nuh przhed·stuh·ve·nyee
play	na hru	nuh hru
pub	do hospody	do hos·po·di
puppet show	na loutkové představení	nuh loht·ko·vair przhed·stuh·ve·nyee
restaurant	do restaurace	do res·tow·ruh·tse

For more on bars, drinks and partying, see **romance**, page 135, and **eating out**, page 159.

In the Czech Republic, it's not only men who get a chance to politely say *Až po vás.* uhzh po vas (lit: After you. **pol**). Of course, good old manners dictate that the man lets the woman enter first when going out to a nice, expensive restaurant. However, the man goes in first if it's a pub, bar or a cheap restaurant – so a girl can have her turn to casually offer *Po tobě.* po to·bye (lit: After you. **inf**).

invitations

pozvání

What are you doing now?
  Co teď děláš?   tso ted' *dye*·lash

What are you doing tonight?
  Co děláš dnes večer?   tso *dye*·lash dnes *ve*·cher

What are you doing this weekend?
  Co budeš dělat   tso *bu*·desh *dye*·luht
  tento víkend?   *ten*·to *vee*·kend

My round.
  To platím já.   to *pluh*·tyim ya

Would you like to go (for a) …?	*Chtěl/Chtěla bys jít …?* m/f	khtyel/*khtye*·luh bis yeet …
I feel like going (for a) …	*Rad bych šel …* m *Rada bych šla …* f	rad bikh shel … *ra*·duh bikh shluh …
dancing	*tancovat*	*tuhn*·tso·vuht
coffee	*na kafe*	nuh *kuh*·fe
drink	*na sklenku*	nuh *sklen*·ku
meal	*na jídlo*	nuh *yeed*·lo
walk	*na vycházku*	nuh *vi*·khaz·ku

Different generations, different jargons – generally speaking, middle-aged and older Czechs say *večírek* ve·chee·rek when referring to a party, while *mejdan* mey·duhn is the word used by younger people. Of course, their ideas of a good party are probably quite different too …

Do you know a good restaurant?
 Znáš dobrou restauraci? znash *dob*·roh res·tow·ruh·tsi

Do you want to come to the concert with me?
 Chceš jít se mnou khtsesh yeet se mnoh
 na koncert? nuh *kon*·tsert

We're having a party.
 Pořádáme večírek/ po·rzha·da·me ve·chee·rek/
 mejdan. mey·duhn

You should come.
 Měl/Měla bys přijít. m/f myel/*mye*·luh bis przhi·yeet

responding to invitations

Sure!
 Jistě! yis·tye

Yes, I'd love to.
 Ano, velmi rád/ráda. m/f uh·no *vel*·mi rad/*ra*·duh

Where shall we go?
 Kam půjdeme? kuhm *pooy*·de·me

No, I'm afraid I can't.
 Ne, obávám se, že nemohu. ne o·ba·vam se zhe *ne*·mo·hu

Sorry, I can't sing/dance.
 Promiň, nemohu pro·min' *ne*·mo·hu
 zpívat/tančit. spee·vuht/*tuhn*·chit

What about tomorrow?
 Co zítra? tso *zee*·truh

arranging to meet

What time will we meet?
V kolik hodin se setkáme?   f *ko*·lik *ho*·dyin se *set*·ka·me

Where will we meet?
Kde se setkáme?   gde se *set*·ka·me

Let's meet at ...	*Setkáme se ...*	*set*·ka·me se ...
(eight) o'clock	*v (osm) hodin*	f (*o*·sm) *ho*·dyin
the (entrance)	*u (vchodu)*	u (*fkho*·du)

---

lonely letters

The single consonants in our coloured pronunciation guides haven't been pushed out of an overcrowded Czech word by mistake. They're Czech versions of some common prepositions (eg 'with', 'in') and are usually joined in pronunciation with the following word. You'll see v or f for the sound of the letter *v*, k for *k* and s or z for the letters *s* and *z*. For more on prepositions, see the **phrasebuilder**, page 25.

OK!
Fajn!   fain

I'll pick you up.
Vyzvednu tě.   *viz*·ved·nu tye

Are you ready?
Jsi připravený/á? **m/f**   ysi *przhi*·pruh·ve·nee/a

I'm ready.
Jsem připravený/á. **m/f**   ysem *przhi*·pruh·ve·nee/a

I'll be coming later.
Přijdu později.   *przhiy*·du *poz*·dye·yi

Where will you be?
Kde budeš?   gde *bu*·desh

If I'm not there by (nine), don't wait for me.
Když tam nebudu do   gdizh tuhm *ne*·bu·du do
(devíti), nečekej na mě.   (*de*·vee·tyi) *ne*·che·key na mye

going out

133

I'll see you then.
Uvidíme se pak.   u·vi·dyee·me se puhk

See you later.
Na shledanou.   nuh·skhle·duh·noh

See you tomorrow.
Na shledanou zítra.   nuh·skhle·duh·noh *zee*·truh

I'm looking forward to it.
Těším se na to.   *tye*·sheem se nuh to

Sorry I'm late.
Promiň jdu pozdě.   *pro*·min' ydu *poz*·dye

Never mind.
Nevadí.   ne·vuh·dyee

drugs

drogy

I don't take drugs.
Neberu drogy.   ne·be·ru *dro*·gi

I take ... occasionally.
Příležitostně si   *przhee*·le·zhi·tost·nye si
vezmu ...   *vez*·mu ...

Do you want to have a smoke?
Chceš si zakouřit?   khtsesh si *zuh*·koh·rzhit

Do you have a light?
Můžu si zapálit?   moo·zhu si *zuh*·pa·lit

If the police are talking to you about drugs, see **police**, page 188, for useful phrases.

> **why, oh why**
>
> Remember that the apostrophe ' in the pronunciation guide is said as a slight 'y' sound after a consonant while the y (eg *jsem* ysem) is always pronounced like the 'y' in 'yes'.

In this chapter, phrases are in the informal *ty* ti (you) form. If you're not sure what this means, see the box **all about you** on page 172 for more details.

asking someone out

pozvat někoho na rande

Where would you like to go (tonight)?
Kam bys chtěl/chtěla   kuhm bis khtyel/*khtye*·luh
jít (dnes večer)? m/f   yeet (dnes *ve*·cher)

Would you like to do something (tomorrow)?
Chtěl/Chtěla bys něco   khtyel/*khtye*·luh bis *nye*·tso
(zítra) podniknout? m/f   (*zee*·truh) *pod*·nyik·noht

Yes, I'd love to.
Ano, rád/ráda. m/f   uh·no rad/*ra*·duh

Sorry, I can't.
Promiň, nemohu.   *pro*·min' *ne*·mo·hu

local talk

He's a babe.	*On je frajer.*	on ye *fruh*·yer
She's a babe.	*Ona je kočka.*	*o*·nuh ye *koch*·kuh
She's hot.	*Ona je rajcovní*	*o*·nuh ye *rai*·tsov·nyee
	ženská.	*zhen*·ska

pick-up lines

Would you like a drink?
Mohu tě pozvat   mo·hu tye *poz*·vuht
na sklenku?   nuh *sklen*·ku

You look like someone I know.
Vypadáš, jako někdo   vi·puh·dash *yuh*·ko *nyek*·do
koho znám.   *ko*·ho znam

You're a fantastic dancer.
Jsi výtečný tanečník. m   ysi *vee*·tech·nee *tuh*·nech·nyeek

You're a fantastic dancer.
Jsi výtečná tanečnice. f   ysi *vee*·tech·na *tuh*·nech·nyi·tse

Can I …?	*Mohu …?*	mo·hu …
dance with you	*si s tebou*	si s *te*·boh
	zatančit	zuh·tuhn·chit
sit here	*si k tobě*	si k *to*·bye
	přisednout	przhi·sed·noht
take you home	*tě pozvat k*	tye *poz*·vuht k
	sobě domů	*so*·bye do·mu

rejections

I'm here with my girlfriend.
Jsem zde s mojí   ysem zde s *mo*·yee
přítelkyní.   *przhee*·tel·ki·nyee

I'm here with my boyfriend.
Jsem zde s mým   ysem zde s meem
přítelem.   *przhee*·te·lem

I'd rather not.
Raději ne.   ruh·dye·yi ne

No, thank you.
Ne, děkuji.   ne *dye*·ku·yi

Excuse me, I have to go now.
  Promiň, ale musím   pro·min' uh·le mu·seem
  teď jít.   ted' yeet

Pity, but I'm doing something else.
  Škoda, ale mám   shko·duh uh·le mam
  jiný program.   yi·nee pro·gruhm

Thank you, but I'm not interested.
  Děkuji, ale nemám zájem.   dye·ku·yi uh·le ne·mam za·yem

local talk

Leave me alone!
  Nech mě na pokoji!   nekh mye nuh po·ko·yi

Don't bother me!
  Neobtěžuj mě!   ne·ob·tye·zhuy mye

Don't touch me!
  Nedotíkej se mě!   ne·do·tee·key se mye

Take a hike!   *Běž k šípku!*   byezh k sheep·ku
Piss off!   *Odprejskni!*   od·preysk·nyi
Get stuffed!   *Jdi se vycpat!*   ydyi se vits·puht

getting closer

I really like you. (man speaking)
  Mám tě moc rád.   mam tye mots rad

I really like you. (woman speaking)
  Mám tě moc ráda.   mam tye mots ra·duh

You're great.
  Jsi báječný/á. m/f   ysi ba·yech·nee/a

Can I kiss you?
  Mohu tě políbit?   mo·hu tye po·lee·bit

Do you want to come inside for a while?
  Chceš jít na chvíli ke mě? khtsesh yeet nuh khvi·li ke mye

romance

137

Do you want a massage?
   Chceš udělat masáž?   khtsesh *u*·dye·luht *muh*·sazh

Would you like to stay over?
   Chceš u mě přespat?   khtsesh u mye *przhes*·puht

Can I stay over?
   Mohu zde přespat?   *mo*·hu zde *przhes*·puht

sex

Kiss me.	*Polib mě.*	*po*·lib mye
I want you.	*Chci tě.*	khtsi tye
Let's go to bed.	*Pojďme do postele.*	poyd'·me do *pos*·te·le
Touch me here.	*Dotkni se mě.*	*dot*·knyi se mye
Do you like this?	*Líbí se ti to?*	*lee*·bee se tyi to

I like that.
   Mám to rád/ráda. m/f   mam to rad/*ra*·duh

I don't like that.
   Nemám to rád/ráda. m/f   *ne*·mam to rad/*ra*·duh

I think we should stop now.
   Myslím si, že by jsme   *mis*·leem si zhe bi ysme
   měli přestat.   *mye*·li *przhes*·tuht

Do you have a (condom)?
   Máš (prezervativ)?   mash (*pre*·zer·vuh·tif)

Let's use a (condom).
   Použijeme (prezervativ).   *po*·u·zhi·ye·me (*pre*·zer·vuh·tif)

I won't do it without protection.
   Nebudu to dělat   *ne*·bu·du to *dye*·luht
   bez ochrany.   bez o·*khruh*·ni

It's my first time.
   Pro mě je to poprvé.   pro mye ye to *po*·pr·vair

Oh my god!	Ó muj bože!	oo muy *bo*·zhe
That's great.	To je skvělé.	to ye skve·lair
Easy tiger!	Zpomal divochu/	*spo*·muhl dyi·vo·khu/
	divoško! **m/f**	dyi·vosh·ko

That was …	To bylo …	to *bi*·lo …
amazing	báječný	ba·yech·nee
romantic	romantický	ro·muhn·tits·kee
wild	divoký	dyi·vo·kee

sweet talk

my bottom	prdelko	pr·del·ko
my darling	můj miláčku	mooy *mi*·lach·ku
my gold	zlatíčko	zluh·tyeech·ko
my sweetheart	srdíčko	sr·dyeech·ko
sweetie	drahoušku	druh·hohsh·ku

love

láska

I think we're good together.
Myslím, že patříme
k sobě.

mis·leem zhe *puht*·rzhee·me
k *so*·bye

Will you go out with me?
Budeš se mnou chodit?

bu·desh se mnoh *kho*·dyit

I love you.
Miluji tě.

mi·lu·yi tye

Will you meet my parents?
Chceš se seznámit
s mými rodiči?

khtsesh se *sez*·na·mit
s *mee*·mi ro·dyi·chi

Will you marry me?
Vezmeš si mě?

vez·mesh si mye

problems

I don't think it's working out.
Myslím, že nám to   mis·leem zhe nam to
nefunguje.   ne·fun·gu·ye

Are you seeing someone else?
Chodíš s někým jiným?   kho·dyeesh s nye·keem yi·neem

He's just a friend.
On je jenom kamarád.   on ye ye·nom kuh·muh·rad

She's just a friend.
Ona je jenom kamarádka.   o·nuh ye ye·nom kuh·muh·rad·kuh

You're just using me for sex.
Jen mně zneužíváš   yen mnye zne·u·zhee·vash
pro sex.   pro seks

I never want to see you again.
Už tě nikdy nechci vidět.   uzh tye nyik·di nekh·tsi vi·dyet

We'll work it out.
Vyřešíme to.   vi·rzhe·shee·me to

leaving

I have to leave (tomorrow).
(Zítra) Odcházím.   (zeet·ruh) od·kha·zeem

I'll keep in touch.
Chci udržovat kontakt.   khtsi u·dr·zho·vuht kon·tuhkt

I'll miss you.
Budeš mi chybět.   bu·desh mye khi·byet

I'll visit you.
Navštívím tě.   nuhf·shtyee·veem tye

beliefs & cultural differences
náboženské víry & kulturní rozdíly

religion

náboženství

Although religion plays little part in urban Czechs' lives (especially in Prague and other major cities), certain rural parts of the country, particularly in the east, are fairly religious.

What's your religion?
Jaká je vaše víra?   yuh·ka ye *vuh*·she vee·ruh

I'm not religious.
Jsem bez vyznání.   ysem bez *viz*·na·nyee

I'm (a) ...	Jsem ...	ysem ...
agnostic	agnostik m	uhg·nos·tik
	agnostička f	uhg·nos·tich·kuh
Buddhist	buddhista m	bud·his·tuh
	buddhistka f	bud·hist·kuh
Catholic	katolík m	kuh·to·leek
	katolička f	kuh·to·lich·kuh
Christian	křesťan m	krzhes·tyuhn
	křesťanka f	krzhes·tyuhn·kuh
Hindu	hind/hindka m/f	hind/*hind*·kuh
Jewish	žid/židovka m/f	zhid/*zhi*·dof·kuh
Muslim	muslim m	mus·lim
	muslimka f	mus·lim·kuh
Protestant	protestant m	pro·tes·tuhnt
	protestantka f	pro·tes·tuhnt·kuh

I believe in ...	Věřím v ...	vye·rzheem f ...
I don't believe in ...	Nevěřím v ...	ne·vye·rzheem f ...
astrology	astrologii	uhs·tro·lo·gi·yi
fate	osud	o·sud
God	Boha	bo·huh

Can I ... here?	Mohu se zde ...?	mo·hu se zde ...
Where can I ...?	Kde se mohu ...?	gde se mo·hu ...
attend a	účastnit	oo·chuhst·nyit
service	bohoslužby	bo·ho·sluzh·bi
attend mass	účastnit mše	oo·chuhst·nyit mshe
pray	modlit	mod·lit

Can I worship here?
Mohu zde uctívat?   mo·hu zde uts·tyee·vuht

Where can I worship?
Kde mohu uctívat?   gde mo·hu uts·tyee·vuht

cultural differences

kulturní rozdíly

Is this a local or national custom?
Je to místní nebo   ye to meest·nyee ne·bo
národní zvyk?   na·rod·nyee zvik

I don't want to offend you.
Nechci vás urazit.   nekh·tsi vas u·ruh·zit

I'm not used to this.
Nejsem na to zvyklí/á. m/f   ney·sem nuh to zvi·klee/a

I'd rather not join in.
Radši se nepřipojím.   ruhd·shi se nep·rzhi·po·yeem

I'll try it.
Zkusím to.   sku·seem to

I'm sorry, it's	Promiňte, je to	pro·min'·te ye to
against my ...	proti ...	pro·tyi ...
beliefs	mojí víře	mo·yee vee·rzhe
religion	mému	mair·mu
	náboženství	na·bo·zhen·stvee

This is ...	Toto je ...	to·to ye ...
different	jiné	yi·nair
fun	legrace	le·gruh·tse
interesting	zajímavé	zuh·yee·muh·vair

When's the gallery/museum open?
V kolik hodin otevírá   f *ko*·lik *ho*·dyin o·te·vee·ra
galerie/muzeum?   *guh*·le·ri·e/*mu*·ze·um

What kind of art are you interested in?
O jaký druh umění   o *yuh*·kee drooh u·mye·nyee
máte zájem?   *ma*·te *za*·yem

What's in the collection?
Co je ve sbírce?   tso ye ve *zbeer*·tse

It's an exhibition of …
To je výstava …   to ye *vees*·tuh·vuh …

What do you think of …?
Co si myslíte o …?   tso si *mis*·lee·te o …

I'm interested in …
Mám zájem o …   mam *zuh*·yem o …

I like the works of …
Mám rád/ráda dílo od … **m/f**   mam rad/*ra*·duh *dyee*·lo od …

It reminds me of …
Připomíná mi to …   *przhi*·po·mee·na mi to …

Art Nouveau a	*secesní*	se·tses·nyee
baroque a	*barokní*	*buh*·rok·nyee
cubist a	*kubistický*	*ku*·bis·tits·kee
Gothic a	*gotický*	*go*·tits·kee
graphic a	*grafický*	*gruh*·fits·kee
impressionist a	*impresionistický*	*im*·pre·si·o·nis·tits·kee
medieval a	*středověký*	*strzhe*·do·vye·kee
modern a	*moderní*	*mo*·der·nyee
performance a	*představení*	*przhed*·stuh·ve·nyee
Renaissance a	*renesanční*	*re*·ne·zuhn·chnyee
rococo a	*rokokový*	*ro*·ko·ko·vee
Romanesque a	*románský*	*ro*·man·skee
Socialist a	*socialistický*	*so*·tsi·uh·lis·tits·kee

architecture	architektura f	uhr·khi·tek·tu·ruh
art	umění n	u·mye·nyee
artwork	umělecké dílo n	u·mye·lets·kair dyee·lo
curator	kustod m	kus·tod
design	vzor m	vzor
etching	lept m	lept
exhibit	exponát m	eks·po·nat
exhibition hall	výstavní hala f	vees·tuhv·nyee huh·luh
installation	instalace f	in·stuh·luh·tse
opening	vernisáž f	ver·nyi·sazh
painter	malíř m	muh·leerzh
painting (artwork)	obraz m	o·bruhz
painting (technique)	malování n	muh·lo·va·nyee
period	období n	ob·do·bee
permanent collection	stálá sbírka f	sta·la sbeer·kuh
print	reprodukce f	re·pro·duk·tse
sculptor	sochař m	so·khuhrzh
sculpture	sochařství n	so·khuhrzh·stvee
statue	socha f	so·khuh
studio	ateliér m	uh·te·li·er
style	sloh m	slokh
technique	metoda f	me·to·duh

SOCIAL

name your castle

Various types of beautiful castles around the Czech Republic are usually called by one of the following two names – *hrad* hruhd, which refers to a medieval defensive structure, or *zámek za·mek*, which is something like a Renaissance or Imperial chateau – a grand manor house.

144

sporting interests

Czechs use both the 'international' names for basketball and volleyball (given in the list below) and the Czech words *košíková* ko·shee·ko·va and *odbíjená* od·bee·ye·na respectively. For more information on the use of the term 'hockey', see the box on page 153.

What sport do you …?	Jaký sport …?	yuh·kee sport …
follow	sledujete	sle·du·ye·te
play	hrajete	hruh·ye·te
I play/do …	Hraji …	hruh·yi …
I follow …	Sleduji …	sle·du·yi …
athletics	atletiku	uht·le·ti·ku
basketball	basketbal	buhs·ket·buhl
football (soccer)	fotbal	fot·buhl
handball	házenou	ha·ze·noh
(ice) hockey	(lední) hokej	(led·nyee) ho·key
karate	karate	kuh·ruh·te
tennis	tenis	te·nis
volleyball	volejbal	vo·ley·buhl
I cycle.	Jezdím na kole.	yez·deem nuh ko·le
I go canoeing.	Jezdím na kánoi.	yez·deem nuh ka·no·i
I go kayaking.	Jezdím na kajaku.	yez·deem nuh kuh·yuh·ku
I run.	Běhám.	bye·ham
I ski.	Lyžuji.	li·zhu·yi
I snowboard.	Snowborduji.	snoh·bor·du·yi
I walk.	Chodím.	kho·dyeem

For more sports, see the **dictionary**.

Do you like (tennis)?
   Máte rád/ráda (tenis)? m/f   *ma*·te rad/*ra*·duh (*te*·nis)

Yes, very much.
   Ano, velmi.   *uh*·no *vel*·mi

Not really.
   Moc ne.   mots ne

I like watching it.
   Rád/Ráda se na to   rad/*ra*·duh se nuh to
   dívám. m/f   *dyee*·vam

Who's your favourite sportsperson?
   Kdo je váš   gdo ye vash
   nejoblíbenější   *ney*·o·blee·be·nyey·shee
   sportovec/sportovkyně? m/f   *spor*·to·vets/*spor*·tof·ki·nye

What's your favourite team?
   Které je vaše   *kte*·rair ye *vuh*·she
   nejoblíbenější   *ney*·o·blee·be·nyey·shee
   mužstvo?   *muzh*·stvo

going to a game

Would you like to go to a game?
   Chcete jít na zápas?   *khtse*·te yeet nuh *za*·puhs

Who are you supporting?
   Komu fandíte?   ko·mu *fuhn*·dyee·te

Who's playing/winning?
   Kdo hraje/vyhrává?   gdo *hruh*·ye/*vi*·hra·va

scoring		
What's the score?	*Kolik je to?*	*ko*·lik ye to
draw/even	*nerozhodně/*	ne·roz·hod·nye/
	remíza	re·mee·zuh
love/nil (zero)	*nula*	*nu*·luh
match-point	*mečbol*	*mech*·bol

What a …!	To je …!	to ye …
goal	gól	gawl
hit	trefa	tre·fuh
kick	střela	strzhe·luh
pass	přihrávka	przhi·hraf·kuh
performance	výkon	vee·kon

That was a … game!	To byl … zápas!	to bil … za·puhs
bad	špatný	shpuht·nee
boring	nudný	nud·nee
great	výborný	vee·bor·nee

playing sport

sportování

Do you want to play?
Chcete hrát?   khtse·te hrat

Can I join in?
Mohu se přidat?   mo·hu se przhi·duht

That would be great.
To je skvělé.   to ye skvye·lair

I can't.
Nemohu.   ne·mo·hu

I have an injury.
Jsem zraněný/á. m/f   ysem zruh·nye·nee/a

Your/My point.
Váš/Můj bod.   vash/mooy bod

Kick/Pass it to me!
Kopni/Přihraj mi to! inf   kop·ni/przhi·hrai mi to

You're a good player.
Jste dobrý hráč.   yste dob·ree hrach

Thanks for the game.
Děkuji za hru.   dye·ku·yi zuh hru

Where's a good place to …?	Kde je dobré místo …?	gde ye *dob*·rair *mees*·to …
fish	*na*	nuh
	rybaření	*ri*·buh·rzhe·nyee
go horse riding	*pro jízdu*	pro *yeez*·du
	na koni	nuh *ko*·nyi
run	*na běhání*	nuh *bye*·ha·nyee
ski	*na lyžování*	nuh *li*·zho·va·nyee

Where's the nearest …?	Kde je nejbližší …?	gde ye *ney*·blizh·shee …
golf course	*golfové*	*gol*·fo·vair
	hřiště	*hrzhish*·tye
gym	*posilovna*	*po*·si·lov·nuh
swimming pool	*bazén*	*buh*·zairn
tennis court	*tenisový kurt*	*te*·ni·so·vee kurt

What's the charge per …?	Kolik stojí …?	*ko*·lik *sto*·yee …
day	*den*	den
game	*hra*	hruh
hour	*hodina*	*ho*·dyi·nuh
visit	*návštěva*	*naf*·shtye·vuh

Can I hire a …?	Mohu si půjčit …?	*mo*·hu si *pooy*·chit …
ball	*míč*	meech
bicycle	*kolo*	*ko*·lo
court	*kurt*	kurt
racquet	*pálku*	*pal*·ku

Do I have to be a member to attend?

Musím být členem	*mus*·eem beet *chle*·nem
abych se mohl/mohla	*uh*·bikh se *mo*·hl/*mo*·hluh
zůčastnit? m/f	*zoo*·chuhst·nyit

Is there a women-only session?

| *Je to někdy vyhrazeno* | ye to *nyek*·di *vi*·hruh·ze·no |
| *jen pro ženy?* | yen pro *zhe*·ni |

Where are the changing rooms?

| *Kde jsou šatny?* | gde ysoh *shuht*·ni |

horse riding

How much is a (one)-hour ride?
*Kolik stojí (jedna)-
hodinová jízda?*

ko·lik *sto*·yee (*yed*·nuh)·
ho·dyi·no·va *yeez*·duh

How long is the ride?
Jak dlouho trvá jízda?

yuhk *dloh*·ho *tr*·va *yeez*·duh

I'm an experienced rider.
*Jsem zkušený/á
jezdec/jezdkyně. m/f*

ysem *sku*·she·nee/a
yez·dets/*yezd*·ki·nye

I'm not an experienced rider.
*Jsem nezkušený/á
jezdec/jezdkyně. m/f*

ysem *ne*·sku·she·nee/a
yez·dets/*yezd*·ki·nye

Can I rent a hat and boots?
*Mohu si půjčit čepici
a boty?*

mo·hu si *pooy*·chit *che*·pi·tsi
uh *bo*·ti

bit	*udidlo* n	*u*·dyi·dlo
bridle	*uzda* f	*uz*·duh
canter v	*lehce cválat*	*lekh*·tse *tsva*·luht
crop n	*bičík* m	*bi*·cheek
gallop v	*cválat*	*tsva*·luht
gelding	*valach* m	*vuh*·luhkh
groom v	*hřebelcovat*	*hrzhe*·bel·tso·vuht
horse	*kůň* m	koon'
pony	*poník* m	*po*·nyeek
reins	*otěže* f pl	*o*·tye·zhe
saddle	*sedlo* n	*sed*·lo
stable	*stáj* m	stai
stallion	*hřebec* m	*hrzhe*·bets
stirrup	*třmen* m	*trzh*·men
trot v	*klusat*	*klu*·suht
walk v	*chodit*	*kho*·dyit

skiing

I'd like to	Chtěl/Chtěla bych	khtyel/khtye·luh bikh
hire (a) ...	si půjčit ... m/f	si pooy·chit ...
boots	přeskáče	przhes·ka·che
gloves	rukavice	ru·kuh·vi·tse
goggles	brýle	bree·le
poles	hůlky	hool·ki
skis	lyže	li·zhe
ski suit	lyžařskou	li·zhuhrzh·skoh
	kombinézu	kom·bi·nair·zu

How much is a pass?
Kolik stojí pernamentka?   ko·lik sto·yee per·nuh·ment·kuh

Can I take lessons?
Mohu si vzít lekce   mo·hu si vzeet lek·tse
lyžování?   li·zho·va·nyee

What level is that slope?
Jakou obtížnost má   *yuh·koh ob·tyeezh·nost ma*
tato sjezdovka?   *tuh·to syez·dof·kuh*

Which are the ... slopes?	*Které svahy jsou pro ...?*	*kte·rair svuh·hi ysoh pro ...*
beginner	*začátečníky*	*zuh·cha·tech·nyee·ki*
intermediate	*pokročilé*	*po·kro·chi·lair*
advanced	*dobré lyžaře*	*dob·rair li·zha·rzhe*

What are the conditions like ...?	*Jaké jsou lyžařské podmínky ...?*	*yuh·kair ysoh li·zharzh·skair pod·meen·ki ...*
at (Špindlerův Mlýn)	*ve (Špindlerově Mlýně)*	*ve (shpind·le·ro·vye mlee·nye)*
higher up	*výš*	*veesh*
on that run	*na této sjezdovce*	*nuh tair·to syez·dov·tse*

Is it possible to go ...?	*Je zde možné ...?*	*ye zde mozh·nair ...*
Alpine skiing	*sjezdové lyžování*	*syez·do·vair li·zho·va·nyee*
cross-country skiing	*lyžovat na běžkách*	*li·zho·vuht nuh byezh·kakh*
snowboarding	*snowbordovat*	*snoh·bor·do·vuht*
tobogganing	*sáňkovat*	*san'·ko·vuht*

cable car	*lanovka* f	*luh·nof·kuh*
chairlift	*sedačková lanovka* f	*se·duch·ko·va luh·nof·kuh*
instructor	*instruktor* m	*in·struk·tor*
resort	*lyžařské středisko* n	*li·zharzh·skair strzhe·dyis·ko*
ski lift	*lyžařský vlek* m	*li·zharzh·skee vlek*
sled	*sáně* f	*sa·nye*

soccer/football

Who plays for (Slavia)?
Kdo hraje za (Slavii)?   gdo *hruh*·ye zuh (*sluh*·vi·yi)

He's a great (player).
Je výborný (hráč).   ye *vee*·bor·nee (hrach)

He played brilliantly in the match against (Italy).
Hrál brilantně v zápase   hral *bri*·luhnt·nye v *za*·puh·se
proti (Itálii).   *pro*·tyi (*i*·ta·li·yi)

Which team is at the top of the league?
Které mužstvo je   *kte*·rair muzh·stvo ye
první v lize?   *prv*·nyee v *li*·ze

What a great/terrible team!
To je výborné/hrozné   to ye *vee*·bor·nair/*hroz*·nair
mužstvo!   muzh·stvo

ball	*míč* m	meech
coach	*trenér* m	*tre*·nair
corner (kick)	*rohový kop* m	*ro*·ho·vee kop
expulsion	*vyloučení* n	*vi*·loh·che·nyee
fan	*fanoušek* m	*fuh*·noh·shek
foul n	*faul* m	fowl
free kick	*volný kop* m	*vol*·nee kop
goal (structure)	*branka* f	*bruhn*·kuh
goalkeeper	*brankář* m	*bruhn*·karzh
manager	*manažer* m	*muh*·nuh·zher
offside	*ofsajd* m	*of*·said
penalty	*penalta* f	*pe*·nuhl·tuh
player	*hráč* m	hrach
red card	*červená karta* f	*cher*·ve·na *kuhr*·tuh
referee	*rozhodčí* m	*roz*·hod·chee
striker	*útočník* m	*oo*·toch·nyeek
throw in v	*vhazovat míč*	*vhuh*·zo·vuht meech
yellow card	*žlutá karta* f	*zhlu*·ta *kuhr*·tuh

Off to see a match? Check out **going to a game**, page 146.

The ice hockey tradition among Czechs goes back to the start of the 20th century. These days they boast one of the world's best national teams, with 17 European titles, 11 world titles and one Olympic Games title in their possession. The Czech ice hockey season runs from September to April.

Just like Canadians and Americans, Czechs refer to ice hockey as simply 'hockey' (*hokej ho*·key), but you can also use the more specific phrase *lední hokej led*·nyee *ho*·key (ice hockey). If they talk about field hockey, they use the term *pozemní hokej po*·zem·nyee *ho*·key. Here's some more hockey terminology:

blue-line offside	*postavení*	*pos*·tuh·ve·nyee
	mimo hru na	*mi*·mo hru nuh
	modré čáře n	*mo*·drair *cha*·rzhe
defender	*obránce* m	*o*·bran·tse
dropping the puck	*vhazování* n	*vhuh*·zo·va·nyee
forward	*útočník* m	*oo*·toch·nyeek
hockey stick	*hokejka* f	*ho*·key·kuh
penalty	*vyloučení* n	*vi*·loh·che·nyee
puck	*puk* m	puk
red-line offside	*zakázané*	*zuh*·ka·zuh·nair
	uvolnění n	*u*·vol·nye·nyee

tennis & table tennis

tenis & stolní tenis

I'd like to …	*Chtěl/Chtěla*	khtyel/*khtye*·luh
	bych si … m/f	bikh si …
book a time to play	*rezervovat hodinu*	*re*·zer·vo·vuht *ho*·dyi·nu
play (table) tennis	*zahrát (stolní) tenis*	*zuh*·hrat (*stol*·nyee) *te*·nis

Can we play at night?
   Můžem hrát v noci?   *moo·zhem hrat v no·tsi*

I need my racquet restrung.
   Potřebuji vyplést   *pot·rzhe·bu·yi vi·plairst*
   moji raketu.   *mo·yi ruh·ke·tu*

ace	*eso* n	*e·so*
advantage	*výhoda* f	*vee·ho·duh*
bat (table tennis)	*pálka* f	*pal·kuh*
clay	*antuka* f	*uhn·tu·kuh*
fault	*chybné podání* n	*khib·nair po·da·nyee*
game, set, match	*hra, sada,*	*hruh suh·duh*
	zápas	*za·puhs*
grass	*tráva* f	*tra·vuh*
hard court	*tvrdý dvorec* m	*tvr·dee dvo·rets*
net	*síť* f	*seet'*
ping-pong ball	*ping-pongový*	*ping·pon·go·vee*
	míček m	*mee·chek*
play doubles v	*hrát čtyřhru*	*hrat chtirzh·hru*
racquet	*raketa* f	*ruh·ke·tuh*
serve n	*podání* n	*po·da·nyee*
serve v	*podávat*	*po·da·vuht*
set	*sada* f	*suh·duh*
tennis ball	*tenisový míč* m	*te·ni·so·vee meech*
table-tennis	*ping-pongový*	*ping·pon·go·vee*
table	*stůl* m	*stool*

hiking

turistika

Where can I ...?	*Kde mohu ...?*	gde mo·hu ...
buy supplies	*koupit zásoby*	koh·pit za·so·bi
find someone	*najít někoho,*	nuh·yeet nye·ko·ho
who knows	*kdo zná tuto*	gdo zna tu·to
the area	*oblast*	o·bluhst
get a map	*dostat mapu*	dos·tuht muh·pu
hire hiking	*půjčit horskou*	pooy·chit hors·koh
gear	*výbavu*	vee·buh·vu

Do we need a guide?
Potřebujeme průvodce?
pot·rzhe·bu·ye·me *proo*·vod·tse

Are there guided treks?
Jsou túry s průvodcem?
ysoh *too*·ri s *proo*·vod·tsem

Is it safe?
Je to bezpečné?
ye to *bez*·pech·nair

Is there a hut?
Je tam chata?
ye tuhm *khuh*·tuh

When does it get dark?
V kolik se stmívá?
f *ko*·lik se stmee·va

How high is the climb?
Jaké je převýšení výstupu?
yuh·kair ye *przhe*·vee·she·nyee vees·tu·pu

How long is the trail?
Jak dlouhá je stezka?
yuhk *dloh*·ha ye stez·kuh

Do we need to take ...?	Musíme si vzít ...?	*mu*·see·me si vzeet ...
bedding	ložní prádlo	*lozh*·nyee *prad*·lo
food	jídlo	*yeed*·lo
water	vodu	*vo*·du

Is the track ...?	Je stezka ...?	ye *stez*·kuh ...
(well-)marked	(dobře) značená	(*dob*·rzhe) *znuh*·che·na
open	otevřená	o·*tev*·rzhe·na
scenic	malebná	*muh*·leb·na

Which is the ... route?	Která trasa je ...?	*kte*·ra *truh*·suh ye ...
easiest	nejlehčí	*ney*·leh·chee
most interesting	nejzajímavější	*ney*·za·yee·muh·vyey·shee
shortest	nejkratší	*ney*·kruht·shee

Where can I find the ...?	Kde mohu najít ... ?	gde *mo*·hu nuh·yeet ...
camping ground	stanový tábor	*stuh*·no·vee *ta*·bor
nearest	nejbližší	*ney*·blizh·shee
village	vesnici	*ves*·nyi·tsi
showers	sprchy	*spr*·khi
toilets	toalety	*to*·uh·le·ti

Where have you come from?
Odkud jste přišli?   *od*·kud yste *przhi*·shli

How long did it take?
Jak to dlouho trvalo?   yuhk to *dloh*·ho *tr*·vuh·lo

Does this path go to (Labská Bouda)?
Vede tato stezka k (Labské Boudě)?   *ve*·de *tuh*·to *stez*·kuh k (*luhp*·skair *boh*·dye)

Can I go through here?
Mohu zde projít?   *mo*·hu zde *pro*·yeet

Is the water OK to drink?
Je ta voda pitná?   ye tuh *vo*·duh *pit*·na

weather

počasí

What's the weather like?
Jaké je počasí?   yuh·kair ye po·chuh·see

What will the weather be like tomorrow?
Jaké bude zítra počasí?   yuh·kair bu·de zee·truh po·chuh·see

It's ...
cloudy	*Je zataženo.*	ye zuh·tuh·zhe·no
cold	*Je chladno.*	ye khluhd·no
fine	*Je krásně.*	ye kras·nye
freezing	*Mrzne.*	mrz·ne
hot	*Je horko.*	ye hor·ko
raining	*Prší.*	pr·shee
snowing	*Sněží.*	snye·zhee
sunny	*Je slunečno.*	ye slu·nech·no
warm	*Je teplo.*	ye tep·lo
windy	*Je větrno.*	ye vye·tr·no

Where can I buy a/an ...?	*Kde mohu koupit ...?*	gde mo·hu koh·pit ...
rain jacket	*pláštěnku*	plash·tyen·ku
umbrella	*deštník*	desht·nyeek

flora & fauna

flóra & fauna

What ... is that?	*Co je to za ...?*	tso ye to zuh ...
animal	*zvíře*	zvee·rzhe
flower	*květinu*	kvye·tyi·nu
plant	*rostlinu*	rost·li·nu
tree	*strom*	strom

What's it used for?
Na co se to používá? nuh tso se to *po*·u·zhee·va

Can you eat the fruit?
Může se toto ovoce jíst? moo·zhe se *to*·to *o*·vo·tse yeest

Is it …?	Je to … ?	ye to …
common	*obecný*	o·bets·nee
dangerous	*nebezpečný*	ne·bez·pech·nee
endangered	*ohrožený*	o·hro·zhe·nee
poisonous	*jedovatý*	ye·do·vuh·tee
protected	*chráněný*	khra·nye·nee

local animals & plants

adder	*zmije* f	*zmi*·ye
badger	*jezevec* m	ye·ze·vets
bear	*medvěd* m	med·vyed
deer	*jelen* m	ye·len
duck	*kachna* f	kuhkh·nuh
eagle	*orel* m	o·rel
lynx	*rys* m	ris
marmot	*svišť* m	svisht'
marten	*kuna* f	ku·nuh
mink	*norek* m	no·rek
otter	*vydra* f	vid·ruh
pheasant	*bažant* m	buh·zhuhnt
roe deer	*srnka* f	srn·kuh
wolf	*vlk* m	vlk
beech	*buk* m	buk
birch	*bříza* f	brzhee·zuh
linden	*lípa* f	lee·puh
oak	*dub* m	dub
spruce	*smrk* m	smrk

For geographical and agricultural terms, and more names of animals and plants, see the **dictionary**.

SOCIAL

basics

breakfast	*snídaně* f	snee·duh·nye
lunch	*oběd* m	o·byed
dinner	*večeře* f	ve·che·rzhe
snack	*občerstvení* n	ob·cherst·ve·nyee
eat v	*jíst*	yeest
drink v	*pít*	peet
I'd like ...	*Chtěl/Chtěla*	khtyel/khtye·luh
	bych ... m/f	bikh ...
I'm starving!	*Jsem*	ysem
	vyhladovělý/á. m/f	vi·hluh·do·vye·lee/a

food glorious food

A Czech breakfast typically consists of a cup of tea or coffee followed by bread or bread rolls with ham, salami, cheese or jam. However, cereals or muesli have also become popular.

No Czech would start lunch without having soup first – for example *dršťková polévka* drsht'·ko·va po·lairf·kuh (tripe soup) or *česnečková polévka* ches·nech·ko·va po·lairf·kuh (garlic soup). This is generally followed by delicacies such as *knedlo* kned·lo (bread dumplings), *zelo* ze·lo (sauerkraut) and *vepřo* vep·rzho (roasted pork).

Most families have dinner at home – usually bread or bread rolls with various types of cold sausage meats, fish or cheese. If they're going to a restaurant or a pub, dinner can mean anything from grilled meats and fish to pasta, pizzas or salads.

Last but not least, open sandwiches (*obložené chlebíčky* o·blo·zhe·nair khle·beech·ki) are a popular snack. There's a wide variety of toppings for these, such as mayonnaise-based salads with vegetables, sausage meats or fish salads.

eating out

finding a place to eat

Can you recommend a ...?	Můžete doporučit ...?	moo·zhe·te do·po·ru·chit ...
café	kavárnu	kuh·var·nu
pub	hospodu	hos·po·du
restaurant	restauraci	res·tow·ruh·tsi
Where would you go for ...?	Kam byste doporučil/ doporučila jít na ...? m/f	kuhm bis·te do·po·ru·chil/ do·po·ru·chi·luh yeet nuh ...
a celebration	oslavu	os·luh·vu
a cheap meal	laciné jídlo	luh·tsi·nair yeed·lo
local specialities	místní speciality	meest·nyee spe·tsi·a·li·ti
I'd like to reserve a table for ...	Chtěl/Chtěla bych rezervovat stůl ... m/f	khtyel/khtye·luh bikh re·zer·vo·vuht stool ...
(two) people	pro (dvě) osoby	pro (dvye) o·so·bi
(eight) o'clock	na (osmou) hodinu	nuh (os·moh) ho·dyi·nu

czech eateries

bageteria f *buh·ge·te·ri·yuh*
sells mainly baguette-style sandwiches

bufet m *bu·fet*
mostly stand-up cheap eatery which serves hot and cold
food, alcoholic and nonalcoholic drinks

jídelna f *yee·del·nuh*
basic and cheap eatery offering hot and cold food,
alcoholic and nonalcoholic drinks

lahůdky f pl *luh·hood·ki*
sells open-bread and other sandwiches, sweets and drinks

FOOD

Are you still serving food?
    Podáváte ještě jídlo?   po·da·va·te *yesh*·tye *yeed*·lo

How long is the wait?
    Jak dlouho budu čekat?   yuhk *dloh*·ho bu·du *che*·kuht

listen for ...		
Máme zavřeno.	*ma*·me *zuhv*·rzhe·no	We're closed.
Máme plno.	*ma*·me *pl*·no	We're full.
Moment.	*mo*·ment	One moment.

at the restaurant

v restauraci

Before Czechs start eating, they say *Dobrou chuť!* do·broh khuť
(Bon appétit!), and before having a drink they toast with *Na
zdraví!* nuh *zdrah*·vee (Cheers!). When making a toast, always
look into the other person's eyes.

What would you recommend?
    Co byste doporučil/   tso *bis*·te do·po·ru·chil/
    doporučila? **m/f**   do·po·ru·chi·luh

What's in that dish?
    Co je v tom pokrmu?   tso ye f tom *po*·kr·mu

What's that called?
    Jak se toto jmenuje?   yuhk se *to*·to *yme*·nu·ye

I'll have that.
    Dám si tohle.   dam si *to*·hle

Does it take long to prepare?
    Jak dlouho to trvá   yuhk *dloh*·ho to *tr*·va
    připravit?   *przhi*·pruh·vit

Is it self-serve?
    Obsloužíme se samy?   ob·sloh·zhee·me se *sa*·mi

Is service included in the bill?
    Je to včetně obsluhy?   ye to *vchet*·nye *op*·slu·hi

eating out

Kam si chcete sednout? kuhm si *khtse*·te *sed*·noht	**Where would you like to sit?**
Co vám mohu přinést? tso vam *mo*·hu *przhi*·nairst	**What can I get for you?**
Tady to máte! *tuh*·di to *ma*·te	**Here you go!**
Nechte si chutnat. *nekh*·te si *khut*·nuht	**Enjoy your meal.**
Přejete si …? *przhe*·ye·te si …	**Do you like …?**
Mohu doporučit … *mo*·hu *do*·po·ru·chit …	**I suggest the …**
Jak byste to chtěl/chtěla uvařit? m/f yuhk *bis*·te to khtyel/ *khtye*·luh *u*·vuh·rzhit	**How would you like that cooked?**

Is there a cover/service charge?
Účtujete couvert/   *ooch*·tu·ye·te *ku*·vert/
přirážku za obsluhu?   *przhi*·razh·ku zuh *op*·slu·hu

Are these complimentary?
Je toto zdarma?   ye *to*·to *zduhr*·muh

Could I please see the wine list?
Můžete mi dát   *moo*·zhe·te mi dat
vinný lístek?   *vi*·nee *lees*·tek

Can you recommend a good local wine?
Můžete mi doporučit   *moo*·zhe·te mi *do*·po·ru·chit
dobré místní víno?   *do*·brair *meest*·nyee *vee*·no

I'd like (a/the) …, please.	*Chtěl/Chtěla bych …, prosím.* m/f	khtyel/*khtye*·luh bikh … *pro*·seem
children's menu	*dětský jídelníček*	*dyets*·kee yee·del·nyee·chek
drink list	*nápojový lístek*	na·po·yo·vee lees·tek
half portion	*poloviční porci*	po·lo·vich·nyee por·tsi
local speciality	*místní specialitu*	meest·nyee spe·tsi·uh·li·tu
meal fit for a king	*královskou hostinu*	kra·lovs·koh hos·tyi·nu
menu (in English)	*jídelníček (v angličtině)*	yee·del·nyee·chek (f uhn·glich·tyi·nye)
nonsmoking section	*nekuřáckou místnost*	ne·ku·rzhats·koh meest·nost
smoking section	*kuřáckou místnost*	ku·rzhats·koh meest·nost
table for (five)	*stůl pro (pět)*	stool pro (pyet)
that dish	*ten pokrm*	ten po·krm

on the menu

The main courses on the menu in inexpensive or ordinary restaurants serving Czech food are often divided into two sections.

Hotová jídla ho·to·va *yeed*·luh (ready-to-serve dishes) are precooked in the morning and served from 11am until sold out that day. *Jídla na objednávku yeed*·luh nuh o·byed·naf·ku (à la carte dishes) are cooked to order – for example, various meats, steaks and fish.

You might also come across the phrase *Bez masá jídla bez* muh·sa *yeed*·luh (dishes without meat). Beware – contrary to what the phrase suggests, these aren't always vegetarian dishes. Some of them may include bacon or are cooked in animal fat, such as *knedlíky s vejci kned*·lee·ki s *vey*·tsi (fried dumplings with eggs) or *omeleta se sýrem a bramborem* o·me·le·tuh se *see*·rem uh *bruhm*·bo·rem (omelette with cheese and potato).

eating out

163

I'd like it with …	Chtěl/Chtěla bych to … m/f	khtyel/*khtye*·luh bikh to …
cheese	se sýrem	se *see*·rem
chilli	s pfeferonkou	s fe·fe·ron·koh
chilli sauce	s pfeferonkovou omáčkou	s fe·fe·ron·ko·voh o·mach·koh
garlic	s česnekem	s ches·ne·kem
ketchup	s kečupem	s ke·chu·pem
nuts	s ořechy	s o·rzhe·khi
oil	s olejem	s o·le·yem
pepper	s pepřem	s pep·rzhem
salt	se solí	se so·lee
tomato sauce	s rajskou omáčkou	s rais·koh o·mach·koh
vinegar	s octem	s ots·tem

I'd like it without …	Chtěl/Chtěla bych to bez … m/f	khtyel/*khtye*·luh bikh to bez …
cheese	sýru	*see*·ru
chilli	pfeferonky	fe·fe·ron·ki
chilli sauce	pfeferonkové omáčky	fe·fe·ron·ko·vair o·mach·ki
garlic	česneku	ches·ne·ku
ketchup	kečupu	ke·chu·pu
nuts	ořechů	o·rzhe·khoo
oil	oleje	o·le·ye
pepper	pepře	pep·rzhe
salt	sole	so·le
tomato sauce	rajské omáčky	rais·kair o·mach·ki
vinegar	octu	ots·tu

For other specific meal requests, see **vegetarian & special meals**, page 177.

Chuťovky	chu·tyof·ki	Appetisers
Polévky	po·lairf·ki	Soups
Studené předkrmy	stu·de·nair przhed·kr·mi	Cold Entrees
Teplé předkrmy	te·plair przhed·kr·mi	Warm Entrees
Saláty	suh·la·ti	Salads
Hlavní jídla	hluhv·nyee yeed·luh	Main Courses
Přílohy	przhee·lo·hi	Side Dishes
Moučníky	mohch·nyee·ki	Desserts
Aperitivy	uh·pe·ri·ti·vi	Apéritifs
Nápoje	na·po·ye	Drinks
Nealkoholické nápoje	ne·uhl·ko·ho·lits·kair na·po·ye	Soft Drinks
Lihoviny	li·ho·vi·ni	Spirits
Piva	pi·vuh	Beers
Šumivá vína	shu·mi·va vee·nuh	Sparkling Wines
Bílá vína	bee·la vee·na	White Wines
Červená vína	cher·ve·na vee·nuh	Red Wines
Dezertní vína	de·zert·nyee vee·nuh	Dessert Wines
Zažívací likéry	zuh·zhee·vuh·tsee li·kair·ri	Digestifs

For additional items, see the **menu decoder**, page 179.

at the table

u stolu

Please bring a/the ...	*Prosím přineste ...*	pro·seem przhi·nes·te ...
bill	*účet*	oo·chet
cutlery	*příbor*	przhee·bor
(wine)glass	*skleničku (na víno)*	skle·nyich·ku (nuh vee·no)
serviette	*ubrousek*	u·broh·sek
tablecloth	*ubrus*	u·brus

I didn't order this.
 *Toto jsem si neobjednal/
 neobjednala.* m/f

*to·to ysem si ne·ob·yed·nuhl/
ne·ob·yed·nuh·la*

There's a mistake in the bill.
 Na účtu je chyba.

nuh ooch·tu ye khi·buh

talking food

I love this dish.
 Mám rád/ráda toto jídlo. m/f

mam rad/*ra*·duh *to*·to *yeed*·lo

I love the local cuisine.
 *Mám rád/ráda místní
 kuchyň.* m/f

mam rad/*ra*·duh
ku·khin'

That was delicious!
 To bylo lahodné!

to *bi*·lo *luh*·hod·nair

My compliments to the chef.
 Poklonu šéfkuchaři.

pok·lo·nu *shairf*·ku·khuh·rzhi

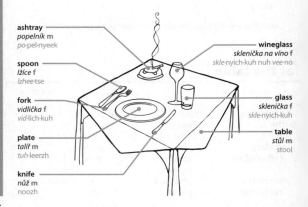

ashtray
popelník m
po·pel·nyeek

spoon
lžíce f
lzhee·tse

fork
vidlička f
vid·lich·kuh

plate
talíř m
tuh·leerzh

knife
nůž m
noozh

wineglass
sklenička na víno f
skle·nyich·kuh nuh *vee*·no

glass
sklenička f
skle·nyich·kuh

table
stůl m
stool

I'm full.	Jsem najedený/á. m/f	ysem nuh·ye·de·nee/a
This is ...	Toto je ...	to·to ye ...
burnt	spálené	spa·le·nair
(too) cold	(moc) studené	(mots) stu·de·nair
(too) spicy	(moc) pálivé	(mots) pa·li·vair
stale	okoralé	o·ko·ruh·lair
superb	výtečné	vee·tech·nair

methods of preparation

I'd like it ...	Chtěl/Chtěla bych ... m/f	khtyel/khtye·luh bikh ...
I don't want it ...	Nechtěl/Nechtěla bych ... m/f	nekh·tyel/nekh·tye·luh bikh ...
boiled	vařené	vuh·rzhe·nair
broiled	grilovaný	gri·lo·vuh·nee
deep-fried	fritovaný	fri·to·vuh·nee
fried	smažený	smuh·zhe·nee
grilled	grilovaný	gri·lo·vuh·nee
mashed	rozmačkané	roz·muhch·ka·nair
medium	středně	strzhed·nye
	propečený	pro·pe·che·nee
rare	krvavý	kr·vuh·vee
reheated	ohřátý	o·hrzha·tee
steamed	dušený	du·she·nee
well-done	propečený	pro·pe·che·nee
without ...	bez ...	bez ...
with the dressing on the side	nálev jako přílohu	na·lev yuh·ko przhee·lo·hu

bramborová placka f	*bruhm·bo·ro·va pluhts·kuh*	potato cake
hamburger m	*huhm·bur·ger*	hamburger
hranolky m	*hruh·nol·ki*	chips
klobása f	*klo·ba·suh*	sausage
párek v rohlíku m	*pa·rek v ro·hlee·ku*	hot dog
smažák m	*smuh·zhak*	fried cheese
smažený sýr m	*smuh·zhe·nee seer*	fried cheese
zmrzlina f	*zmr·zli·nuh*	ice cream

nonalcoholic drinks

nealkoholické nápoje

(cup of) coffee ...	*(šálek) kávy ...*	*(sha·lek) ka·vi ...*
(cup of) tea ...	*(šálek) čaje ...*	*(sha·lek) chuh·ye ...*
with (milk)	*s (mlékem)*	*s (mlair·kem)*
without (sugar)	*bez (cukru)*	*bez (tsu·kru)*
... mineral water	*... minerální voda*	*... mi·ne·ral·nyee vo·duh*
sparkling	*perlivá*	*per·li·va*
still	*neperlivá*	*ne·per·li·va*
(hot) water	*(horká) voda* f	*(hor·ka) vo·duh*
orange juice	*pomerančový džus* m	*po·me·ruhn·cho·vee dzhus*
soft drink	*nealkoholický nápoj* m	*ne·uhl·ko·ho·lits·kee na·poy*

black	*černá*	*cher·na*
iced	*ledová*	*le·do·va*
strong	*silná*	*sil·na*
weak	*slabá*	*sluh·ba*
white	*bílá*	*bee·la*

alcoholic drinks

beer	pivo n	pi·vo
brandy	brandy f	bruh·di
champagne	šampaňské n	shuhm·puhn'·skair
cocktail	koktejl m	kok·teyl

a shot of …	panák …	puh·nak …
gin	ginu	dzhi·nu
rum	rumu	ru·mu
tequila	tequily	te·ki·li
vodka	vodky	vod·ki
whisky	whisky	vis·ki

a bottle/glass	láhev/skleničku	la·hef/skle·nyich·ku
of … wine	… vína	… vee·nuh
dessert	dezertního	de·zert·nyee·ho
red	červeného	cher·ve·nair·ho
rosé	růžového	roo·zho·vair·ho
sparkling	šumivého	shu·mi·vair·ho
white	bílého	bee·lair·ho

a … of beer	… piva	… pi·vuh
glass	sklenička	skle·nyich·kuh
jug	džbán	dzhban
large bottle	velká láhev	vel·ka la·hef
small bottle	malá láhev	muh·la la·hef

how much beer can you drink?

There's no equivalent to a pint in Czech, as metric units are used, not imperial. People don't ask for a glass of beer either: just ask for *pivo* pi·vo (a beer) and you'll get a half-litre glass or mug of the amber liquid. If you're not such a big drinker and want to order less than this, ask for *malé pivo* muh·lair pi·vo and you'll get a small glass (roughly 300ml). Among Czech beer drinkers, it's a no-no to pour the remainder of beer from the old glass into a fresh glass of beer.

absinth m	*uhb*·sint	absinthe
Becherovka f	*be*·khe·rof·kuh	herb schnapps
borovička f	*bo*·ro·vich·kuh	juniper berry liquor
griotka f	*gri*·ot·kuh	cherry liqueur
meruňkovice f	me·run'·ko·vi·tse	apricot liquor
slivovice f	*sli*·vo·vi·tse	plum brandy

For additional items, see the **menu decoder**, page 179, and the **dictionary**.

in the bar

v baru

In a bar or pub, before you take a seat ask *Je tu volno?* ye tu *vol*·no (Is the seat free?). Normally, you don't pay straight away for drinks – a tab is run for you on a slip of paper placed on the table next to your drink. The tipping is the same as in a restaurant – the final sum is rounded up to the next whole number to about 5 to 10%.

Excuse me!
Promiňte! pro·min'·te

I'm next.
Teď jsem na řadě já. ted' ysem nuh rzhuh·dye ya

I'll have a (Becherovka).
Dám si (Becherovku). dam si (be·khe·rof·ku)

Same again, please.
To samé, prosím. to suh·mair pro·seem

No ice, thanks.
Bez ledu, děkuji. bez le·du dye·ku·yi

I'll buy you a drink.
Zvu vás na sklenku. zvu vas nuh sklen·ku

What would you like?
Co byste si přál/přála? m/f tso bis·te si przhal/przha·la

I don't drink alcohol.
   Nepiji alkohol.   ne·pi·yi *uhl*·ko·hol

It's my round.
   To je moje runda.   to ye *mo*·ye *run*·duh

How much is that?
   Kolik to stojí?   *ko*·lik to *sto*·yee

Do you serve meals here?
   Podáváte zde jídlo?   po·da·va·te zde *yeed*·lo

drinking up

In the Czech Republic, you can go for a drink at either a *pivnice* piv·ni·tse (a pub or beer hall that doesn't serve food), or a *vinárna* vi·nar·nuh (a wine bar). If you want something to take away, note that all food shops and supermarkets sell alcohol. There's also a store which sells only wine – *vinotéka* vi·no·tair·kuh.

Cheers!
   Na zdraví!   nuh *zdruh*·vee

This is hitting the spot.
   To mi bodlo.   to mi *bod*·lo

I feel fantastic!
   Cítím se fantasticky!   *tsee*·tyeem se *fuhn*·tuhs·tits·ki

listen for ...

Co si dáte?	
tso si *da*·te	**What are you having?**
Myslím že jste měl/měla dost. m/f	
mis·leem zhe yste	**I think you've had enough.**
myel/*mye*·luh dost	
Poslední objednávky.	
pos·led·nyee ob·yed·naf·ki	**Last orders.**

I think I've had one too many.
Myslím si, že mám dost.   mis·leem si zhe mam dost

I'm feeling drunk.
Cítím se opilý/á. m/f   tsee·tyeem se o·pi·lee/a

I feel ill.
Je mi zle.   ye mi zle

Where's the toilet?
Kde je toaleta?   gde ye to·uh·le·tuh

I'm tired, I'd better go home.
Jsem unavený/á,   ysem u·nuh·ve·nee/a
měl/měla bych jít   myel/mye·luh bikh yeet
domů. m/f   do·moo

Can you call a taxi for me?
Můžete mi zavolat   moo·zhe·te mi zuh·vo·luht
taxi?   tuhk·si

I don't think you should drive.
Myslím, že byste neměl/   mis·leem zhe bis·te ne·myel/
neměla řídit. m/f   ne·mye·luh rzhee·dyit

all about you

In Czech, there are two forms of the singular 'you', the informal *ty* ti and the polite *vy* vi. They're often omitted though,
because the verb endings (singular and plural respectively)
already indicate which form is intended.

Czechs address their friends, family and children with the
informal *ty*, while strangers, older people and people in
authority are always addressed with the formal *vy*. It's very
important to use *vy* with a stranger, as the use of *ty* is con-
sidered rude and disrespectful.

Czechs will generally offer to use the familiar instead of
the respectful form of speech by saying something like
Můžeme si tykat moo·zhe·me si ti·kuht (We can use the informal speech). Throughout this phrasebook, the polite form
has normally been used unless marked otherwise.

FOOD

buying food

What's the local speciality?
Co je místní specialita?   tso ye *meest*·nyee *spe*·tsi·uh·li·tuh

What's that?
Co to je?   tso to ye

Can I taste it?
Mohu to ochutnat?   *mo*·hu to o·khut·nuht

Can I have a bag, please?
Můžete mi dát   moo·zhe·te mi dat
tašku, prosím?   *tuhsh*·ku *pro*·seem

I don't need a bag, thanks.
Nepotřebuji tašku,   ne·pot·rzhe·bu·yi *tuhsh*·ku
děkuji.   *dye*·ku·yi

How much is (500 grams of cheese)?
Kolik stojí (padesát   ko·lik *sto*·yee (*puh*·de·sat
deka sýra)?   de·kuh *see*·ruh)

---

underweight

When you go food shopping in the Czech Republic, you'll notice that prices are calculated according to weight. However, Czechs use decagrams (*deka de*·kuh), not grams, for food – for example, 100 grams equals 10 decagrams, or *deset deka de*·set *de*·kuh in Czech.

I'd like …	Chtěl/Chtěla bych … m/f	khtyel/khtye·luh bikh …
200 grams	dvacet deka	dvuh·tset de·kuh
half a dozen	půl tuctu	pool tuts·tu
a dozen	tucet	tu·tset
half a kilo	půl kila	pool ki·luh
a kilo	kilo	ki·lo
(two) kilos	(dvě) kila	(dvye) ki·luh
a bottle	láhev	la·hef
a jar	sklenici	skle·nyi·tsi
a packet	sáček	sa·chek
a piece	kus	kus
(three) pieces	(tři) kusy	(trzhi) ku·si
a slice	krajíc	kruh·yeets
(six) slices	(šest)	(shest)
	krajíců	kruh·yee·tsoo
a tin	plechovku	ple·khof·ku
(just) a little	(jen) trochu	(yen) tro·khu
more	více	vee·tse
some	několik	nye·ko·lik
that one	tamten	tuhm·ten
this one	tento	ten·to

food stuff

cooked	uvařený	u·vuh·rzhe·nee
cured	naložený	nuh·lo·zhe·nee
dried	sušený	su·she·nee
fresh	čerstvý	cherst·vee
frozen	mražený	mruh·zhe·nee
raw (uncooked)	syrový	si·ro·vee
raw (unprocessed)	surový	su·ro·vee
smoked	uzený	u·ze·nee

slice it up

The Czech word *krajíc* kruh·yeets (slice) is only used to refer to a slice of bread. A slice of salami or lemon is called *kolečko* ko·lech·ko, and a 'piece of cake' is *kus dortu* kus *dor*·tu.

Less.	Méně.	*mair*·nye
A bit more.	Trochu více.	*tro*·khu *vee*·tse
Enough.	Stačí.	*stuh*·chee
Do you have ...?	Máte ...?	*ma*·te ...
anything	něco	*nye*·tso
cheaper	levnějšího	*lev*·nyey·shee·ho
other kinds	jiné druhy	*yi*·nair *dru*·hi
Where can I find the ... section?	Kde mohu najít regál s ...?	gde *mo*·hu *nuh*·yeet *re*·gal s ...
dairy	mléčnými produkty	*mlairch*·nee·mi *pro*·duk·ti
fish	rybami	*ri*·buh·mi
frozen goods	mraženým zbožím	*mruh*·zhe·neem *zbo*·zheem
fruit and vegetable	ovocem a zeleninou	*o*·vo·tsem uh *ze*·le·nyi·noh
meat	masem	*muh*·sem
poultry	drůbeží	*droo*·be·zhee

For food items, see the **menu decoder**, page 179, and the dictionary.

listen for ...

Mohu vám pomoci? *mo*·hu vam *po*·mo·tsi	Can I help you?
Přejete si něco? *przhe*·ye·te si *nye*·tso	What would you like?
Přejete si ještě něco? *przhe*·ye·te si *yesh*·tye *nye*·tso	Anything else?
Žádný nemáme. *zhad*·nee *ne*·ma·me	There isn't any.

self-catering

cooking utensils

Could I please	Mohu si prosím	mo·hu si pro·seem
borrow a ...?	půjčit ...?	pooy·chit ...
I need a ...	Potřebuji ...	pot·rzhe·bu·yi ...
chopping board	prkýnko	pr·keen·ko
frying pan	pánev	pa·nef
knife	nůž	noozh
saucepan	kastrol	kuhs·trol

For more cooking implements, see the **dictionary**.

---

festival flavour

The festivities that accompany the two main religious holidays in the Czech Republic have a specific local flavour:

Velikonoce   ve·li·ko·no·tse   Easter
In villages, a figure made of sticks and cloth symbolising death is thrown into a river to drown. This ritual, called 'carrying of death' (*vynášení smrti* vi·na·she·nyee smr·tyi), is a symbolic cleansing act at the start of spring. The rite of *pomlázka* pom·las·kuh (lit: rejuvenation), which was originally meant to rid women of evil spirits, is still popular on Easter Monday. Men splash women with water and lightly whip them around the ankles with willow branches. Women give painted eggs (*kraslice* kruh·sli·tse) in return.

Vánoce   va·no·tse   Christmas
One of the most common Christmas rituals is the slicing of the apple. If the core is in the shape of a star (*hvězda* hvyez·duh), the whole family will be present next year, but if it's in the form of a cross (*kříž* krzheezh), there might be a death in the family. Pouring molten lead into a bowl of water is an old way of telling the future for the following year. The shape of a ball (*kulička* ku·lich·kuh) means a long journey, a cylinder (*ovál* o·val) brings friendship, and a jug (*džbán* dzhban) shape indicates a wedding.

FOOD

176

ordering food

Do you have ... food?	Máte ... jídla?	ma·te ... yeed·luh
halal	halal	huh·luhl
kosher	košer	ko·sher
vegetarian	vegetariánská	ve·ge·tuh·ri·ans·ka

I don't eat ...	Nejím ...	ne·yeem ...
butter	máslo	mas·lo
eggs	vejce	vey·tse
fish	ryby	ri·bi
fish stock	rybí vývar	ri·bee vee·vuhr
meat stock	bujón	bu·yawn
oil	olej	o·ley
pork	vepřové	vep·rzho·vair
poultry	drůbež	droo·bezh
red meat	tmavé maso	tmuh·vair muh·so

Is this ...?	Je to ...?	ye to ...
decaffeinated	bez kofeinu	bez ko·fey·nu
free of animal produce	bez zvířecích produktů	bez zvee·rzhe·tseekh pro·duk·too
free-range	z volného výběhu	z vol·nair·ho vee·bye·hu
genetically modified	geneticky modifikované	ge·ne·tits·ki mo·di·fi·ko·va·nair
gluten-free	bez glutenu	bez glu·te·nu
low-fat	nízkotučné	nyees·ko·tuch·nair
low in sugar	s omezeným cukrem	s o·me·ze·neem tsu·krem
organic	organické	or·guh·nits·kair
salt-free	bez soli	bez so·li

special diets & allergies

I'm on a special diet.
Držím speciální dietu. dr·zheem spe·tsi·al·nyee di·ye·tu

I'm a vegan.
Jsem vegan/veganka. m/f ysem ve·guhn/ve·guhn·kuh

I'm a vegetarian.
Jsem vegetarián/ ysem ve·ge·tuh·ri·an/
vegetariánka. m/f ve·ge·tuh·ri·an·ka

Could you prepare a meal without …?
Mohl/Mohla by jste mo·hl/mo·hluh bi yste
připravit jídlo bez …? m/f przhi·pruh·vit yeed·lo bez …

I'm allergic to … Mám alergii na … mam uh·ler·gi·yi nuh …
  dairy mléčné mlair·chnair
   produce výrobky vee·rob·ki
  eggs vejce vey·tse
  gelatine želatinu zhe·luh·ti·nu
  gluten lepek le·pek
  honey med med
  MSG glutaman glu·tuh·muhn
   sodný sod·nee
  nuts ořechy o·rzhe·khi
  peanuts arašídy uh·ruh·shee·di
  seafood plody moře plo·di mo·rzhe
  shellfish korýše a ko·ree·she uh
   měkkýše mye·kee·she

To explain your dietary restrictions with reference to religious
beliefs, see **beliefs & cultural differences**, page 141.

This guide to Czech cuisine is in Czech alphabetical order (shown below). It's designed to help you find your way around Czech menus and markets. Czech nouns have their gender marked as ⓜ masculine, ⓕ feminine or ⓝ neuter. If it's a plural noun, you'll also see pl. Adjectives are given in the masculine form only – for more information on gender, see the **phrasebuilder**, page 20.

alphabet

Aa	Áá	Bb	Cc	Čč	Dd	Ďď	Ee	Éé	Ěě	Ff	Gg	Hh	Ch ch
Ii	Íí	Jj	Kk	Ll	Mm	Nn	Ňň	Oo	Óó	Pp	Qq	Rr	Řř
Ss	Šš	Tt	Ťť	Uu	Úú	Ůů	Vv	Ww	Xx	Yy	Ýý	Zz	Žž

A

absinth ⓜ *uhb*·sint *absinthe*
ananas ⓜ *uh*·nuh·nuhs *pineapple*
angrešt ⓜ *uhn*·gresht *gooseberry*
arašídy pl *uh*·ruh·shee·di *peanuts*
avokádo ⓝ *uh*·vo·ka·do *avocado*

B

baklažán ⓜ *buh*·kluh·zhan
　aubergine (eggplant)
banán ⓜ *buh*·nan *banana*
bažant ⓜ *buh*·zhuhnt *pheasant*
Becherovka ⓕ *be*·khe·rof·kuh
　herb schnapps
bez kofeinu bez *ko*·fey·nu *decaffeinated*
bez ledu bez *le*·du *without ice*
bez masá jídla ⓝ pl bez muh·sa *yeed*·luh
　dishes without meat
biftek ⓜ *bif*·tek *beef steak*
bílá káva ⓕ *bee*·la *ka*·vuh *white coffee*
bílé víno ⓝ *bee*·lair vee·no *white wine*
borovička ⓕ *bo*·ro·vich·kuh
　juniper berry liquor
boršč ⓜ *borshch beetroot soup*
borůvky ⓕ pl *bo*·roof·ki *blueberries*

borůvkové knedlíky ⓜ pl *bo*·roof·ko·vair
　kned·lee·ki *blueberry dumplings*
brambor ⓜ *bruhm*·bor *potato*
bramboračka ⓕ *bruhm*·bo·ruhch·kuh
　thick soup of potatoes & mushrooms
bramborák ⓜ *bruhm*·bo·rak *potato cake*
bramborová kaše ⓕ *bruhm*·bo·ro·va
　kuh·she *mashed potatoes often served
　with diced onions fried in butter*
bramborová placka ⓕ
　bruhm·bo·ro·va *pluhts*·kuh *potato cake*
bramborová polévka ⓕ
　bruhm·bo·ro·va *po*·lairf·kuh *potato soup*
bramborové knedlíky ⓜ pl
　bruhm·bo·ro·vair *kned*·lee·ki
　potato dumplings
bramborový salát ⓜ *bruhm*·bo·ro·vee
　suh·lat *potato salad – mayonnaise-
　based with yogurt, diced potatoes,
　carrots, peas, dill pickles, onions & corn*
brokolice ⓕ *bro*·ko·li·tse *broccoli*
broskev ⓕ *bros*·kef *peach*
bujón ⓜ *bu*·yawn *broth with egg*
burčák ⓜ *bur*·chak *young & sweet wine*
bylinkový čaj ⓜ *bi*·lin·ko·vee chai
　herbal tea

C

celer ⓜ *tse·ler celery*
celozrný chléb ⓜ *tse·lo·zr·nee khlairb*
  wholemeal bread
cereálie ⓕ *tse·re·a·li·ye cereal (breakfast)*
cibulačka ⓕ *tsi·bu·luhch·kuh onion soup*
cibule ⓕ *tsi·bu·le onion*
císařský lusk ⓜ *tsee·suhrzh·skee lusk*
  snow pea
citrón ⓜ *tsi·trawn lemon*
cizrna ⓕ *tsi·zr·nuh chickpea*
cuketa ⓕ *tsu·ke·tuh zucchini (courgette)*
cukr ⓜ *tsu·kr sugar*
cukroví ⓜ pl *tsu·kro·vee sweet biscuits*

Č

čaj ⓜ *chai tea*
čaj s citrónem ⓜ *chai s tsi·traw·nem*
  tea with lemon
čaj s mlékem ⓜ *chai s mlair·kem*
  tea with milk
černá káva ⓕ *cher·na ka·vuh black coffee*
černé pivo ⓝ *cher·nair pi·vo dark beer*
čerstvý *cherst·vee fresh*
červená řepa ⓕ *cher·ve·na rzhe·puh*
  beetroot
červené víno ⓝ *cher·ve·nair vee·no*
  red wine
česnek ⓜ *ches·nek garlic*
česnečková polévka ⓕ
  ches·nech·ko·va po·lairf·kuh garlic soup
čevapčiči ⓝ *che·vuhp·chi·chi*
  fried or grilled minced veal, pork &
  mutton made into cone-like shapes
čočka ⓕ *choch·kuh lentil*
čočková polévka ⓕ
  choch·ko·va po·lairf·kuh lentil soup
čokoláda ⓕ *cho·ko·la·duh chocolate*

D

ďábelská topinka ⓕ
  dya·bel·ska to·pin·kuh
  a piquant toast with meat & cheese
datl ⓜ *duh·tl date*
dezertní víno ⓝ *de·zert·nyee vee·no*
  dessert wine

divoký *dyi·vo·kee wild*
domácí *do·ma·tsee homemade*
dort ⓜ *dort cake*
dortík ⓜ *dor·tyeek tart*
dršťková polévka ⓕ
  drsht'·ko·va po·lairf·kuh spicy tripe soup
dršťky ⓕ *drsht·ki sliced tripe*
dušená mrkev ⓕ *du·she·na mr·kev*
  stewed carrots
dušená roštěnka ⓕ
  du·she·na rosh·tyen·kuh
  braised beef slices in sauce
dušené fazole ⓜ pl *du·she·nair fuh·zo·le*
  stewed beans
dušený *du·she·nee steamed • stewed*
dýně ⓕ *dee·nye pumpkin*
džem ⓜ *dzhem jam*
džin ⓜ *dzhin gin*

F

fazole ⓕ *fuh·zo·le bean*
fazolová polévka ⓕ
  fuh·zo·lo·va po·lairf·kuh bean soup
fazolové klíčky ⓜ pl
  fuh·zo·lo·vair kleech·ki bean sprouts
fazolové lusky ⓜ pl *fuh·zo·lo·vair lus·ki*
  beans
fazolový salát ⓜ *fuh·zo·lo·vee suh·lat*
  bean salad
fík ⓜ *feek fig*
filé ⓝ *fi·lair fillet*
fritovaný *fri·to·vuh·nee deep-fried*

G

grilovaný *gri·lo·vuh·nee broiled • grilled*
  or on the spit
griotka ⓕ *gri·ot·kuh cherry liqueur*
guláš ⓜ *gu·lash thick, spicy stew, usually*
  made with beef & potatoes, sometimes
  with venison or mushrooms
gulášová polévka ⓕ *gu·la·sho·va*
  po·lairf·kuh beef goulash soup

H

hlávkový salát ⓜ *hlaf·ko·vee suh·lat*
  green salad in vinegar • lettuce

hlavní jídla ⓝ pl *hluhv-nyee yeed-luh*
   main courses
hodně vypečený *hod-nye vi-pe-che-nee*
   well-done (of meat)
horký *hor-kee hot*
hořčice ⓕ *horzh-chi-tse mustard*
hotová jídla ⓝ pl *ho-to-va yeed-luh*
   ready-to-serve dishes
houba ⓕ *hoh-buh mushroom*
houbová polévka ⓕ
   hoh-bo-va po-lairf-kuh mushroom soup
houska ⓕ *hohs-kuh oval bread roll*
houskové knedlíky ⓜ pl
   hohs-ko-vair kned-lee-ki bread dumplings
hovězí (maso) ⓝ *ho-vye-zee (muh-so)*
   beef
hovězí guláš ⓜ *ho-vye-zee gu-lash beef*
   stew, sometimes served with dumplings
hovězí vývar s játrovými knedlíčky ⓝ
   ho-vye-zee vee-vuhr s ya-tro-vee-mi
   kned-leech-ki beef broth with little
   dumplings of seasoned liver
hrách ⓜ *hrakh dried peas*
hrachová polévka ⓕ *hra-kho-va*
   po-lairf-kuh thick pea soup with bacon
hrachová polévka s uzeným ⓕ
   hra-kho-va po-lairf-kuh s u-ze-nyeem
   pea soup with smoked pork
hranolky ⓝ pl *hruh-nol-ki French fries*
hrášek ⓜ *hra-shek peas*
hrozny ⓜ pl *hroz-ni grapes*
hruška ⓕ *hrush-kuh pear*
humr ⓜ *hu-mr lobster*
husa ⓕ *hu-suh goose*

Ch

chléb ⓜ *khlairb bread*
chřest ⓜ *khrzhest asparagus*

J

jablečný džus ⓜ *yuh-blech-nee dzhus*
   apple juice
jablečný závin ⓜ *yuh-blech-nee za-vin*
   apple strudel
jablko ⓝ *yuh-bl-ko apple*
jahoda ⓕ *yuh-ho-duh strawberry*
játra ⓝ *yat-ruh liver*

jehněčí (maso) ⓝ *yeh-nye-chee (muh-so)*
   lamb
jelení (maso) ⓝ *ye-le-nyee (muh-so)*
   venison
jelito ⓝ *ye-li-to black pudding*
jídla na objednávku ⓝ pl
   yeed-luh nuh o-byed-naf-ku
   à la carte dishes (cooked as ordered)
jitrnice ⓕ *yi-tr-nyi-tse white pudding*
jogurt ⓜ *yo-gurt yogurt*

K

kachna ⓕ *kuhkh-nuh duck*
kakao ⓝ *kuh-kuh-o hot chocolate (drink)*
kanec ⓜ *kuh-nets boar*
kantalup ⓜ *kuhn-tuh-lup cantaloupe*
kapr ⓜ *kuh-pr carp*
kapučíno ⓝ *kuh-pu-chee-no cappuccino*
kapusta ⓕ *ka-pus-tuh cabbage*
karbanátek ⓜ *kuhr-buh-na-tek*
   hamburger with breadcrumbs, egg,
   diced white bread roll & onions
kari ⓝ *kuh-ri curry*
kaštan ⓜ *kuhsh-tuhn chestnut*
káva ⓕ *ka-vuh coffee*
káva bez kofeinu ⓕ *ka-vuh bez*
   ko-fey-nu decaffeinated coffee
káva se smetanou ⓕ *ka-vuh se*
   sme-tuh-noh coffee with cream
kaviár ⓜ *kuh-vi-ar caviar*
kečup ⓜ *ke-chup ketchup*
kedluben ⓜ *ked-lu-ben kohlrabi*
kešů ⓝ *ke-shoo cashew*
klobása ⓕ *klo-ba-suh thick sausage*
kmín ⓜ *kmeen caraway*
knedlíky ⓜ pl *kned-lee-ki dumplings*
knedlíky s vejci ⓜ pl *kned-lee-ki s vey-tsi*
   fried dumplings with eggs
kobliha ⓕ *kob-li-huh doughnut*
kokos ⓝ *ko-kos coconut*
koláč ⓜ *ko-lach*
   pastry with various toppings)
koňak ⓜ *ko-nyuhk brandy*
kopr ⓜ *ko-pr dill*
koprová polévka ⓕ *kop-ro-va*
   po-lairf-kuh dill & sour cream soup
kotleta ⓕ *kot-le-tuh chop • cutlet*
krajíc ⓜ *kruh-yeets slice of bread*

králík ⑩ *kra-leek rabbit*
krevety ① pl *kre-ve-ti prawns (shrimps)*
krokety ① pl *kro-ke-ti*
  deep-fried mashed potato balls
krvavý *kr-vuh-vee rare (of meat)*
krůta ① *kroo-tuh turkey*
křen ⑩ *krzhen horseradish*
křenová rolka ① *krzhe-no-va rol-kuh*
  ham & horseradish roll
kukuřice ① *ku-ku-rzhi-tse corn*
kukuřičné lupínky ① pl
  ku-ku-rzhich-nair lu-peen-ki cornflakes
kuře ⑩ *ku-rzhe chicken*
kuřecí polévka s nudlemi ①
  ku-rzhe-tsee po-lairf-kuh s nud-le-mi
  chicken noodle soup
kuře na paprice ① *ku-rzhe nuh*
  puh-pri-tse chicken boiled in spicy
  paprika cream sauce
kuskus ⑩ *kus-kus couscous*
květák ⑩ *kvye-tak cauliflower*
kyselá smetana ① *ki-se-la sme-tuh-nuh*
  sour cream

L

lečo ⑩ *le-cho stewed onions, capsicums,*
  tomatoes, eggs & sausage
led ⑩ *led ice*
ledová káva ① *le-do-va ka-vuh iced coffee*
ledový čaj ⑩ *le-do-vee chai iced tea*
ležák ⑩ *le-zhak lager*
lilek ⑩ *li-lek aubergine • eggplant*
limeta ① *li-me-tuh lime*
limonáda ①
  li-mo-na-duh
  lemonade • soft drink
lískový oříšek ⑩ *lees-ko-vee o-rzhee-shek*
  hazelnut
losos ⑩ *lo-sos salmon*
luštěnina ① *lush-tye-nyi-nuh legume*

M

majonéza ① *muh-yo-nair-zuh mayonnaise*
makový koláč ⑩ *muh-ko-vee ko-lach*
  poppy seed pastry
makrela ① *muh-kre-luh mackerel*

malina ① *muh-li-nuh raspberry*
mandarinka ① *muhn-duh-rin-kuh*
  mandarin
mandle ① *muhnd-le almond*
mango ⑩ *muhn-go mango*
margarín ⑩ *muhr-guh-reen margarine*
máslo ⑩ *mas-lo butter*
maso ⑩ *muh-so meat*
med ⑩ *med honey*
meloun ⑩ *me-lohn*
  melon • watermelon
meruňka ① *me-run'-kuh apricot*
meruňkovice ① *me-run'-ko-vi-tse*
  apricot liquor
míchaná vejce ① pl *mee-khuh-na vey-tse*
  scrambled eggs
míchaná vejce s klobásou ① pl
  mee-khuh-na vey-tse s klo-ba-soh
  scrambled eggs with sausage
míchaný *mee-khuh-nee mixed*
minerálka ① *mi-ne-ral-kuh mineral water*
mléko ⑩ *mlair-ko milk*
mleté maso ⑩ *mle-tair muh-so*
  minced meat
moučník ⑩ *mohch-nyeek dessert*
mouka ① *moh-kuh flour*
mrkev ① *mr-kev carrot*
mrkvový salát ⑩ *mrk-vo-vee suh-lat*
  carrot salad

N

nadívaný *nuh-dyee-vuh-nee stuffed*
nakládaná okurka ①
  nuh-kla-duh-na o-kur-kuh dill pickle
nakládaná zelenina ①
  nuh-kla-duh-na ze-le-nyi-nuh pickles
nápoj ⑩ *na-poy drink*
na roštu *nuh rosh-tu grilled*
natvrdo uvařený *nuht-vr-do*
  u-vuh-rzhe-nee hard-boiled (egg)
nealkoholický nápoj ⑩
  ne-uhl-ko-ho-lits-kee na-poy soft drink
nektarínka ① *nek-tuh-reen-kuh nectarine*
neperlivá minerálka ① *ne-per-li-va*
  mi-ne-ral-kuh still mineral water
nudle ① pl *nud-le noodles*

nudlová polévka ① *nud·lo·va po·lairf·kuh* noodle soup made from chicken broth with vegetables

O

obložené chlebíčky ⓜ pl *o·blo·zhe·nair khle·beech·ki* open sandwiches on French bread, with cold meat, eggs, cheese and/or mayonnaise-based salads such as lobster, fish, potatoes or ham

ocet ⓜ *o·tset* vinegar

odstředěné mléko ⓝ *od·strzhe·dye·nair mlair·ko* skim milk

okurka ① *o·kur·kuh* cucumber or dill pickle

okurkový salát ⓜ *o·kur·ko·vee suh·lat* cucumber salad

olej ⓜ *o·ley* oil

oliva ① *o·li·vuh* olive

olivový olej ⓜ *o·li·vo·vee o·ley* olive oil

omáčka ① *o·mach·kuh* sauce

omeleta ① *o·me·le·tuh* omelette

omeleta se sýrem a bramborem ① *o·me·le·tuh se see·rem uh bruhm·bo·rem* cheese & potato omelette

opékané brambory ① pl *o·pair·kuh·nair bruhm·bo·ri* roasted potatoes

oplatka ① *o·pluht·kuh* large paper-thin waffle

ořechy ⓜ pl *o·rzhe·khi* nuts

oříšek ⓜ *o·rzhee·shek* nut

oves ⓜ *o·ves* oats

ovoce ⓝ *o·vo·tse* fruit

ovocná šťáva ① *o·vots·na shtya·vuh* fruit juice

ovocné knedlíky ⓜ pl *o·vots·nair kned·lee·ki* fruit dumplings (the dough has a potato, cottage cheese or yeast flour base & the fillings are usually plums, apricots, strawberries or blueberries)

ovocný čaj ⓜ *o·vots·nee chai* fruit tea

P

palačinka ① *puh·luh·chin·kuh* crepe • pancake

pálivý *pa·li·vee* spicy

paprika ① *puh·pri·kuh* capsicum (bell pepper)

párek ⓜ *pa·rek* thin sausage

párek v rohlíku ⓜ *pa·rek v ro·hlee·ku* hot dog

pasiflora ① *puh·si·flo·ruh* passionfruit

paštika ① *puhsh·tyi·kuh* paté

pečená husa ① *pe·che·na hu·suh* roast goose

pečená kachna ① *pe·che·na kuhkh·nuh* roast duck (often served with cabbage or sauerkraut & dumplings)

pečená šunka s vejci ① *pe·che·na shun·kuh s vey·tsi* fried ham with eggs

pečený *pe·che·nee* baked • roasted

pečivo ⓝ *pe·chi·vo* bread rolls

pepř ⓜ *pe·przh* black pepper

perlivá minerálka ① *per·li·va mi·ne·ral·kuh* carbonated mineral water

perlivý *per·li·vee* carbonated

perník ⓜ *per·nyeek* gingerbread

pfereron ⓜ *fe·fe·ron* chilli

pfereronová omáčka ① *fe·fe·ro·no·va o·mach·kuh* chilli sauce

piroh ⓜ *pi·roh* pastry (with a filling)

pistácie ① *pis·ta·tsi·ye* pistachio

pivo ⓝ *pi·vo* beer

plněná paprika ① pl *pl·nye·na puh·pri·kuh* capsicum stuffed with minced meat & rice, served with tomato sauce

plody moře ⓜ pl *plo·di mo·rzhe* seafood

podzemnice olejná ① *pod·zem·nyi·tse o·ley·na* groundnut

polévka ① *po·lairf·kuh* soup

pomeranč ⓜ *po·me·ruhnch* orange

pomerančový džus ⓜ *po·me·ruhn·cho·vee dzhus* orange juice

pórek ⓜ *paw·rek* leek

povidla ⓝ *po·vid·luh* plum purée

povidlový koláč ⓜ *po·vid·lo·vee ko·lach* plum purée pastry

Pražská šunka ① *pruhzh·ska shun·kuh* Prague ham – ham pickled in brine & spices & smoked over a beechwood fire

Pražská šunka s okurkou ① *pruhzh·ska shun·kuh s o·kur·koh* Prague ham with gherkins

předkrmy ⓜ pl *przhed*-kr-mi *entrées*

přílohy ⓕ pl *przhee*-lo-hi *side dishes*

přírodně sycená minerálka ⓕ
*przhee-rod-nye si-*tse-na *mi*-ne-ral-kuh
still mineral water

přírodní řízek ⓜ *przhee-rod-nyee
rzhee-*zek *pork or veal schnitzel without
breadcrumbs*

propečený *pro-pe-*che-nee
well-done (of meat)

pstruh ⓜ pstrooh *trout*

pstruh na másle ⓜ pstrooh nuh *mas*-le
grilled trout with butter

pudink ⓜ *pu*-dink *custard*

R

rajčatový protlak ⓜ
rai-chuh-to-vee *prot*-luhk *tomato purée*

rajčatový salát ⓜ *rai*-chuh-to-vee *suh*-lat
tomato salad with onions

rajče ⓝ *rai*-che *tomato*

rajská omáčka ⓕ *rais*-ka o-mach-kuh
*tomato sauce – a sweeter version of the
original Italian sauce, served with meat
& rice or noodles*

rajské jablko ⓝ *rais*-kair yuh-bl-ko
tomato

rakvička ⓕ *ruhk*-vich-kuh *'coffin' –
meringues topped with whipped cream*

rizoto ⓝ *ri*-zo-to
a mixture of pork, onions, peas & rice

rohlík ⓜ *roh*-leek *long bread roll*

roštěný *rosh*-tye-nee *broiled*

rozinky ⓕ pl *ro*-zin-ki *raisins • sultanas*

rozmačkané *roz*-muhch-ka-nair *mashed*

ruské vejce ⓝ *rus*-kair vey-tse
*hard-boiled eggs & ham, covered with
mayonnaise & topped with caviar*

růžové víno ⓝ *roo-*zho-vair vee-no
rosé (wine)

ryba ⓕ *ri*-buh *fish*

rybí filé ⓝ *ri*-bee fi-lair *fish fillet*

rybí polévka ⓕ *ri*-bee po-lairf-kuh
*fish soup usually made with carp & some
carrots, potatoes & peas*

rýže ⓕ *ree*-zhe *rice*

Ř

ředkvička ⓕ *rzhed*-kvich-kuh *radish*

S

salám ⓜ *suh*-lam *salami*

salát ⓜ *suh*-lat *salad*

salát z červené řepy ⓜ *suh*-lat s
cher-ve-nair rzhe-pi *beetroot salad*

sardinka ⓕ *suhr*-din-kuh *sardine*

segedínský guláš ⓜ *se*-ge-deens-kee
gu-lash *goulash with beef, pork, lamb &
sauerkraut in a paprika cream sauce,
served with dumplings*

sekaná ⓕ *se*-kuh-na *meatloaf*

sendvič ⓜ *send*-vich *sandwich*

skopové (maso) ⓝ *sko*-po-vair (*muh*-so)
mutton

sladký ⓜ *sluhd*-kee *sweet*

slanina ⓕ *sluh*-nyi-nuh *bacon*

slávka jedlá ⓕ *slaf*-kuh yed-la *mussels*

sleď ⓜ sled' *herring*

slivovice ⓕ *sli*-vo-vi-tse *plum brandy*

smažené žampiony ⓜ pl *smuh*-zhe-nair
zhuhm-pi-yo-ni *fried mushrooms often
mixed with onions & eggs*

smažený *smuh*-zhe-nee *fried*

smažený kapr ⓜ *smuh*-zhe-nee *kuh*-pr
pieces of carp fried in breadcrumbs

smažený květák ⓜ *smuh*-zhe-nee *kve*-tak
fried cauliflower in breadcrumbs

smažený květák s bramborem ⓜ
smuh-zhe-nee *kve*-tak s *bruhm*-bo-rem
*vegetarian dish of cauliflower florets
fried in breadcrumbs & served with
boiled potatoes & tartar sauce*

smažený sýr ⓜ *smuh*-zhe-nee seer
fried cheese in breadcrumbs

smažená vejce ⓝ pl
smuh-zhe-na vey-tse *fried eggs*

smažený vepřový řízek ⓜ
smuh-zhe-nee ve-przho-vee *rzhee*-zek
*schnitzel with potatoes or potato
salad*

smetana ⓕ *sme*-tuh-nuh *cream*

sójová omáčka ⓕ *saw*-yo-va o-mach-kuh
soy sauce

sójové mléko ⓝ *saw-yo-vair mlair-ko*
soy milk

sójový tvaroh ⓜ *saw-yo-vee tvuh-rawh*
tofu

sterilizované zelí ⓝ *ste-re-li-zo-vuh-nair ze-lee* pickled cabbage

středně propečený *strzhed-nye pro-pe-che-nee medium rare (of meat)*

studený *stu-de-nee cold*

sůl ⓕ *sool salt*

sušené ovoce ⓝ *su-she-nair o-vo-tse* dried fruit

svíčková ⓕ *sveech-ko-va sirloin*

svíčková na smetaně ⓕ
sveech-ko-va nuh sme-ta-nye
roast beef in carrot cream sauce with dumplings, topped with lemon, cranberries & whipped cream

sýr ⓜ *seer cheese*

syrový *si-ro-vee raw*

sýrový nářez ⓜ *see-ro-vee na-rzhez* cheeseboard

Š

šampaňské ⓝ *shuhm-puhn'-skair* champagne

šlehačka ⓕ *shle-huhch-kuh* whipped cream

šopský salát ⓜ *shop-skee suh-lat* lettuce, tomato, onion & cheese salad

španělský ptáček ⓜ *shpuh-nyel-skee pta-chek slice of beef rolled up & filled with onions, capsicums, dill pickle, bacon & sausage – cooked in beef sauce & served with rice*

špenát ⓜ *shpe-nat spinach*

(se) špenátem ⓜ *(se) shpe-na-tem finely chopped spinach, cooked with onions, garlic & cream (often served with potato dumplings & meat)*

šťáva ⓕ *shtya-vuh juice*

šumivé víno ⓝ *shu-mi-vair vee-no* sparkling wine

šumivý *shu-mi-vee carbonated*

šunka ⓕ *shun-kuh ham*

šunka lesnická ⓕ *shun-kuh les-nits-ka Prague ham cooked with red wine, tomatoes, mushrooms, bacon & butter*

šunka v aspiku ⓕ *shun-kuh f uhs-pi-ku ham in aspic*

šunkové závitky s pórem ⓜ
shun-ko-vair za-vit-ki s paw-rem
rolled ham with cheese & leek

švestka ⓕ *shvest-kuh plum*

švestkové knedlíky ⓕ pl *shvest-ko-vair kned-lee-ki sweet dumplings filled with fresh plums & sprinkled with poppy seeds, sugar & melted butter*

T

tatarská omáčka ⓕ *tuh-tuhrs-ka o-mach-kuh a mayonnaise-based tartar sauce with diced onions & spices*

tatarský biftek ⓜ *tuh-tuhrs-kee bif-tek raw steak*

telecí (maso) ⓝ *te-le-tsee (muh-so) veal*

telecí kotleta ⓕ *te-le-tsee kot-le-tuh veal cutlet*

telecí pečeně ⓕ *te-le-tsee pe-che-nye roast veal*

teplý *tep-lee warm*

těstovina ⓕ *tyes-to-vi-na pasta*

tlačenka ⓕ *tluh-chen-kuh jellied meat loaf – pieces of pork pressed together with additional ingredients*

tlačenka s octem a cibulí ⓕ
tluh-chen-kuh s ots-tem a tsi-bu-lee jellied meat loaf, served with vinegar & brown onions

treska ⓕ *tres-kuh cod*

třešně ⓕ pl *trzhesh-nye cherries*

tuňák ⓜ *tu-nyak tuna*

tvaroh ⓜ *tvuh-rawkh cottage cheese*

tvarohový koláč ⓜ
*tvuh-ro-ho-vee ko-lach
pastry with cottage cheese & raisins*

U

uherský salám s okurkou ⓜ
u-hers-kee suh-lam s o-kur-koh Hungarian salami with gherkins

ústřice ⓕ *oost-rzhi-tse oyster*

utopenci ⓜ *u-to-pen-tsi 'the drowned one' – sliced pickled pork sausage with onions & capsicums*

uzené koleno ⑩ *u·ze·nair ko·le·no*
smoked hock
uzené se zelím a knedlíky ⑩ *u·ze·nair*
se ze·leem uh kned·lee·ki smoked pork
with cooked sauerkraut & dumplings
uzený *u·ze·nee smoked*
uzený jazyk ⑩ *u·ze·nee yuh·zik*
smoked tongue

V

vajíčko ⑩ *vuh·yeech·ko egg*
vanilka ① *vuh·nil·kuh vanilla*
vařené brambory ① pl *vuh·rzhe·nair*
bruhm·bo·ri boiled potatoes
vařené vejce ① pl *vuh·rzhe·nair vey·tse*
boiled eggs
vařený *vuh·rzhe·nee boiled*
vařit ve skle *vuh·rzhit ve skle*
poached (egg)
vejce ⑩ pl *vey·tse eggs*
vejce na měkko ⑩ pl *vey·tse nuh mye·ko*
soft-boiled eggs
vejce se slaninou ⑩ pl
vey·tse se sluh·nyi·noh bacon & eggs
vejce se šunkou ⑩ pl *vey·tse se shun·koh*
ham & eggs
veka ① *ve·kuh French bread stick*
vepřová játra ① *vep·rzho·va yat·ruh*
pork liver fried with onions
vepřová pečeně ①
vep·rzho·va pe·che·nye
roast pork with caraway seeds
vepřová pečeně s knedlíky a zelím ①
vep·rzho·va pe·che·nye s kned·lee·ki uh
ze·leem roast pork with dumplings &
cooked sauerkraut
vepřové (maso) ⑩ *vep·rzho·vair (muh·so)*
pork
víno ⑩ *vee·no wine*
víno rozlévané ⑩ *vee·no roz·lair·vuh·nair*
wine by the glass

višně ① pl *vish·nye sour cherries*
vlašský salát ⑩ *vluhsh·skee suh·lat*
mayonnaise salad with ham, dill pickles,
celery, peas, carrots & potatoes
voda ① *vo·duh water*
voda s ledem ① *vo·duh s le·dem*
water with ice cubes
vuřt ⑩ *vurzht pork sausage*

Z

zajíc ⑩ *zuh·yeets hare*
zajíc na smetaně ① *zuh·yeets nuh*
sme·tuh·nye hare in cream sauce
zažívací likéry ⑩ pl
zuh·zhee·vuh·tsee li·kair·ri digestifs
zapečená šunka plněná chřestem ①
zuh·pe·che·na shun·kuh pl·nye·na
khrzhes·tem Prague ham baked with
asparagus, breadcrumbs & cheese
zavináč ⑩ *zuh·vi·nach*
rolled pickled herring fillets
zelenina ① *ze·le·nyi·nuh vegetables*
zeleninová polévka ① *ze·le·nyi·no·va*
po·lairf·kuh vegetable soup
zeleninový míchaný salát ⑩
ze·le·nyi·no·vee mee·khuh·nee suh·lat
mixed vegetable salad
zelí ⑩ *ze·lee sauerkraut*
zelňačka ① *zel·nyuhch·kuh*
thick sauerkraut, potatoes & cream soup
zmrzlí *zmrz·lee frozen*
zmrzlina ① *zmrz·li·nuh ice cream*
zmrzlinový pohár ⑩
zmrz·li·no·vee po·har ice cream sundae
znojemská pečeně ① *zno·yem·ska*
pe·che·nye sliced roast beef in gherkin
sauce, often served with rice
zvěřinový guláš ⑩ *zvye·rzhi·no·vee*
gu·lash goulash made from any game
meat or any combination of game
meats

emergencies

nouzové situace

Help!	*Pomoc!*	*po·mots*
Stop!	*Zastav!*	*zuhs·tuhf*
Go away!	*Běžte pryč!*	*byezh·te prich*
Thief!	*Zloděj!*	*zlo·dyey*
Fire!	*Hoří!*	*ho·rzhee*
Watch out!	*Pozor!*	*po·zor*

signs

Nemocnice	*ne·mots·nyi·tse*	**Hospital**
Policie	*po·li·tsi·ye*	**Police**
Pohotovostní	*po·ho·to·vost·nye*	**Emergency**
oddělení	*od·dye·le·nyee*	**Department**

Call ...!	*Zavolejte ...!*	*zuh·vo·ley·te ...*
a doctor	*lékaře*	*lair·kuh·rzhe*
an ambulance	*sanitku*	*suh·nit·ku*
the police	*policii*	*po·li·tsi·yi*

It's an emergency.
To je naléhavý   to ye *nuh·lair·huh·vee*
případ.   *przhee·*puhd

There's been an accident.
Došlo k nehodě.   *dosh·*lo k *ne·*ho·dye

Could you please help?
Můžete prosím pomoci? moo·zhe·te pro·seem po·mo·tsi

Can I use your phone?
Mohu si zatelefonovat? mo·hu si zuh·te·le·fo·no·vuht

I'm going to call the police.
Jdu zavolat policii. ydu zuh·vo·luht po·li·tsi·yi

I'm lost.
Zabloudil/Zabloudila zuh·bloh·dyil/zuh·bloh·dyi·luh
jsem. m/f ysem

Where are the toilets?
Kde jsou toalety? gde ysoh to·uh·le·ti

Is it safe at night?
Je to v noci bezpečné? ye to v no·tsi bez·pech·nair

Is it safe ...?	*Je to*	ye to
	bezpečné pro ...?	bez·pech·nair pro ...
for gay people	*teplý*	tep·lee
for travellers	*cestovatele*	tses·to·vuh·te·le
for women	*ženy*	zhe·ni
on your own	*samotnou*	suh·mot·noh
	osobu	o·so·bu

police

policie

Where's the police station?
Kde je policejní gde ye po·li·tsey·nyee
stanice? stuh·nyi·tse

Please telephone the Tourist Police.
Prosím zavolejte pro·seem zuh·vo·ley·te
turistickou policii. tu·ris·tits·koh po·li·tsi·yi

I want to report an offence.
Chci nahlásit trestný čin. khtsi nuh·hla·sit trest·nee chin

It was him/her.
To byl on/ona. to bil on/o·nuh

I've been ...	... mě.	... mye
assaulted	Přepadli	*przhe*·puhd·li
raped	Znásilnili	*zna*·sil·nyi·li
robbed	Okradli	*o*·kruhd·li

My ... was/were stolen.	Ukradli mě ...	*u*·kruhd·li mye ...

I've lost my ...	Ztratil/Ztratila jsem ... m/f	*ztruh*·tyil/*ztruh*·tyi·luh ysem ...
backpack	batoh	*buh*·tawh
bag	zavazadlo	*zuh*·vuh·zuhd·lo
credit card	kreditní kartu	*kre*·dit·nyee *kuhr*·tu
handbag	kabelku	*kuh*·bel·ku
jewellery	šperky	*shper*·ki
money	peníze	*pe*·nyee·ze
papers	doklady	*dok*·luh·di
passport	pas	puhs
travellers cheques	cestovní šeky	*tses*·tov·nyee *she*·ki
wallet	peněženku	*pe*·nye·zhen·ku

I want to contact my ...	Potřebuji se obrátit na ...	*pot*·rzhe·bu·yi se *o*·bra·tyit nuh ...
consulate	můj konzulát	mooy *kon*·zu·lat
embassy	mé velvyslanectví	mair *vel*·vi·sluh·nets·tvee

I have insurance.
Jsem pojištěný/á. m/f — ysem *po*·yish·tye·nee/a

What am I accused of?
Z čeho jsem obžalován/obžalována? m/f — z *che*·ho ysem *ob*·zhuh·lo·van/*ob*·zhuh·lo·va·nuh

I didn't do it.
Neudělal/Neudělala jsem to. m/f — *ne*·u·dye·luhl/*ne*·u·dye·luh·luh ysem to

Can I pay an on-the-spot fine?
Mohu zaplatit pokutu na místě? — *mo*·hu *zuh*·pluh·tyit *po*·ku·tu nuh *mees*·tye

Can I make a phone call?
Mohu si zavolat? — *mo*·hu si *zuh*·vo·luht

Can I have an English interpreter?

Můžete mi poskytnout	moo·zhe·te mi pos·kit·noht
tlumočníka	tlu·moch·nyee·ka
angličtiny?	uhn·glich·tyi·ni

Can I have a lawyer (who speaks English)?

Můžete mi poskytnout	moo·zhe·te mi pos·kit·noht
(anglickomluvícího)	(uhn·glits·kom·lu·vee·tsee·ho)
právníka?	prav·nyee·kuh

This drug is for personal use.

Tyto léky jsou pro mé	ti·to lair·ki ysoh pro mair
vlastní použití.	vluhst·nyee po·u·zhi·tyee

I have a prescription for this drug.

Mám lékařský	mam lair·kuhrzh·skee
předpis pro tento lék.	przhed·pis pro ten·to lairk

<table>
<tr><th colspan="3">the police may say …</th></tr>
<tr><td>*Jste obžalován/*
obžalována
z … m/f</td><td>yste ob·zhuh·lo·van/
ob·zhuh·lo·vuh·nuh
z …</td><td>**You're charged**
with …</td></tr>
<tr><td>*krádeže v*
obchodě</td><td>kra·de·zhe v
ob·kho·dye</td><td>**shoplifting**</td></tr>
<tr><td>*napadení*</td><td>nuh·puh·de·nyee</td><td>**assault**</td></tr>
<tr><td>*nelegálního*
prodloužení
pobytu</td><td>ne·le·gal·nyee·ho
pro·dloh·zhe·nyee
po·bi·tu</td><td>**overstaying**
a visa</td></tr>
<tr><td>*nelegálního*
vstupu</td><td>ne·le·gal·nyee·ho
fstu·pu</td><td>**not having**
a visa</td></tr>
<tr><td>*nezákoné*
držení
(omamných
látek)</td><td>ne·za·ko·nair
dr·zhe·nyee
(o·mam·neekh
la·tek)</td><td>**possession**
(of illegal
substances)</td></tr>
<tr><td>*porušování*
klidu</td><td>po·ru·sho·va·nyee
kli·du</td><td>**disturbing**
the peace</td></tr>
<tr><td>*To je pokuta za …*</td><td>to ye po·ku·tuh zuh …</td><td>**It's a … fine.**</td></tr>
<tr><td>*parkování*</td><td>puhr·ko·va·nyee</td><td>**parking**</td></tr>
<tr><td>*překročení*
povolené
rychlosti</td><td>przhe·kro·che·nyee
po·vo·le·nair
rikh·los·tyi</td><td>**speeding**</td></tr>
</table>

SAFE TRAVEL

doctor

lékař

Male and female doctors are addressed as *pane doktore* puh·ne *dok·to·re* (Mr Doctor) and *pani doktorko* puh·nyi *dok·tor·ko* (Mrs Doctor) respectively. These forms are also used for dentists.

Where's the nearest …?	*Kde je nejbližší …?*	gde ye ney·blizh·shee …
dentist	*zubař*	zu·buhrzh
doctor	*lékař*	lair·kuhrzh
emergency department	*pohotovost*	po·ho·to·vost
hospital	*nemocnice*	ne·mots·nyi·tse
optometrist	*optik*	op·tik
(night) pharmacist	*(non-stop) lékárník*	*(non-*stop) lair·kar·nyeek

I need a doctor (who speaks English).

Potřebuji (anglickomluvícího) doktora.

pot·rzhe·bu·yi (uhn·glits·kom·lu·vee·tsee·ho) dok·to·ruh

Could I see a female doctor?

Mohla bych být vyšetřená lékařkou?

mo·hluh bikh beet vi·shet·rzhe·na lair·kuhrzh·koh

Could the doctor come here?

Může lékař přijít k nám?

moo·zhe lair·kuhrzh przhi·yeet k nam

Jaký máte problém?
yuh·kee ma·te pro·blairm — **What's the problem?**

Kde to bolí?
gde to bo·lee — **Where does it hurt?**

Máte teplotu?
ma·te tep·lo·tu — **Do you have a temperature?**

Jak dlouho již máte tyto příznaky?
yuhk dloh·ho yizh ma·te
ti·to przheez·nuh·ki — **How long have you been like this?**

Už jste měl/měla někdy něco podobného? m/f
uzh yste myel/mye·luh
nyek·di nye·tso po·dob·nair·ho — **Have you had this before?**

Jaký je váš intimní život?
yuh·kee ye vash
in·tim·nyee zhi·vot — **Are you sexually active?**

Měl/Měla jste nechráněný pohlavní styk? m/f
myel/mye·luh yste
ne·khra·nye·nee
po·hluhv·nyee stik — **Have you had unprotected sex?**

Pijete alkoholické nápoje?
pi·ye·te uhl·ko·ho·lits·kair
na·po·ye — **Do you drink?**

Kouříte?
koh·rzhee·te — **Do you smoke?**

Užíváte nějaké návykové látky?
u·zhee·va·te nye·yuh·kair
na·vi·ko·vair lat·ki — **Do you take drugs?**

Jste na něco alergický?
yste nuh nye·tso
uh·ler·gits·kee — **Are you allergic to anything?**

Berete nějaké léky?
be·re·te nye·yuh·kair lair·ki — **Are you on medication?**

Jak dlouho cestujete?
yuhk dloh·ho tses·tu·ye·te — **How long are you travelling for?**

Potřebujete být hospitalizován.

pot·rzhe·bu·ye·te beet
hos·pi·tuh·li·zo·van

**You need to be
admitted to hospital.**

Po návratu domu byste si měl/měla zajít na kontrolu. m/f

po *na*·vruh·tu *do*·mu *bis*·te
si myel/*mye*·luh zuh·yeet
nuh *kon*·tro·lu

**You should have it
checked when you
go home.**

Váš zdravotní stav vyžaduje léčení ve vaší zemi.

vash *zdruh*·vot·nyee stuhv
vi·zhuh·du·ye *lair*·che·nyee
ve *vuh*·shee *ze*·mi

**You should return
home for treatment.**

Jste hypochondr.

yste *hi*·po·khon·dr

You're a hypochondriac.

Is there an after-hours emergency number?

Máte non-stop	*ma*·te *non*·stop
pohotovostní	po·ho·to·*vost*·nyee
telefonní číslo?	te·le·fo·nyee *chees*·lo

I've run out of my medication.

Došly mi léky.	*dosh*·li mi *lair*·ki

This is my usual medicine.

Toto jsou mé obvyklé léky.	*to*·to ysoh mair *ob*·vik·lair *lair*·ki

My child weighs (20 kilos).

Mé dítě váží	mair *dyee*·tye *va*·zhee
(dvacet kilo).	(*dvuh*·tset *ki*·lo)

What's the correct dosage?

Jaká je přesná dávka?	*yuh*·ka ye *przhes*·na *daf*·kuh

I don't want a blood transfusion.
  Nechci transfúzi krve.   nekh·tsi truhns·foo·zi kr·ve

Please use a new syringe.
  Prosím použijte   pro·seem po·u·zhiy·te
  novou stříkačku.   no·voh strzhee·kuhch·ku

I have my own syringe.
  Mám svojí stříkačku.   mam svo·yee strzhee·kuhch·ku

My prescription is …
  Můj lékařský   mooy lair·kuhrzh·skee
  předpis je …   przhed·pis ye …

Can I have a receipt for my insurance?
  Můžete mi dát účtenku   moo·zhe·te mi dat ooch·ten·ku
  pro moji pojišťovnu?   pro mo·yi po·yish·tyov·nu

I've been	Byl/Byla jsem	bil/bi·luh ysem
vaccinated	*očkovaný/á*	och·ko·vuh·nee/a
against …	*proti …* m/f	pro·tyi …
hepatitis	*žloutence*	zhloh·ten·tse
A/B/C	*A/B/C*	a/bair/tsair
lyme disease	*lymské*	lim·skair
	borelióze	bo·re·li·aw·ze
rabies	*vzteklině*	vzte·kli·nye
tetanus	*tetanusu*	te·tuh·nu·su
tick-borne	*meningo-*	me·nin·go·
encephalitis	*kokové*	ko·ko·vair
	encefalitidě	en·tse·fuh·li·ti·dye
typhoid	*tyfu*	ti·fu
I need new …	*Potřebuji …*	pot·rzhe·bu·yi …
contact lenses	*kontaktní*	kon·tuhkt·nyee
	čočky	choch·ki
glasses	*brýle*	bree·le

symptoms & conditions

I'm sick.
Jsem nemocný/á. **m/f** ysem *ne*·mots·nee/a

My child is sick.
Moje dítě je nemocné. mo·ye *dyee*·tye ye *ne*·mots·nair

I've been injured.
Byl/Byla jsem zraněný/á. **m/f** bil/*bi*·luh ysem *zruh*·nye·nee/a

I've been vomiting.
Zvracel/Zvracela jsem. **m/f** *zvruh*·tsel/*zvruh*·tse·luh ysem

He/She has been ...	*Byl/Byla ...* **m/f**	bil/*bi*·luh ...
injured	*zraněný/á* **m/f**	*zruh*·nye·nee/a
vomiting	*zvracel* **m**	*zvruh*·tsel
	zvracela **f**	*zvruh*·tse·luh

He/She is having a/an ...	*On/Ona má ...*	on/*o*·nuh ma ...
allergic reaction	*alergickou reakci*	*uh*·ler·gits·koh re·*uhk*·tsi
asthma attack	*astmatický záchvat*	*uhst*·muh·tits·kee *zakh*·vuht
epileptic fit	*epileptický záchvat*	*e*·pi·lep·tits·kee *zakh*·vuht
heart attack	*infarkt*	*in*·fuhrkt

I feel ...		
anxious	*Pociťuji úzkost.*	po·tsi·tyu·yi *oos*·kost
better	*Cítím se lépe.*	*tsee*·tyeem se *lair*·pe
depressed	*Mám depresi.*	mam *de*·pre·si
dizzy	*Mám závratě.*	mam *za*·vruh·tye
hot and cold	*Polévá mě horko a zima.*	po·*lair*·va mye *hor*·ko uh *zi*·muh
nauseous	*Je mi nevolno.*	ye mi *ne*·vol·no
shivery	*Třesu se.*	*trzhe*·su se
strange	*Je mi divně.*	ye mi *dyiv*·nye
weak	*Jsem slabý/á.* **m/f**	ysem *sluh*·bee/a
worse	*Cítím se hůř.*	*tsee*·tyeem se hoorzh

195

It hurts here.
Tady to bolí. — tuh·di to bo·lee

I'm dehydrated.
Jsem dehydratovaný/á. m/f — ysem de·hid·ruh·to·vuh·nee/a

I can't sleep.
Nemohu spát. — ne·mo·hu spat

I'm on medication for …
Užívám léky na … — u·zhee·vam lair·ki nuh …

He/She is on medication for …
On/Ona užívá — on/o·nuh u·zhee·va
léky na … — lair·ki nuh …

I have (a/an) …
Mám … — mam …

He/She has (a/an) …
On/Ona má … — on/o·nuh ma …

I've recently had (a/an) …
Nedávno jsem — ne·dav·no ysem
měl/měla … m/f — myel/mye·luh …

He/She has recently had (a/an) …
Nedávno měl/měla … m/f — ne·dav·no myel/mye·luh …

asthma	*astma* n	uhst·muh
cold n	*nachlazení* n	nuh·khluh·ze·nyee
constipation	*zácpa* f	zats·puh
cough n	*kašel* m	kuh·shel
diabetes	*cukrovka* f	tsu·krof·kuh
diarrhoea	*průjem* m	proo·yem
fever	*horečka* f	ho·rech·kuh
headache	*bolesti hlavy* f	bo·les·tyi hluh·vi
nausea	*nevolnost* f	ne·vol·nost
pain n	*bolest* f	bo·lest
sore throat	*bolest v krku* f	bo·lest f kr·ku

women's health

(I think) I'm pregnant.
(Myslím že) Jsem těhotná. *(mis·leem zhe) ysem tye·hot·na*

I'm on the pill.
Užívám *u·zhee·vam*
antikoncepční pilulky. *uhn·ti·kon·tsep·chnyee pi·lul·ki*

I haven't had my period for (six) weeks.
Moje poslední *mo·ye pos·led·nye*
menstruace byla *mens·tru·uh·tse bi·luh*
před (šesti) týdny. *przhed (shes·tyi) teed·ni*

I've noticed a lump here.
Nahmatala jsem si bulku. *nuh·hmuh·tuh·luh ysem si bul·ku*

Do you have something for (period pain)?
Máte něco na *ma·te nye·tso nuh*
(menstruační bolesti)? *(men·stru·uhch·nyee bo·les·tyi)*

I have a …	Mám …	mam …
urinary tract infection	*infekci močových cest*	*in·fek·tsi mo·cho·veech tsest*
yeast infection	*kvasinkovou infekci*	*kvuh·sin·ko·voh in·fek·tsi*

---

the doctor may say …

Užíváte antikoncepci?
   u·zhee·va·te
   uhn·ti·kon·tsep·tsi
Are you using contraception?

Máte právě menstruaci?
   ma·te prav·ye mens·tru·uh·tsi
Are you menstruating?

Jste těhotná?
   yste tye·hot·na
Are you pregnant?

Kdy jste naposledy měla menstruaci?
   gdi yste nuh·pos·le·di
   mye·luh mens·tru·uh·tsi
When did you last have your period?

Jste těhotná.
   yste tye·hot·na
You're pregnant.

health

197

I need (a/the) ...	Potřebuji ...	pot·rzhe·bu·yi ...
contraception	anti-koncepční prostředek	uhn·ti· kon·tsep·chnyee pros·trzhe·dek
morning-after pill	postinor	pos·ti·nor
pregnancy test	těhotenský test	tye·ho·tens·kee test

allergies

I have a skin allergy.
Mám kožní alergii. mam *kozh*·nyee uh·ler·gi·yi

I'm allergic to ...	Jsem alergický/á na ... m/f	ysem uh·ler·gits·kee/a nuh ...
He/She is allergic to ...	Je alergický/á na ... m/f	ye uh·ler·gits·kee/a nuh ...
antibiotics	antibiotika	uhn·ti·bi·o·ti·kuh
anti-inflammatories	proti-zánětlivé léky	pro·tyi· za·nyet·li·vair lair·ki
aspirin	aspirin	uhs·pi·rin
bees	včely	fche·li
codeine	kodein	ko·deyn
penicillin	penicilin	pe·ni·tsi·lin
pollen	pyl	pil
sulphur-based drugs	léky obsahující síru	lair·ki ob·suh·hu·yee·tsee see·ru

antihistamines	anti-histaminikum m	uhn·ti· his·tuh·mi·ni·kum
inhaler	inhalátor m	in·huh·la·tor
injection	injekce f	in·yek·tse

For food-related allergies, see **special diets & allergies**, page 178.

parts of the body

My ... hurts.
   Bolí mě ...   *bo·*lee mye ...

I can't move my ...
   Nemohu hýbat s ...   *ne·*mo·hu *hee·*but s ...

I have a cramp in my ...
   Mám křeč v ...   mam krzhech v ...

My ... is swollen.
   Mám oteklý ...   mam o·tek·lee ...

For other parts of the body, see the **dictionary**.

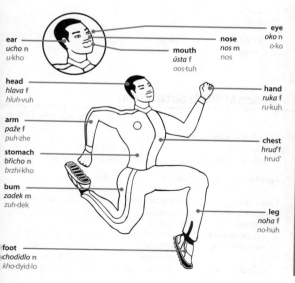

ear
ucho n
*u·*kho

eye
oko n
*o·*ko

nose
nos m
nos

mouth
ústa f
*oos·*tuh

head
hlava f
*hluh·*vuh

hand
ruka f
*ru·*kuh

arm
paže f
*puh·*zhe

chest
hruď f
hrud'

stomach
břicho n
*brzhi·*kho

bum
zadek m
*zuh·*dek

leg
noha f
*no·*huh

foot
chodidlo n
*kho·*dyid·lo

soft talk

You'll notice from our coloured pronunciation guides that the Czech consonants *d*, *n* and *t*, when followed in writing by the vowels *ě*, *i* or *í*, are pronounced softly, with a slight 'y' sound after them – just like the letters *ď*, *ň* and *ť* are always pronounced, regardless of the letter following them. You don't need to think about this in most cases, as we've used the symbol y to help you pronounce these sounds naturally. However, to avoid mispronunciation (ie reading it as an ee after the consonant) when it appears at the end of a syllable or a word, we've used an apostrophe (') instead of the y symbol. For example:

thousand	tisíc	*tyi*·seets
rain	déšť	dairsht'
Sunday	neděle	ne·dye·le
now	teď	ted'
breakfast	snídaně	snee·duh·nye
Sorry.	Promiňte.	pro·min'·te

alternative treatments

alternativní léčbu

I use (alternative treatments).

| Používám | po·u·zhee·vam |
| (alternativní léčbu). | (uhl·ter·na·tiv·nyee lairch·bu) |

I prefer ...	Dávám přednost ...	da·vam przhed·nost ...
Can I see someone who practises ...?	Mohu navštívit někoho, kdo provozuje ...?	mo·hu nav·shtyee·vit nye·ko·ho gdo pro·vo·zu·ye ...
acupuncture	akupunkturu	uh·ku·punk·tu·ru
naturopathy	přírodní medicínu	przhee·rod·nyee me·di·tsee·nu
reflexology	reflexní terapii	re·fleks·nee te·ruh·pi·i

pharmacist

I need something for (a headache).
Potřebuji něco na *pot*·rzhe·bu·yi *nye*·tso nuh
(bolest hlavy). (*bo*·lest *hluh*·vi)

Do I need a prescription for (antihistamines)?
Potřebuji předpis na *pot*·rzhe·bu·yi *przhed*·pis nuh
(antihistaminikum)? (uhn·ti·his·tuh·mi·ni·kum)

I have a prescription.
Mám recept. mam *re*·tsept

How many times a day?
Kolikrát denně? ko·li·krat *de*·nye

Will it make me drowsy?
Budu potom ospalý/á? m/f bu·du po·tom os·puh·lee/a

antiseptic	antiseptický prostředek m	uhn·ti·sep·tits·kee prost·rzhe·dek
contraceptives	antikoncepce f	uhn·ti·kon·tsep·tse
painkillers	prášky proti bolesti m pl	prash·ki pro·tyi bo·les·tyi
rehydration salts	iontový nápoj m	yon·to·vee *na*·poy
thermometer	teploměr m	te·plo·myer

the pharmacist may say ...

Dvakrát/Třikrát denně. dvuh·krat/trzhi·krat *de*·nye	Twice/Three times a day.
Před jídlem/Při jídle/Po jídle. przhed *yeed*·lem/ przhi *yeed*·le/po *yeed*·le	Before/With/After food.
Užívali jste tento lék? u·zhe·va·li yste *ten*·to lairk	Have you taken this before?
Musíte využívat celé balení. mu·see·te *vi*·u·zhe·vuht tse·lair buh·le·nyee	You must complete the course.

For more pharmaceutical items, see the **dictionary**.

dentist

I have a ...	*Mám ...*	mam ...
broken tooth	*zlomený zub*	*zlo*·me·nee zub
cavity	*kaz*	kuhz
toothache	*bolavý zub*	*bo*·luh·vee zub

I've lost a filling.
Vypadla mi plomba.   vi·puhd·luh mi *plom*·buh

My dentures are broken.
Zubní protéza se mi   zub·nyee pro·tair·zuh se mi
rozbila.   roz·bi·luh

My gums hurt.
Bolí mě dásně.   bo·lee mye *das*·nye

I don't want it extracted.
Nechci to vytrhnout.   nekh·tsi to vi·trh·noht

I need a/an ...	*Potřebuji ...*	pot·rzhe·bu·yi ...
anaesthetic	*znecitlivění*	zne·tsit·li·vye·nyee
filling	*plombu*	*plom*·bu

---

the dentist may say ...

Hodně otevřete ústa. hod·nye o·tev·rzhe·te oos·tuh	**Open wide.**
Nebude to vůbec bolet. ne·bu·de to voo·bets bo·let	**This won't hurt a bit.**
Skousněte. skohs·nye·te	**Bite down on this.**
Nehýbejte se. ne·hee·bey·te se	**Don't move.**
Vypláchněte si. vi·plakh·nye·te si	**Rinse.**
Vraťte se, neskončil/neskončila jsem. m/f vruht'·te se nes·kon·chil/ nes·kon·chi·luh ysem	**Come back, I haven't finished.**

Czech nouns in the **dictionary** have their gender indicated by ⓜ (masculine), ⓕ (feminine) or ⓝ (neuter). If it's a plural noun, you'll also see pl. When a word that could be either a noun or a verb has no gender indicated, it's a verb. For added clarity, certain words are marked as adjectives a or verbs v. Adjectives, however, are given in the masculine form only. Both nouns and adjectives are provided in the nominative case only. For information on case and gender, refer to the **phrasebuilder**.

A

aboard *na palubě* nuh puh·lu·bye
abortion *potrat* ⓜ po·truht
about *o* o
above *nad* nuhd
abroad *v cizině* v tsi·zi·nye
accident *nehoda* ⓕ ne·ho·duh
accommodation *ubytování* ⓝ u·bi·to·va·nyee
account (bill) *účet* ⓜ oo·chet
acid rain *kyselý déšť* ki·se·lee deshtʼ
across *přes* przhez
activist *aktivista/aktivistka* ⓜ/ⓕ uhk·ti·vis·tuh/uhk·ti·vist·kuh
actor *herec/herečka* ⓜ/ⓕ he·rets/he·rech·kuh
acupuncture *akupunktura* ⓕ uh·ku·punk·tu·ruh
adaptor *adaptor* ⓜ uh·duhp·tor
addiction *závislost* ⓕ za·vis·lost
address *adresa* ⓕ uh·dre·suh
administration *správa* ⓕ spra·vuh
administrator *správce* ⓜ spraf·tse
admission (price) *vstupné* ⓝ fstup·nair
admit (let in) *vpustit* fpus·tyit
adult *dospělý/á* ⓜ/ⓕ dos·pye·lee/a
advertisement *inzerát* ⓜ in·ze·rat
advice *rada* ⓕ ruh·duh
aerobics *aerobik* ⓜ uh·e·ro·bik
aeroplane *letadlo* ⓝ le·tuhd·lo
Africa *Afrika* ⓕ uh·fri·kuh
after *po* po
afternoon *odpoledne* ⓝ ot·po·led·ne
aftershave *voda po holení* ⓕ vo·duh po ho·le·nyee
again *znovu* zno·vu
age *věk* ⓜ vyek

(three days) ago *před (třemi dny)* przhed (trzhe·mi dni)
agree *souhlasit* soh·hluh·sit
agriculture *zemědělství* ⓝ ze·mye·dyels·tvee
ahead *vpředu* fprzhe·du
AIDS *AIDS* ⓕ eyds
air *vzduch* ⓜ vzdukh
air-conditioned *klimatizovaný* kli·muh·ti·zo·vuh·nee
air conditioning *klimatizace* ⓕ kli·muh·ti·zuh·tse
airline *aerolinie* ⓕ uh·e·ro·li·ni·ye
airmail *letecká pošta* ⓕ le·tets·ka posh·tuh
airplane *letadlo* ⓝ le·tuhd·lo
airport *letiště* ⓝ le·tyish·tye
airport tax *letištní poplatek* ⓜ le·tyisht·nyee po·pluh·tek
aisle (on plane) *ulička* ⓕ u·lich·kuh
alarm clock *budík* ⓜ bu·dyeek
alcohol *alkohol* ⓜ uhl·ko·hol
all *všichni* vshikh·nyi
allergy *alergie* ⓕ uh·ler·gi·ye
almond *mandle* ⓕ muhn·dle
almost *skoro* sko·ro
alone *sám* sam
already *již* yizh
also *také* tuh·kair
altar *oltář* ⓜ ol·tarzh
altitude *nadmořská výška* ⓕ nuhd·morzh·ska veesh·kuh
always *vždy* vzhdi
ambassador *velvyslanec/velvyslankyně* ⓜ/ⓕ vel·vis·luh·nets/vel·vis·luhn·ki·nye
ambulance *ambulance* ⓕ uhm·bu·luhn·tse
American football *americký fotbal* ⓜ uh·me·rits·kee fot·buhl

anaemia *chudokrevnost* ①
  khu·do·kref·nost

anarchist *anarchista/anarchistka* ⓜ/①
  uh·nuhr·khis·tuh/uh·nuhr·khist·kuh

ancient *starodávný* stuh·ro·dav·nee

and *a* uh

angry *rozhněvaný* roz·hnye·vuh·nee

animal *zvíře* ⓝ zvee·rzhe

ankle *kotník* ⓜ kot·nyeek

another *další* duhl·shee

answer *odpověď* ① ot·po·vyed'

answer v *odpovědět* ot·po·vye·dyet

ant *mravenec* ⓜ mruh·ve·nets

antibiotics *antibiotika* ⓜ pl
  uhn·ti·bi·o·ti·kuh

antinuclear *protiatomový*
  pro·tyi·uh·to·mo·vee

antique *starožitnost* ① stuh·ro·zhit·nost

antiseptic *antiseptikum* ⓜ
  uhn·ti·sep·ti·kum

any *nějaký* nye·yuh·kee

apartment *byt* ⓜ bit

appendix (body) *slepé střevo* ⓝ
  sle·pair strzhe·vo

apple *jablko* ⓝ yuh·bl·ko

appointment *schůzka* ① skhooz·kuh

apricot *meruňka* ① me·run'·kuh

April *duben* ⓜ du·ben

archaeological *archeologický*
  uhr·khe·o·lo·gits·kee

architect *architekt/architektka* ⓜ/①
  uhr·khi·tekt/uhr·khi·tet·kuh

architecture *architektura* ①
  uhr·khi·tek·tu·ruh

argue *hádat se* ha·duht se

arm (body) *paže* ① puh·zhe

aromatherapy *aromaterapie* ①
  uh·ro·muh·te·ruh·pi·ye

arrest v *zatknout* zuht·knoht

arrivals *příjezd* ⓜ przhee·yezd

arrive *přijít* przhi·yeet

art *umění* ⓝ u·mye·nyee

art gallery *galerie* ① guh·le·ri·ye

artist *umělec/umělkyně* ⓜ/①
  u·mye·lets/u·myel·ki·nye

ashtray *popelník* ⓜ po·pel·nyeek

Asia *Asie* ① a·si·ye

ask (a question) *ptát se* ptat se

ask (for something) *požádat* po·zha·duht

asparagus *chřest* ⓜ khrzhest

aspirin *aspirin* ⓜ uhs·pi·rin

asthma *astma* ⓝ uhst·muh

at *na* nuh

athletics *lehká atletika* ①
  leh·ka uht·le·ti·kuh

atmosphere *atmosféra* ① uht·mos·fair·ruh

aubergine *lilek* ⓜ li·lek

August *srpen* ⓜ sr·pen

aunt *teta* ① te·tuh

Australia *Austrálie* ① ow·stra·li·ye

Austria *Rakousko* ① ruh·kohs·ko

automated teller machine (ATM)
  bankomat ⓜ buhn·ko·muht

autumn *podzim* ⓜ pod·zim

avenue *třída* ① trzhee·duh

avocado *avokádo* ① uh·vo·ka·do

awful *hrozný* hroz·nee

B

B&W (film) *černobílý* cher·no·bee·lee

baby *nemluvně* ⓝ nem·luv·nye

baby food *dětská výživa* ①
  dyets·ka vee·zhi·vuh

baby powder *dětský pudr* ⓜ
  dyets·kee pu·dr

babysitter *chůva* ① khoo·vuh

back (body) *záda* ① za·duh

back (position) *opěradlo* ⓝ o·pye·ruhd·lo

backpack *batoh* ⓜ buh·tawh

bacon *slanina* ① sluh·nyi·nuh

bad *špatný* shpuht·nee

bag *taška* ① tuhsh·kuh

baggage *zavazadlo* ⓝ zuh·vuh·zuhd·lo

baggage allowance
  povolená váha zavazadel ①
  po·vo·le·na va·huh zuh·vuh·zuh·del

baggage claim *výdej zavazadel* ⓜ
  vee·dey zuh·vuh·zuh·del

bakery *pekárna* ① pe·kar·nuh

balance (account) *zůstatek* ⓜ
  zoo·stuh·tek

balcony *balkón* ⓜ buhl·kawn

ball (sport) *míč* ⓜ meech

ballet *balet* ⓜ buh·let

banana *banán* ⓜ buh·nan

band (music) *skupina* ⓜ sku·pi·nuh

bandage *obvaz* ⓜ ob·vuhz

Band-Aid *leukoplast* ① le·u·ko·pluhst

bank *banka* ① buhn·kuh

bank account *bankovní účet* ⓜ
  buhn·kov·nyee oo·chet

banknote *bankovka* ① buhn·kof·kuh

baptism *křest* ⓜ krzhest

bar *bar* ⓜ buhr

barber *holič* ⓜ ho·lich

bar work *práce v baru* ⓕ *pra*·tse f *buh*·ru
baseball *baseball* ⓜ *beys*·bawl
basket *koš* ⓜ kosh
basketball *košíková* ⓕ *ko*·shee·ko·va
bath *koupel* ⓕ *koh*·pel
bathing suit *plavky* ⓕ *pluhf*·ki
bathroom *koupelna* ⓕ *koh*·pel·nuh
battery *baterie* ⓕ *buh*·te·ri·ye
be *být* beet
beach *pláž* ⓕ plazh
beach volleyball *plážový volejbal* ⓜ
   pla·zho·vee vo·ley·bvl
bean *fazole* ⓕ *fuh*·zo·le
bean sprouts *fazolové klíčky* ⓜ pl
   fuh·zo·lo·vair kleech·ki
beautician *kosmetička* ⓕ kos·me·tich·kuh
beautiful *krásný* kras·nee
beauty salon *kosmetický salón* ⓜ
   kos·me·tits·kee suh·lawn
because *protože* pro·to·zhe
bed *postel* ⓕ pos·tel
bedding *lůžkoviny* ⓕ loozh·ko·vi·ni
bed linen *ložní prádlo* ⓕ lozh·nyee prad·lo
bedroom *ložnice* ⓕ lozh·nyi·tse
bee *včela* ⓕ fche·luh
beef *hovězí* ⓕ ho·vye·zee
beer *pivo* ⓕ pi·vo
beetroot *červená řepa* ⓕ
   cher·ve·na rzhe·puh
before *před* prhed
beggar *žebrák* ⓕ zheb·rak
behind *za* zuh
Belgium *Belgie* ⓕ bel·gi·ye
below *pod* pod
Berlin *Berlín* ⓜ ber·leen
berth *kotviště* ⓕ kot·vish·tye
beside *vedle* ved·le
best *nejlepší* ney·lep·shee
bet *sázka* ⓕ saz·kuh
bet v *sázet* sa·zet
better *lepší* lep·shee
between *mezi* me·zi
Bible *Bible* ⓕ bib·le
bicycle *kolo* ⓕ ko·lo
big *velký* vel·kee
bigger *větší* vyet·shee
biggest *největší* ney·vyet·shee
bike *kolo* ⓕ ko·lo
bike chain *řetěz na kolo* ⓕ
   rzhe·tyez nuh ko·lo
bike lock *zámek na kolo* ⓕ
   za·mek nuh ko·lo
bike path *cyklostezka* ⓕ tsi·klo·stez·kuh

bike shop *obchod s kolama* ⓜ
   op·khod s ko·luh·muh
bill (restaurant) *účet* ⓕ oo·chet
binoculars *dalekohled* ⓜ duh·le·ko·hled
bird *pták* ⓜ ptak
birth certificate *rodný list* ⓜ rod·nee list
birthday *narozeniny* ⓕ pl nuh·ro·ze·nyi·ni
biscuit *sušenka* ⓕ su·shen·kuh
bite (dog) *kousnutí* ⓕ kohs·nu·tyee
bite (insect) *štípnutí* ⓕ shtyeep·nu·tyee
bitter *hořký* horzh·kee
black *černý* cher·nee
black market *černý trh* ⓜ cher·nee trh
bladder *močový měchýř* ⓜ
   mo·cho·vee mye·kheerzh
blanket *deka* ⓕ de·kuh
blind a *slepý* sle·pee
blister *puchýř* ⓜ pu·kheerzh
blocked *ucpaný* uts·puh·nee
blood *krev* ⓕ kref
blood group *krevní skupina* ⓕ
   krev·nyee sku·pi·nuh
blood pressure *krevní tlak* ⓕ
   krev·nyee tluhk
blood test *krevní zkouška* ⓕ
   krev·nyee skohsh·kuh
blue *modrý* mod·ree
board (plane, ship) v *nastoupit*
   nuhs·toh·pit
boarding house *penzion* ⓜ pen·zi·on
boarding pass *palubní vstupenka* ⓕ
   puh·lub·nyee fstu·pen·kuh
boat *člun* ⓜ chlun
body *tělo* ⓕ tye·lo
boiled *vařený* vuh·rzhe·nee
bone *kost* ⓕ kost
book *kniha* ⓕ knyi·huh
book (make a booking) v *objednat*
   ob·yed·nuht
booked out *obsazeno* op·suh·ze·no
book shop *knihkupectví* ⓜ
   knih·ku·pets·tvee
boot (footwear) *bota* ⓕ bo·tuh
boots (footwear) *boty* ⓕ pl bo·ti
border *hranice* ⓕ hruh·nyi·tse
bored *unuděný* u·nu·dye·nee
boring *nudný* nud·nee
borrow *půjčit* pooy·chit
botanic garden *botanická zahrada* ⓕ
   bo·tuh·nits·ka zuh·hruh·duh
both *oba* o·buh
bottle *láhev* ⓕ la·hef

bottle opener otvírák na láhve ⓜ
ot-vee-rak nuh lah-ve
bottom (body) zadek ⓜ zuh-dek
bottom (position) dno ⓝ dno
bowl (plate) miska ⓕ mis-kuh
box krabice ⓕ kruh-bi-tse
boxer shorts trenýrky ⓕ pl tre-neer-ki
boxing box ⓜ boks
boy chlapec ⓜ khluh-pets
boyfriend přítel ⓜ przhee-tel
bra podprsenka ⓕ pod-pr-sen-kuh
brakes brzdy ⓕ pl brz-di
brandy brandy ⓕ bruhn-di
Bratislava Bratislava ⓕ bruh-tyi-sluh-vuh
brave odvážný od-vazh-nee
bread chléb ⓜ khlairb
bread rolls pečivo ⓝ pe-chi-vo
break v zlomit zlo-mit
break down v porouchat po-roh-khuht
breakfast snídaně ⓕ snee-duh-nye
breast (body) prso ⓝ pr-so
breathe dýchat dee-khuht
bribe úplatek ⓜ oo-pluh-tek
bribe v podplatit pod-pluh-tyit
bridge (structure) most ⓜ most
briefcase aktovka ⓕ uhk-tof-kuh
bring přinést przhi-nairst
broccoli brokolice ⓕ bro-ko-li-tse
brochure brožura ⓕ bro-zhu-ruh
broken zlomený zlo-me-nee
broken down rozbitý roz-bi-tee
bronchitis zánět průdušek ⓜ
za-nyet proo-du-shek
brother bratr ⓜ bruh-tr
brown hnědý hnye-dee
bruise modřina ⓕ mod-rzhi-nuh
brush kartáč ⓜ kuhr-tach
bucket kbelík ⓜ kbe-leek
Buddhist buddhista/buddhistka ⓜ/ⓕ
bud-his-tuh/bud-hist-kuh
budget rozpočet ⓜ roz-po-chet
buffet bufet ⓜ bu-fet
bug brouk ⓜ brohk
build v stavět stuh-vyet
builder stavbař ⓜ stuhf-buhrzh
building budova ⓕ bu-do-vuh
bumbag ledvinka ⓕ led-vin-kuh
burn spálenina ⓕ spa-le-nyi-nuh
burnt spálený spa-le-nee
bus autobus ⓜ ow-to-bus
business obchod ⓜ op-khod
business class business třída ⓕ
biz-nis trzhee-duh

businessperson obchodník ⓜ&ⓕ
ob-khod-nyeek
business trip služební cesta ⓕ
slu-zheb-nyee tses-tuh
busker pouliční muzikant ⓜ
po-u-lich-nyee mu-zi-kuhnt
bus station autobusové nádraží ⓝ
ow-to-bu-so-vair nad-ruh-zhee
bus stop autobusová zastávka ⓕ
ow-to-bu-so-va zuhs-taf-kuh
busy zaneprázdněný zuh-ne-prazd-nye-nee
but ale uh-le
butcher řezník ⓜ rzhez-nyeek
butcher's shop řeznictví ⓝ rzhez-nyits-tvee
butter máslo ⓝ mas-lo
butterfly motýl ⓜ mo-teel
button knoflík ⓜ knof-leek
buy v koupit koh-pit

C

cabbage kapusta ⓕ kuh-pus-tuh
cable car kabinová lanovka ⓕ
kuh-bi-no-va luh-nof-kuh
café kavárna ⓕ kuh-var-nuh
cafeteria jídelna ⓕ yee-del-nuh
cake dort ⓜ dort
cake shop cukrárna ⓕ tsu-krar-nuh
calculator kalkulačka ⓕ kuhl-ku-luhch-kuh
calendar kalendář ⓜ kuh-len-darzh
call (phone) v telefonovat te-le-fo-no-vuht
camera fotoaparát ⓜ fo-to-uh-puh-rat
camera shop foto potřeby ⓕ pl
fo-to pot-rzhe-bi
camp v tábořit ta-bo-rzhit
camping ground stanový tábor ⓜ
stuh-no-vee ta-bor
camping store obchod s kempingovými
potřebami ⓜ op-khod s
kem-pin-go-vee-mi pot-rzhe-buh-mi
camp site autokempink ⓜ ow-to-kem-pink
can plechovka ⓕ ple-khof-kuh
can (be able) umět u-myet
can (have permission) moci mo-tsi
Canada Kanada ⓕ kuh-nuh-duh
cancel zrušit zru-shit
cancer rakovina ⓕ ruh-ko-vi-nuh
candle svíčka ⓕ sveech-kuh
candy kandovaný cukr ⓜ
kuhn-do-vuh-nee tsu-kr
canoeing kanoistika ⓕ kuh-no-is-ti-kuh
can opener otvírák na konzervy ⓜ
ot-vee-rak nuh kon-zer-vi

cantaloupe *kantalup* ⓜ kuhn·tuh·lup
capsicum *paprika* ⓕ puh·pri·kuh
car *auto* ⓝ ow·to
caravan *karavan* ⓜ kuh·ruh·vuhn
cardiac arrest *zdstava srdce* ⓕ
   zas·tuh·vuh srd·tse
cards (playing) *karty* ⓕ pl kuhr·ti
care (for someone) v *starat se (o)*
   stuh·ruht se (o)
car hire *půjčovna aut* ⓕ
   pooy·chov·nuh owt
car owner's title *doklad o vlastnictví auta*
   ⓜ *dok·luhd o vluhst·nyits·tvee·ow·tuh*
car park *parkoviště* ⓝ puhr·ko·vish·tye
carpenter *tesař* ⓜ te·suhrzh
car registration *osvědčení o registraci* ⓝ
   os·vyed·che·nyee o re·gis·truh·tsi
carrot *mrkev* ⓕ mr·kef
carry *nosit* no·sit
carton *kartón* ⓜ kuhr·tawn
cash *hotovost* ⓕ ho·to·vost
cash (a cheque) v *inkasovat šek*
   in·kuh·so·vuht shek
cashew *kešů* ⓝ ke·shoo
cashier *pokladník/pokladní* ⓜ/ⓕ
   po·kluhd·nyeek/po·kluhd·nyee
cash register *pokladna* ⓕ po·kluhd·nuh
casino *kasino* ⓝ kuh·si·no
cassette *kazeta* ⓕ kuh·ze·tuh
castle (classical) *zámek* ⓜ za·mek
castle (medieval) *hrad* ⓜ hruhd
casual work *příležitostní práce* ⓕ
   przhe·le·zhi·tost·nyee pra·tse
cat *kočka* ⓕ koch·kuh
cathedral *katedrála* ⓕ ka·te·dra·luh
Catholic *katolík* ⓜ kuh·to·leek
cauliflower *květák* ⓜ kvye·tak
cave *jeskyně* ⓕ yes·ki·nye
CD *CD* ⓝ tsair·dairch·ko
celebration *oslava* ⓕ o·sluh·vuh
cell phone *mobil* ⓜ mo·bil
cemetery *hřbitov* ⓜ hrzh·bi·tov
cent *cent* ⓜ tsent
centimetre *centimetr* ⓜ tsen·ti·me·tr
centre *střed* ⓜ strzhed
ceramics *keramika* ⓕ ke·ruh·mi·kuh
cereal (breakfast) *cereálie* ⓕ tse·re·a·li·ye
certificate *osvědčení* ⓝ os·vyed·che·nyee
chain *řetěz* ⓜ rzhe·tyez
chair *židle* ⓕ zhid·le
chairlift (skiing) *sedačka* ⓕ se·duhch·kuh
champagne *šampaňské* ⓝ
   shuhm·puhn'·skair

championships *mistrovství* ⓝ
   mis·trofs·tvee
chance *náhoda* ⓕ na·ho·duh
change *změna* ⓕ zmye·nuh
change (coins) *drobné* ⓝ drob·nair
change (money) v *vyměnit* vi·mye·nyit
changing room *šatna* ⓕ shuht·nuh
charming *okouzlující* o·koh·zlu·yee·tsee
chat up v *balit* buh·lit
cheap *levný* lev·nee
cheat *podvod* ⓜ pod·vod
check (banking) *šek* ⓜ shek
check (bill) *účet* ⓜ oo·chet
check v *kontrolovat* kon·tro·lo·vuht
check-in (desk) *recepce* ⓕ re·tsep·tse
checkpoint *kontrolní stanoviště* ⓝ
   kon·trol·nyee stuh·no·vish·tye
cheese *sýr* ⓜ seer
cheese shop *obchod se sýrem* ⓜ
   op·khod se see·rem
chef *šéfkuchař(ka)* ⓜ/ⓕ
   shairf·ku·khuhrzh(·kuh)
chemist (pharmacist) *lékárník* ⓜ
   lair·kar·nyeek
chemist (pharmacy) *lékárna* ⓕ
   lair·kar·nuh
cheque (banking) *šek* ⓜ shek
cherry *třešeň* ⓕ trzhe·shen'
chess *šachy* ⓕ shuh·khi
chessboard *šachovnice* ⓕ
   shuh·khov·nyi·tse
chest (body) *hruď* ⓜ hrud'
chestnut *kaštan* ⓜ kuhsh·tuhn
chewing gum *žvýkačka* ⓕ
   zhvee·kuhch·kuh
chicken *kuře* ⓝ ku·rzhe
chicken pox *plané neštovice* ⓕ
   pluh·nair nesh·to·vi·tse
chickpea *cizrna* ⓕ tsi·zr·nuh
child *dítě* ⓝ dyee·tye
child-minding service
   služba pro hlídání dětí ⓕ
   sluzh·buh pro hlee·da·nyee dye·tyee
children *děti* ⓕ pl dye·tyi
child seat *autosedačka* ⓝ
   ow·to·se·duhch·kuh
chilli *feferon* ⓜ pfe·fe·ron
chilli sauce *feferonová omáčka* ⓕ
   pfe·fe·ro·no·va o·mach·kuh
China *Čína* ⓕ chee·nuh
chiropractor *chiropraktik* ⓜ
   khi·ro·pruhk·tik
chocolate *čokoláda* ⓕ cho·ko·la·duh

choose *vybrat si* vi-bruht si
chopping board *prkénko na krájení* ⓝ
pr-kairn-ko nuh kra-ye-nyee
chopsticks *hůlky* ① pl hool-ki
Christian *křesťan* ⓜ krzhes-tyuhn
Christian name *křestní jméno* ⓝ
krzhest-nyee ymair-no
Christmas *Vánoce* ⓝ pl va-no-tse
Christmas Day *Boží hod vánoční* ⓜ
bo-zhee hod va-noch-nyee
Christmas Eve *Štědrý večer* ⓜ
shtyed-ree ve-cher
church *kostel* ⓜ kos-tel
cider *mošt* ⓜ mosht
cigar *doutník* ⓜ doht-nyeek
cigarette *cigareta* ① tsi-guh-re-tuh
cigarette lighter *zapalovač* ⓜ
zuh-puh-lo-vuhch
cinema *kino* ⓝ ki-no
circus *cirkus* ⓜ tsir-kus
citizenship *občanství* ⓝ ob-chuhn-stvee
city *město* ⓝ myes-to
city centre *střed města* ⓝ
strzhed myes-tuh
civil rights *občanská práva* ⓝ pl
ob-chuhns-ka pra-vuh
clarinet *klarinet* ⓜ kluh-ri-net
class (category) *třída* ① trzhee-duh
class system *třídní systém* ⓜ
trzheed-nyee sis-tairm
classical *antický* uhn-tits-kee
clean a *čistý* chis-tee
clean v *čistit* chis-tyit
cleaning *úklid* ⓜ oo-klid
client *zákazník/zákaznice* ⓜ/①
za-kuhz-nyeek/za-kuhz-nyi-tse
cliff *skála* ① ska-luh
climb v *šplhat* shpl-hut
cloakroom *šatna* ① shuht-nuh
clock *hodiny* ① pl ho-dyi-ni
close a *blízký* bleez-kee
close v *zavírat* zuh-vee-ruht
closed *zavřený* zuh-vrzhe-nee
clothesline *prádelní šňůra* ①
pra-del-nyee shnyoo-ruh
clothing *šaty* ⓜ pl shuh-ti
clothing store *obchod s oblečením* ⓜ
op-khod s-o-ble-che-nyeem
cloud *mrak* ⓜ mruhk
cloudy *zataženo* zuh-tuh-zhe-no
clutch (car) *spojka* ① spoy-kuh
coach (bus) *autokar* ⓜ ow-to-kuhr

coach (trainer) *trenér* ⓜ tre-ner
coach v *trénovat* trair-no-vuht
coast *pobřeží* ⓝ pob-rzhe-zhee
coat *kabát* ⓜ kuh-bat
cocaine *kokain* ⓜ ko-kain
cockroach *šváb* ⓜ shvab
cocktail *koktejl* ⓜ kok-teyl
cocoa *kakao* ⓝ kuh-kow
coconut *kokos* ⓜ ko-kos
coffee *káva* ① ka-vuh
coins *mince* ① min-tse
cold (illness) *nachlazení* ⓝ
nuh-khluh-ze-nyee
cold (weather) *zima* ① zi-muh
cold a *chladný* khluhd-nee
colleague *kolega/kolegině* ⓜ/①
ko-le-guh/ko-le-gi-nye
collect call *hovor na účet volaného* ⓜ
ho-vor nuh oo-chet vo-luh-nair-ho
college *vysoká škola* ① vi-so-ka shko-luh
colour *barva* ① buhr-vuh
comb *hřeben* ⓜ hrzhe-ben
come *přijít* przhi-yeet
comedy *komedie* ① ko-me-di-ye
comfortable *pohodlný* po-ho-dl-nee
commission *zakázka* ① zuh-kaz-kuh
communion *přijímání svátosti oltářní* ⓝ
przhi-yee-ma-nyee sva-tos-tyi
ol-tarzh-nyee
communist *komunista/komunistka* ⓜ/①
ko-mu-nis-tuh/ko-mu-nist-kuh
companion *společník/společnice* ⓜ/①
spo-lech-nyeek/spo-lech-nyi-tse
company (firm) *společnost* ①
spo-lech-nost
compass *kompas* ⓜ kom-puhs
complain *stěžovat si* stye-zho-vuht si
complaint *stížnost* ① styeezh-nost
complimentary (free) *bezplatný*
bez-pluht-nee
computer *počítač* ⓜ po-chee-tuhch
computer game *počítačová hra* ①
po-chee-tuh-cho-va hruh
concert *koncert* ⓜ kon-tsert
concussion *otřes mozku* ⓜ
ot-rzhes moz-ku
conditioner (hair) *kondicionér* ⓜ
kon-di-tsi-o-ner
condom *prezervativ* ⓜ pre-zer-vuh-tif
conference (big) *konference* ①
kon-fe-ren-tse
conference (small) *porada* ① po-ruh-duh

confession (religious) zpověď ① spo-vyed'
confirm (a booking) potvrdit pot-vr-dyit
congratulations blahopřání
  bluh-ho-przha-nyee
conjunctivitis zánět spojivek ⓜ
  za-nyet spo-yi-vek
connection (transport) spojení ⓝ
  spo-ye-nyee
conservative konzervativec ⓜ&①
  kon-zer-vuh-ti-vets
constipation zácpa ① zats-puh
consulate konzulát ⓜ kon-zu-lat
contact lenses kontaktní čočky ① pl
  kon-tuhkt-nyee choch-ki
contact lens solution fjozologický roztok
  ⓜ fyo-zo-lo-gits-kee roz-tok
contraceptives
  antikoncepční prostředky ⓜ pl
  uhn-ti-kon-tsep-chnyee prost-rzhed-ki
contract smlouva ① smloh-vuh
convenience store (milk bar) večerka ①
  ve-cher-kuh
convent klášter ⓜ klash-ter
cook kuchař(ka) ⓜ/① ku-kharzh(-kuh)
cook v vařit vuh-rzhit
cookie sušenka ① su-shen-kuh
cooking vaření ⓝ v uh-rzhe-nyee
cool (groovy) žůžo zhoo-zho
cool (temperature) chladný khluhd-nee
corkscrew vývrtka ① vee-vrt-kuh
corn kukuřice ① ku-ku-rzhi-tse
corner roh ⓜ rawh
cornflakes kukuřičné lupínky ⓜ pl
  ku-ku-rzhich-nair lu-peen-ki
corrupt a zkorumpovaný
  zko-rum-po-vuh-nee
corruption korupce ① ko-rup-tse
cost cena ① tse-nuh
cost v stát stat
cotton bavlna ① buh-vl-nuh
cotton balls kosmetické polštářky ⓜ pl
  kos-me-tits-kair polsh-tarzh-ki
cotton buds vatové tyčinky ① pl
  vuh-to-vair ti-chin-ki
couchette lehátko ⓝ le-hat-ko
cough kašel ⓜ kuh-shel
cough v kašlat kuhsh-luht
cough medicine lék proti kašli ⓜ
  lairk pro-tyi kuhsh-li
count v počítat po-chee-tat
counter (at bar) pult ⓜ pult
country země ① ze-mye
countryside venkov ⓜ ven-kof

coupon kupón ⓜ ku-pawn
courgette cuketa ① tsu-ke-tuh
court (legal) soud ⓜ sohd
court (tennis) kurt ⓜ kurt
couscous kuskus ⓜ kus-kus
cover charge vstupné ⓝ vstup-nair
cow kráva ① kra-vuh
cracker kreker ⓜ kre-ker
crafts umělecké řemesla ⓝ pl
  u-mye-lets-kair rzhe-mes-luh
crash srážka ① srazh-kuh
crazy bláznivý blaz-nyi-vee
cream (food) smetana ① sme-tuh-nuh
cream (lotion) krém ⓜ krairm
crèche jesle ① pl yes-le
credit úvěr ⓜ oo-vyer
credit card kreditní karta ①
  kre-dit-nyee kuhr-tuh
cricket (sport) kriket ⓜ kri-ket
crop (riding) bičík ⓜ bi-cheek
cross (religious) kříž ⓜ krzheezh
crowded nacpaný nuhts-puh-nee
crystal krystal ⓜ kris-tuhl
cucumber okurka ① o-kur-kuh
cup šálek ⓜ sha-lek
cupboard kredenc ① kre-dents
currency exchange směnárna ①
  smye-nar-nuh
current (electricity) elektrický proud ⓜ
  e-lek-trits-kee prohd
current affairs aktuální události ① pl
  uhk-tu-al-nyee u-da-los-tyi
curry kari ⓝ kuh-ri
custom zvyk ⓜ zvik
customs celnice ① tsel-ni-tse
cut říznutí ⓝ rzheez-nu-tyee
cut (with knife) v říznout rzheez-noht
cut (with scissors) v stříhat strzhee-huht
cutlery příbory ⓜ pl przhee-bo-ri
CV životopis ⓜ zhi-vo-to-pis
cycle (ride) v jezdit na kole
  yez-dit nuh ko-le
cycling jízda na kole ① yeez-duh nuh ko-le
cyclist cyklista ⓜ tsi-klis-tuh
cystitis zánět močového měchýře ⓜ
  za-nyet mo-cho-vair-ho mye-khee-rzhe
Czech a český ches-kee
Czech (language) čeština ① chesh-tyi-nuh
Czech (nationality) Čech/Češka ⓜ/①
  chekh/chesh-kuh
Czech Republic Česká republika ①
  ches-ka re-pu-bli-kuh

D

dad *táta* ⓜ *ta·tuh*
daily adv *denně* *de·nye*
dance *tanec* ⓜ *tuh·nets*
dance v *tancovat* *tuhn·tso·vuht*
dancing *tanec* ⓜ *tuh·nets*
dangerous *nebezpečný* *ne·bez·pech·nee*
dark (colour) *tmavý* *tmuh·vee*
dark (night) *černý* *cher·nee*
date (appointment) *schůzka* ⓕ
    skhooz·kuh
date (day) *datum* ⓝ *duh·tum*
date (fruit) *datle* ⓝ *duht·le*
date (night out) *rande* ⓝ *ruhn·de*
date of birth *datum narození* ⓝ
    duh·tum nuh·ro·ze·nye
daughter *dcera* ⓕ *dtse·ruh*
dawn *svítání* *svee·ta·nyee*
day *den* *den*
day after tomorrow *pozítří* ⓝ
    po·zeet·rzhee
day before yesterday *předevčírem* ⓝ
    przhe·def·chee·rem
dead *mrtvý* *mrt·vee*
deaf *hluchý* *hlu·khee*
deal (cards) v *rozdávat* *roz·da·vat*
December *prosinec* ⓜ *pro·si·nets*
decide *rozhodnout* *roz·hod·noht*
deep (water) *hluboký* *hlu·bo·kee*
deforestation *odlesňování* ⓝ
    od·les·nyo·va·nyee
degrees (temperature) *stupeň* ⓜ *stu·pen'*
delay *zpoždění* ⓝ *zpozh·dye·nyee*
delicatessen *lahůdky* ⓕ pl *luh·hood·ki*
deliver *dovézt* *do·vairzt*
democracy *demokracie* ⓕ
    de·mo·kruh·tsi·ye
demonstration (display) *předvedení* ⓝ
    przhed·ve·de·nyee
demonstration (rally) *demonstrace* ⓕ
    de·mons·truh·tse
Denmark *Dánsko* ⓝ *dans·ko*
dental floss *dentální nit* ⓕ
    den·tal·nyee nyit
dentist *zubař(ka)* ⓜ/ⓕ *zu·buhrzh(·kuh)*
deodorant *deodorant* ⓝ *de·o·do·ruhnt*
depart *odjet* *od·yet*
department store *obchodní dům* ⓜ
    op·khod·nyee doom
departure *odjezd* ⓜ *od·yezd*
departure gate *východ k letadlům* ⓕ
    vee·khod k le·tuhd·loom

deposit *vklad* ⓜ *fkluhd*
derailleur *přesmykač* ⓜ *przhes·mi·kuhch*
descendent *potomek* ⓜ *po·to·mek*
desert *poušť* *pohshť*
design *vzor* ⓜ *vzor*
dessert *moučník* ⓜ *mohch·nyeek*
destination *cíl cesty* ⓜ *tseel tses·ti*
details *podrobnosti* ⓕ *po·drob·nos·tyi*
diabetes *cukrovka* ⓕ *tsu·krof·kuh*
dial tone *oznamovací tón* ⓜ
    oz·nuh·mo·vuh·tsee tawn
diaper *plénka* ⓕ *plairn·kuh*
diaphragm (contraceptive) *pesar* ⓜ
    pe·suhr
diarrhoea *průjem* ⓜ *proo·yem*
diary *denník* ⓜ *de·nyeek*
dice *kostka* ⓕ *kost·kuh*
dictionary *slovník* ⓜ *slov·nyeek*
die v *zemřít* *zem·rzheet*
diet *strava* ⓕ *struh·vuh*
different *odlišný* *od·lish·nee*
difficult *těžký* *tyezh·kee*
digital *digitální* *di·gi·tal·nee*
dining car *jídelní vůz* ⓜ *yee·del·nye vooz*
dinner *večeře* ⓕ *ve·che·rzhe*
direct *přímý* *przhee·mee*
direct-dial *přímé volání* ⓝ
    przhee·mair vo·la·nye
direction *směr* ⓜ *smyer*
director *ředitel(ka)* ⓜ/ⓕ *rzhe·dyi·tel(·kuh)*
dirty *špinavý* *shpi·nuh·vee*
disabled *invalidní* *in·vuh·lid·nye*
disco *disko* ⓝ *dis·ko*
discount *sleva* ⓕ *sle·vuh*
discrimination *diskriminace* ⓕ
    dis·kri·mi·nuh·tse
disease *nemoc* ⓕ *ne·mots*
dish *pokrm* ⓜ *po·krm*
disk (CD-ROM) *disk* ⓜ *disk*
disk (floppy) *disketa* ⓕ *dis·ke·tuh*
diving *potápění* ⓝ *po·ta·pye·nyee*
diving equipment *výzbroj na potápění* ⓝ
    veez·broy na po·ta·pye·nyee
divorced *rozvedený* *roz·ve·de·nee*
dizzy *závratný* *za·vruht·nee*
do *dělat* *dye·luht*
doctor *doktor(ka)* ⓜ/ⓕ *dok·tor(·kuh)*
documentary *dokumentární* ⓝ
    do·ku·men·tar·nye
dog *pes* ⓜ *pes*
dole *podpora v nezaměstnanosti* ⓕ
    pod·po·ruh v ne·zuh·myest·nuh·nos·tyi
doll *panenka* ⓕ *puh·nen·kuh*

dollar *dolar* ⓜ do·luhr
door *dveře* ⓕ pl dve·rzhe
dope (drugs) *hřup* ⓜ hnyup
double a *dvojitý* dvo·yi·tee
double bed *manželská postel* ⓕ
    muhn·zhels·ka pos·tel
double room *dvoulůžkový pokoj* ⓜ
    dvoh·loozh·ko·vee po·koy
down *dolů* do·loo
downhill *z kopce* s kop·tse
dozen *tucet* ⓜ tu·tset
drama *činohra* ⓕ chi·no·hruh
dream *sen* ⓜ sen
dress *šaty* ⓜ pl shuh·ti
dried *sušený* su·she·nee
dried fruit *sušené ovoce* ⓝ
    su·she·nair o·vo·tse
drink *nápoj* ⓜ na·poy
drink v *pít* peet
drink (alcoholic) *alkoholický nápoj* ⓜ
    uhl·ko·ho·lits·kee na·poy
drive v *řídit* rzhe·dyit
drivers licence *řidičský průkaz* ⓜ
    rzhi·dyich·skee proo·kuhz
drug *lék* ⓜ lairk
drug addiction *narkomanie* ⓕ
    nuhr·ko·muh·ni·ye
drug dealer *překupník drog* ⓜ
    przhe·kup·nyeek drog
drugs (illicit) *drogy* ⓕ pl dro·gi
drug trafficking *pašování drog* ⓝ
    puh·sho·va·nyee drog
drug user *narkoman(ka)* ⓜ/ⓕ
    nuhr·ko·muhn(·kuh)
drum *buben* ⓜ bu·ben
drums (kit) *bicí souprava* ⓕ pl
    bi·tsee soh·pruh·vuh
drunk *opilý* o·pi·lee
dry a *suchý* su·khee
dry (clothes) v *sušit* su·shit
dry (oneself) v *utřít se* ut·rzheet se
duck *kachna* ⓕ kuhkh·nuh
dummy (pacifier) *dudlík* ⓜ dud·leek
duty-free *bez cla* bez tsluh
DVD *DVD* ⓝ dee·vee·deech·ko

E

each *každý* kuhzh·dee
ear *ucho* ⓝ u·kho
early adv *časně* chuhs·nye
earn *vydělat* vi·dye·luht

earplugs *ucpávky do ucha* ⓕ pl
    uts·paf·ki do u·khuh
earrings *náušnice* ⓕ pl na·ush·nyi·tse
Earth *Země* ⓕ ze·mye
earthquake *zemětřesení* ⓝ
    ze·myet·rzhe·se·nyee
east *východ* ⓜ vee·khod
Easter *Velikonoce* ve·li·ko·no·tse
easy *lehký* leh·kee
eat v *jíst* yeest
economy class *turistická třída* ⓕ
    tu·ris·tits·ka trzhee·duh
ecstasy (drug) *extáze* ⓕ eks·ta·ze
eczema *ekzém* ⓜ ek·zairm
education *vzdělání* ⓝ vzde·la·nyee
egg *vajíčko* ⓝ vuh·yeech·ko
eggplant *lilek* ⓜ li·lek
election *volby* ⓕ pl vol·bi
electrical store *elektro obchod* ⓜ
    e·lek·tro op·khod
electrician *elektrikář* e·lek·tri·karzh
electricity *elektřina* ⓕ e·lek·trzhi·nuh
elevator *výtah* ⓜ vee·tuh
email *email* ⓜ ee·meyl
embarrassed *rozpačitý* roz·puh·chi·tee
embassy *velvyslanectví* ⓝ
    vel·vi·sluh·nets·tvee
emergency *pohotovost* ⓕ po·ho·to·vost
emotional *citový* tsi·to·vee
employee *zaměstnanec/zaměstnankyně*
    ⓜ/ⓕ zuh·myest·nuh·nets/
    zuh·myest·nuhn·ki·nye
employer *zaměstnavatel(kyně)* ⓜ/ⓕ
    zuh·myest·nuh·vuh·tel(·ki·nye)
empty a *prázdný* prazd·nee
encephalitis (tick-borne)
    meningokoková encefalitida ⓕ
    me·nin·go·ko·ko·va en·tse·fuh·li·ti·duh
end *konec* ⓜ ko·nets
endangered species *ohrožené druhy*
    ⓜ pl o·hro·zhe·nair dru·hi
engaged (phone) *obsazeno* ob·suh·ze·no
engaged (to be married) *zasnoubený*
    zuh·snoh·be·nee
engagement (to marry) *zasnoubení* ⓝ
    zuh·snoh·be·nyee
engine *motor* ⓜ mo·tor
engineer *inženýr(ka)* ⓜ/ⓕ
    in·zhe·neer(·kuh)
engineering *strojírenství* ⓝ
    stro·yee·rens·tvee
England *Anglie* ⓕ uhn·gli·ye

English (language) *angličtina* ①
uhn·glich·tyi·nuh

English (nationality) *Angličan(ka)* ⑩/①
uhn·gli·chuhn(·kuh)

enjoy (oneself) *užívat* u·zhee·vuht

enough *dost* dost

enter *vstoupit* vstoh·pit

entertainment guide
přehled kulturních pořadů ⑩
przhe·hled kul·tur·nyeekh po·rzha·doo

entry *vstup* ⑩ vstup

envelope *obálka* ① o·bal·kuh

environment *prostředí* ⑩ prost·rzhe·dee

epilepsy *epilepsie* ① e·pi·lep·si·ye

equality *rovnost* ① rov·nost

equal opportunity *rovné příležitosti* ① pl
rov·nair przhe·le·zhi·tos·tyi

equipment *výstroj* ① vees·troy

escalator *eskalátor* ⑩ es·kuh·la·tor

estate agency *realitní kancelář* ①
re·uh·lit·nyee kuhn·tse·larzh

euro *euro* ⑩ e·u·ro

Europe *Evropa* ① e·vro·puh

European Union *Evropská unie* ①
e·vrops·ka u·ni·ye

euthanasia *euthanasie* ①
e·u·tuh·nuh·si·ye

evening *večer* ⑩ ve·cher

every a *každý* kuzh·dee

everyone *všichni* vshikh·nyi

everything *všechno* ⑩ vshekh·no

exactly *přesně* przhes·nye

example *příklad* ⑩ przhee·kluhd

excellent *výborný* vee·bor·nee

excess baggage *nadměrné zavazadlo* ⑩
nuhd·myer·nair zuh·vuh·zuhd·lo

exchange *výměna* ① vee·mye·nuh

exchange v *vyměnit* vi·mye·nyit

exchange rate *směnný kurs* ⑩
smye·nee kurz

excluded *vynechaný* vi·ne·khuh·nee

exhaust (car) *výfuk* ⑩ vee·fuk

exhibition *výstava* ① vees·tuh·vuh

exit *východ* ⑩ vee·khod

expensive *drahý* druh·hee

experience *zkušenost* ① sku·she·nost

exploitation *vykořisťování* ⑩
vi·ko·rzhis·tyo·va·nye

export permit *vývozní povolení* ⑩
vee·voz·nyee po·vo·le·nyee

express a *expresní* eks·pres·nye

express mail *expresní zásilka* ①
eks·pres·nye za·sil·kuh

extension (visa) *prodloužení* ⑩
prod·loh·zhe·nyee

eye *oko* ⑩ o·ko

eye drops *oční kapky* ① pl
och·nyee kuhp·ki

F

fabric *látka* ① lat·kuh

face *obličej* ⑩ ob·li·chey

face cloth *žínka* ① zheen·kuh

factory *továrna* ① to·var·nuh

factory worker *dělník* ⑩ dyel·nyeek

fall (autumn) *podzim* ⑩ pod·zim

fall (down) *pád* ⑩ pad

family *rodina* ① ro·dyi·nuh

family name *příjmení* ⑩ przheey·me·nyee

famous *slavný* sluhv·nee

fan (machine) *větrák* ⑩ vye·trak

fan (sport) *fanoušek* ⑩ fuh·noh·shek

fan belt *klínový řemen* ⑩
klee·no·vee rzhe·men

far *daleko* duh·le·ko

fare *jízdné* ① yeezd·nair

farm *statek* ⑩ stuh·tek

farmer *zemědělec/zemědělkyně* ⑩/①
ze·mye·dye·lets/ze·mye·dyel·ki·nye

fashion *móda* ① maw·duh

fast a *rychlý* rikh·lee

fat a *tlustý* tlus·tee

father *otec* ⑩ o·tets

father-in-law *tchán* ⑩ tkhan

faucet *kohoutek* ⑩ ko·hoh·tek

fault (someone's) *chyba* ① khi·buh

faulty *vadný* vuhd·nee

fax machine *fax* ⑩ fuhks

February *únor* ⑩ oo·nor

feed *krmit* kr·mit

feel (touch) v *sáhnout* sah·noht

feeling (physical) *cit* ⑩ tsit

feelings *city* ⑩ pl tsi·ti

female a *ženský* zhens·kee

fence *plot* ⑩ plot

fencing (sport) *šerm* ⑩ sherm

ferry *trajekt* ⑩ truh·yekt

festival *festival* ⑩ fes·ti·vuhl

fever *horečka* ① ho·rech·kuh

few *málo* ma·lo

fiancé *snoubenec* ⑩ snoh·be·nets

fiancée *snoubenka* ① snoh·ben·kuh

fiction *beletrie* ① be·le·tri·ye

fig *fík* ⑩ feek

fight *rvačka* ① rvuhch·kuh

fill v *plnit* pl·nyit
fillet *filé* ⓕ fi·lair
film (cinema) *film* ⓜ film
film (for camera) *film* ⓜ film
film speed *citlivost* ⓕ tsit·li·vost
filtered *filtrovaný* fil·tro·vuh·nee
find v *najít* nuh·yeet
fine a *vynikající* vi·nyi·kuh·yee·tsee
fine *pokuta* ⓕ po·ku·tuh
finger *prst* ⓜ prst
finish *konec* ⓜ ko·nets
finish v *dokončit* do·kon·chit
Finland *Finsko* ⓝ fin·sko
fire *oheň* ⓜ o·hen'
firewood *palivové dřevo* ⓝ
   puh·li·vo·vair drzhe·vo
first a *první* prv·nyee
first-aid kit *lékárnička* ⓕ lair·kar·nyich·kuh
first class *první třída* ⓕ
   prv·nyee trzhee·duh
first name *křestní jméno* ⓝ
   krzhest·nyee ymair·no
fish *ryba* ⓕ ri·buh
fishing *rybolov* ⓜ ri·bo·lov
fishmonger *prodavač ryb* ⓜ
   pro·duh·vuhch rib
fish shop *obchod s rybami* ⓕ
   op·khod s ri·buh·mi
flag *vlajka* ⓕ vlai·kuh
flannel (face cloth) *žínka* ⓕ zheen·kuh
flash (camera) *blesk* ⓜ blesk
flashlight *baterka* ⓕ buh·ter·kuh
flat (apartment) *byt* ⓜ bit
flat a *rovný* rov·nee
flea *blecha* ⓕ ble·khuh
fleamarket *bleší trh* ⓕ ble·shee trh
flight *let* ⓜ let
flood *povodeň* ⓕ po·vo·den'
floor *podlaha* ⓕ pod·luh·huh
floor (storey) *poschodí* ⓝ pos·kho·dyee
florist *květinář* ⓜ kvye·tyi·narzh
flour *mouka* ⓕ moh·kuh
flower *květina* ⓕ kvye·tyi·nuh
flu *chřipka* ⓕ khrzhip·kuh
flute *flétna* ⓕ flairt·nuh
fly *moucha* ⓕ moh·khuh
fly v *létat* lair·tuht
foggy *mlhavý* ml·huh·vee
follow *následovat* nas·le·do·vuht
food *jídlo* ⓝ yeed·lo
food supplies *zásoby potravin* ⓕ pl
   za·so·bi po·truh·vin
foot (body) *chodidlo* ⓝ kho·dyid·lo

football (soccer) *fotbal* ⓜ fot·buhl
footpath *chodník* ⓜ khod·nyeek
foreign *cizí* tsi·zee
forest *les* ⓜ les
forever *navždy* nuhv·zhdi
forget *zapomenout* zuh·po·me·noht
forgive *prominout* pro·mi·noht
fork *vidlička* ⓕ vid·lich·kuh
fortnight *čtrnáct dní* chtr·natst dnye
fortune teller *věštkyně* ⓕ vyesht·ki·nye
foul (soccer) *faul* ⓜ fowl
foyer *předsíň* ⓕ przhed·seen'
fragile *křehký* krzheh·kee
France *Francie* ⓕ fruhn·tsi·ye
free (available) a *volný* vol·nee
free (gratis) a *bezplatný* bez·pluht·nee
free (not bound) a *svobodný* svo·bod·nee
freeze v *zmrznout* zmrz·noht
fresh *čerstvý* cherst·vee
Friday *pátek* ⓜ pa·tek
fridge *lednička* ⓕ led·nyich·kuh
fried *smažený* smuh·zhe·nee
friend *přítel* ⓜ przhee·tel
from z z
frost *mráz* ⓜ mraz
frozen *zmrzlý* zmrz·lee
fruit *ovoce* ⓝ o·vo·tse
fruit picking *trhání ovoce* ⓝ
   tr·ha·nyee o·vo·tse
fry v *smažit* smuh·zhit
frying pan *pánev* ⓕ pa·nef
full *plný* pl·nee
full-time *na plný úvazek*
   nuh pl·nee oo·vuh·zek
fun a *zábavný* za·buhv·nee
funeral *pohřeb* ⓜ po·hrzheb
funny *legrační* le·gruhch·nyee
furniture *nábytek* ⓜ na·bi·tek
future *budoucnost* ⓕ bu·dohts·nost

G

game (general) *hra* ⓕ hruh
game (sport) *zápas* ⓜ za·puhs
garage *garáž* ⓕ guh·razh
garbage *odpadky* ⓜ pl od·puhd·ki
garbage can *popelnice* ⓕ po·pel·nyi·tse
garden *zahrada* ⓕ zuh·hruh·duh
gardener *zahradník* ⓜ zuh·hrud·nyeek
gardening *zahradničení* ⓝ
   zuh·hruhd·nyi·che·nyee
garlic *česnek* ⓜ ches·nek
garnet *granát* ⓜ gruh·nat

gas (for cooking) plyn ⓜ plin
gas (petrol) benzín ⓜ ben-zeen
gas cartridge plynová bomba ⓕ
    pli-no-va bom-buh
gastroenteritis gastroenteritida ⓕ
    guhs-tro-en-te-ri-ti-duh
gate (airport) výstup k letadlům ⓜ
    vees-tup k le-tuhd-loom
gauze gáza ⓕ ga-zuh
gay (homosexual) homosexuální
    ho-mo-sek-su-al-nyee
gearbox rychlostní skříň ⓕ
    ri-khlost-nyee skrzheen'
Germany Německo ⓝ nye-mets-ko
get dostat do-stuht
get off (bus, train) vystoupit vis-toh-pit
gift dar ⓜ duhr
gig koncert ⓜ kon-tsert
gin džin dzhin
girl dívka ⓕ dyeef-kuh
girlfriend přítelkyně ⓕ przhee-tel-ki-nye
give dát dat
given name křestní jméno ⓝ
    krzhest-nyee ymair-no
glandular fever mononukleóza ⓕ
    mo-no-nu-kle-aw-zuh
glass (drinking) sklenička ⓕ skle-nyich-kuh
glasses (spectacles) brýle ⓕ pl bree-le
glassware skleněné zboží ⓝ
    skle-nye-nair zbo-zhee
gloves (clothing) rukavice ⓕ pl
    ru-kuh-vi-tse
gloves (latex) gumové rukavice ⓕ pl
    gu-mo-vair ru-kuh-vi-tse
glue lepidlo ⓝ le-pid-lo
go jít yeet
goal (sport) gól ⓜ gawl
goalkeeper brankář ⓜ bruhn-karzh
goat koza ⓕ ko-zuh
god (general) bůh ⓜ booh
goggles (skiing) lyžařské brýle ⓕ pl
    li-zharzh-skair bree-le
goggles (swimming) plavecké brýle ⓕ pl
    pluh-vets-kair bree-le
gold zlato ⓝ zluh-to
golf ball golfový míček ⓜ
    gol-fo-vee mee-chek
golf course golfové hřiště ⓝ
    gol-fo-vair hrzhish-tye
good dobrý do-bree
goodbye na shledanou nuh-skhle-duh-noh
go out vyjít vi-yeet
go out with (date) chodit s kho-dyit s

go shopping jít na nákupy
    yeet nuh na-ku-pi
government vláda ⓕ vla-duh
gram gram ⓜ gruhm
grandchild vnuk/vnučka ⓜ/ⓕ
    vnuk/vnuch-kuh
grandfather dědeček ⓜ dye-de-chek
grandmother babička ⓕ buh-bich-kuh
grapes hrozny ⓜ pl hroz-ni
grass (lawn) tráva ⓕ tra-vuh
grateful vděčný vdyech-nee
grave hrob ⓜ hrob
great (fantastic) báječný ba-yech-nee
green zelený ze-le-nee
greengrocer zelinář ⓜ ze-li-narzh
grey šedivý she-dyi-vee
grocery potravina ⓕ pot-ruh-vi-nuh
grocery store konzum ⓜ kon-zum
groundnut podzemnice olejná ⓕ
    pod-zem-nyi-tse o-ley-na
grow růst roost
guarantee záruka ⓕ za-ru-kuh
guess v odhadovat od-huh-do-vuht
guesthouse penzion ⓜ pen-zi-on
guide (audio) audio guide ⓜ ow-di-o gaid
guide (person) průvodce ⓜ proo-vod-tse
guidebook průvodce ⓜ proo-vod-tse
guide dog slepecký pes ⓜ sle-pets-kee pes
guided tour okružní jízda ⓕ
    o-kruzh-nyee yeez-duh
guilty vinný vi-nee
guitar kytara ⓕ ki-tuh-ruh
gum dáseň ⓕ da-sen'
gun (pistol) pistole ⓕ pis-to-le
gun (rifle) puška ⓕ push-kuh
gym (place) tělocvična ⓕ tye-lots-vich-nuh
gymnastics gymnastika ⓕ gim-nuhs-ti-kuh
gynaecologist gynekolog ⓜ gi-ne-ko-log

H

hair vlasy ⓜ pl vluh-si
hairbrush kartáč na vlasy ⓜ
    kuhr-tach nuh vluh-si
haircut ostříhání vlasů ⓝ
    ost-rzhee-ha-nyee vluh-soo
hairdresser (for men) holič ⓜ ho-lich
hairdresser (for women)
    kadeřník/kadeřnice ⓜ/ⓕ
    kuh-derzh-nyeek/kuh-derzh-nyi-tse
halal halal huh-luhl
half polovina ⓕ po-lo-vi-nuh

hallucination *halucinace* ①
  huh·lu·tsi·nuh·tse
ham *šunka* ① *shun·kuh*
hammer *kladivo* ⓝ *kluh·dyi·vo*
hammock *hamak* ⓜ *huh·muhk*
hand *ruka* ① *ru·kuh*
handbag *kabelka* ① *kuh·bel·kuh*
handball *házená* ① *ha·ze·na*
handicraft *umělecké řemeslo* ⓝ
  u·mye·lets·kair rzhe·mes·lo
handkerchief *kapesník* ⓜ *kuh·pes·nyeek*
handlebars *řidítka* ① *rzhi·dyeet·kuh*
handmade *ručně vyrobeno*
  ruch·nye vi·ro·be·no
handsome *hezký* *hez·kee*
happy *šťastný* *shtyast·nee*
harassment *obtěžování* ⓝ
  ob·tye·zho·va·nyee
harbour *přístav* ⓜ *przhee·stuhf*
hard (not soft) *tvrdý* *tvr·dee*
hard-boiled *natvrdo uvařený*
  nuh·tvr·do u·vuh·rzhe·nee
hardware store *železářství* ⓝ
  zhe·le·zarzh·stve·
hashish *hašiš* ⓜ *huh·shish*
hat (hard) *klobouk* ⓜ *klo·bohk*
hat (soft) *čepice* ① *che·pi·tse*
have *mít* *meet*
have a cold *být nastydlý* *beet nuh·stid·lee*
have fun *bavit se* *buh·vit se*
hay fever *senná rýma* ① *se·na ree·muh*
hazelnut *lískový oříšek* ⓜ
  lees·ko·vee o·rzhee·shek
he *on* *on*
head *hlava* ① *hluh·vuh*
headache *bolení hlavy* ①
  bo·le·nyee hluh·vi
headlights *reflektor* ⓜ *re·flek·tor*
health *zdraví* ⓝ *zdra·vee*
hear *slyšet* *sli·shet*
hearing aid *naslouchátko* ⓝ
  nuh·sloh·khat·ko
heart *srdce* ① *srd·tse*
heart attack *srdeční infarkt* ⓜ
  sr·dech·nyee in·fuhrkt
heart condition *srdeční porucha* ①
  sr·dech·nyee po·ru·khuh
heat *horko* ⓝ *hor·ko*
heated *vytápěný* *vi·ta·pye·nee*
heater *ohřívač* ⓜ *o·hrzhee·vuhch*
heating *topení* ⓝ *to·pe·nyee*
heavy (weight) *těžký* *tyezh·kee*
helmet *helma* ① *hel·muh*

help *pomoc* ① *po·mots*
help v *pomoci* *po·mo·tsi*
hepatitis *žloutenka* ① *zhloh·ten·kuh*
her (possessive) *její* *ye·yee*
herb *bylina* ① *bi·li·nuh*
herbalist *kořenář* ⓜ *ko·rzhe·narzh*
here *tady* *tuh·di*
heroin *heroin* ⓜ *he·ro·in*
herring *sleď* ① *sled'*
high (height) *vysoký* *vi·so·kee*
highchair *dětská stolička* ①
  dyet·ska sto·lich·kuh
high school *střední škola* ①
  strzhed·nyee shko·luh
highway *dálnice* ① *dal·nyi·tse*
hike v *trampovat* *truhm·po·vuht*
hiking *turistika* ① *tu·ris·ti·kuh*
hiking boots *trekingová obuv* ①
  tre·kin·go·va o·buf
hiking route *turistická stezka* ①
  tu·ris·tits·ka stez·kuh
hill *kopec* ⓜ *ko·pets*
Hindu *hind/hindka* ⓜ/① *hind/hind·kuh*
hire v *vypůjčit* *vi·pooy·chit*
his *jeho* *ye·ho*
historical *historický* *his·to·rits·kee*
history *dějiny* ① pl *dye·yi·ni*
hitchhike *stopovat* *sto·po·vuht*
HIV *HIV* ⓝ *ha·ee·vair*
hockey *hokej* ⓝ *ho·key*
holiday *svátek* ⓜ *sva·tek*
holidays *dovolená* ① *do·vo·le·na*
home *domov* ⓜ *do·mof*
homeless (person) *bezdomovec* ⓜ&①
  bez·do·mo·vets
homemaker *manželka* ① *muhn·zhel·kuh*
homeopathy *homeopatie* ①
  ho·me·o·puh·ti·ye
homesick *tesknící po domově*
  tesk·nyee·tsee po do·mo·vye
homosexual *homosexuál* ⓜ
  ho·mo·sek·su·al
honey *med* ⓝ *med*
honeymoon *svatební cesta* ①
  svuh·teb·nyee tses·tuh
horoscope *horoskop* ⓜ *ho·ros·kop*
horse *kůň* ⓜ *koon'*
horse racing *dostihy* ⓜ pl *dos·tyi·hi*
horse riding *jízda na koni* ①
  yeez·duh nuh ko·nyi
hospital *nemocnice* ① *ne·mots·nyi·tse*
hospitality *pohostinství* ⓝ
  po·hos·tyins·tve·

hot *horký* hor·kee
hotel *hotel* m ho·tel
hot water *teplá voda* ① tep·la vo·duh
hot water bottle *ohřívací láhev* ①
  o·hrzhee·vuh·tsee la·hef
hour *hodina* ① ho·dyi·nuh
house *dům* m doom
housework *práce v domácnosti* ①
  pra·tse v do·mats·nos·tyi
how *jak* yuhk
how much *kolik* ko·lik
hug v *obejmout* o·bey·moht
huge *ohromný* o·hrom·nee
humanities *humanitní vědy* ① pl
  hu·muh·nit·nyee vye·di
human resources *lidské zdroje* m pl
  lid·skair zdro·ye
human rights *lidská práva* ① pl
  lid·ska pra·vuh
hundred *sto* m sto
hungry *hladový* hluh·do·vee
hunting *lov* m lov
hurt v *uhodit se* u·ho·dyit se
husband *manžel* m muhn·zhel

I

I *já* ya
ice *led* m led
ice axe *cepín* m tse·peen
ice cream *zmrzlina* ① zmrz·li·nuh
ice-cream parlour
  cukrárna ①/*ovocný bar* m
  tsu·krar·nuh/o·vots·nee buhr
ice hockey *lední hokej* m led·nyee ho·key
identification *osobní doklad* ①
  o·sob·nyee dok·luhd
identification card (ID) *doklad totožnosti*
  m dok·luhd to·tozh·nos·tyi
if *jestliže* yest·li·zhe
ill *nemocný* ne·mots·nee
immigration *imigrace* ① i·mi·gruh·tse
important *důležitý* doo·le·zhi·tee
impossible *nemožný* ne·mozh·nee
in v v
in a hurry *spěšně* spyesh·nye
included *včetně* fchet·nye
income tax *daň z příjmu* ①
  duhn' z przheey·mu
indicator *blinkr* m blin·kr

indigestion *zažívací poruchy* ① pl
  zuh·zhee·vuh·tsee po·ru·khi
indoor *halový* huh·lo·vee
industry *průmysl* m proo·mi·sl
infection *infekce* ① in·fek·tse
inflammation *zánět* m za·nyet
influenza *chřipka* ① khrzhip·kuh
information *informace* ① in·for·muh·tse
in front of *před* przhed
ingredient *příměs* ① przhe·myes
inject *aplikovat injekci*
  uh·pli·ko·vuht in·yek·tsi
injection *injekce* ① in·yek·tse
injured *zraněný* zruh·nye·nee
injury *zranění* m zruh·nye·nyee
inner tube *duše* ① du·she
innocent *nevinný* ne·vi·nee
insect *hmyz* m hmiz
insect repellent *repelent (prostředek
  na hubení hmyzu)* m re·pe·lent
  (prost·rzhe·dek nuh hu·be·nyee hmi·zu)
inside adv *vnitřní* vnyi·trzh·nyee
instructor *instruktor(ka)* m/①
  ins·truk·tor(·kuh)
insurance *pojištění* m po·yish·tye·nyee
interesting *zajímavý* zuh·yee·muh·vee
intermission *přestávka* ① przhe·staf·kuh
international *mezinárodní*
  me·zi·na·rod·nyee
Internet *internet* m in·ter·net
Internet café *internetová kavárna* ①
  in·ter·ne·to·va kuh·var·nuh
interpreter *tlumočník/tlumočnice* m/①
  tlu·moch·nyeek/tlu·moch·nyi·tse
interview *pohovor* m po·ho·vor
invite *pozvat* poz·vuht
Ireland *Irsko* m ir·sko
iron (for clothes) *žehlička* ①
  zheh·lich·kuh
island *ostrov* m os·trov
it *to* to
IT (information technology) *IT
  (informuční technologie)* ① ee·tair
  (in·for·muhch·nyee tekh·no·lo·gi·ye)
Italy *Itálie* ① i·ta·li·ye
itch *svědění* m svye·dye·nyee
itemised *rozepsaný* ro·zep·suh·nee
itinerary *itinerář* m i·ti·ne·rarzh
IUD *nitroděložní tělísko* m
  nyi·tro·dye·lozh·nyee tye·lees·ko

J

jacket *sako* ⓝ suh-ko
jail *věznice* ⓕ vyez-ni-tse
jam *džem* ⓝ dzhem
January *leden* ⓜ le-den
Japan *Japonsko* ⓝ yuh-pon-sko
jar *sklenice* ⓕ skle-nyi-tse
jaw *čelist* ⓕ che-list
jealous *žárlivý* zhar-li-vee
jeans *džíny* ⓟⓛ dzhee-ni
jeep *džíp* ⓜ dzheep
jet lag *pásmová nemoc* ⓕ
  pas-mo-va ne-mots
jewellery *šperky* ⓜ ⓟⓛ shper-ki
Jewish *židovský* zhi-dof-skee
job *zaměstnání* ⓝ zuh-myest-na-nyee
jogging *kondiční běh* ⓜ
  kon-dich-nyee byeh
joke *vtip* ⓜ ftyip
journalist *novinář(ka)* ⓜ/ⓕ
  no-vi-narzh(-kuh)
journey *cesta* ⓕ tses-tuh
judge *soudce* ⓜ sohd-tse
juice *šťáva* ⓕ shtya-vuh
July *červenec* ⓜ cher-ve-nets
jump v *skočit* sko-chit
jumper (sweater) *svetr* ⓜ sve-tr
jumper leads *startovací kabely* ⓜ
  stuhr-to-vuh-tsee kuh-be-li
June *červen* ⓜ cher-ven

K

kayaking *kajakování* ⓝ
  kuh-yuh-ko-va-nyee
ketchup *kečup* ⓜ ke-chup
key (door etc) *klíč* ⓜ kleech
keyboard *klávesnice* ⓕ kla-ves-nyi-tse
kick v *kopat* ko-puht
kidney *ledvina* ⓕ led-vi-nuh
kill v *zabít* zuh-beet
kilogram *kilogram* ⓜ ki-lo-gruhm
kilometre *kilometr* ⓜ ki-lo-me-tr
kind (nice) *laskavý* luhs-kuh-vee
kindergarten *školka* ⓕ shkol-kuh
king *král* ⓜ kral
kiosk *stánek* ⓜ sta-nek
kiss *polibek* ⓜ po-li-bek
kiss v *líbat* lee-buht
kitchen *kuchyň* ⓕ ku-khin'

knee *koleno* ⓝ ko-le-no
knife *nůž* ⓜ noozh
know *vědět* vye-dyet
kosher *košer* ko-sher

L

labourer *pomocný dělník* ⓜ
  po-mots-nee dyel-nyeek
lace (fabric) *krajka* ⓕ krai-kuh
lake *jezero* ⓝ ye-ze-ro
lamb (meat) *jehněčí* ⓝ yeh-nye-chee
land *země* ⓕ ze-mye
landlady *paní domácí* ⓕ
  puh-nyee do-ma-tsee
landlord *pan domácí* puhn do-ma-tsee
language *jazyk* ⓜ yuh-zik
laptop *notebook* ⓝ noht-buk
large *velký* vel-kee
last (final) *poslední* pos-led-nyee
last (previous) *předešlý* przhe-desh-lee
late adv *pozdě* poz-dye
later *později* poz-dye-yi
laugh v *smát se* smat se
launderette (samoobslužná) pradlenka ⓕ
  (suh-mo-ob-sluzh-na) pruhd-len-kuh
laundry (clothes) *prádlo* ⓝ prad-lo
laundry (place/room) *prádelna* ⓕ
  pra-del-nuh
law (legislation) *zákon* ⓜ za-kon
law (study/profession) *právo* ⓝ pra-vo
lawyer *advokát(ka)* ⓜ/ⓕ uhd-vo-kat(-kuh)
laxative *projímadlo* ⓝ pro-yee-muhd-lo
lazy *líný* lee-nee
leader *vůdce/vůdkyně* ⓜ/ⓕ
  vood-tse/vood-ki-nye
leaf *list* ⓜ list
learn *učit se* u-chit se
leather *kůže* ⓕ koo-zhe
lecturer *lektor(ka)* ⓜ/ⓕ lek-tor(-kuh)
ledge *lišta* ⓕ lish-tuh
left (direction) *levý* le-vee
left luggage *zavazadlo v úschovně* ⓝ
  zuh-vuh-zuhd-lo v oos-khov-nye
left-luggage office *úschovna zavazadel*
  ⓕ oos-khov-nuh zuh-vuh-zuh-del
left-wing *levicový* le-vi-tso-vee
leg (body) *noha* ⓕ no-huh
legal *legální* le-gal-nyee
legislation *legislativa* ⓕ le-gis-luh-ti-vuh
legume *luštěnina* ⓕ lush-tye-nyi-nuh
lemon *citron* ⓜ tsi-tron
lemonade *limonáda* ⓕ li-mo-na-duh

lens (camera) objektiv ⓜ ob-yek-tif
lentil čočka ⓕ choch-ka
lesbian lesbička ⓕ les-bich-kuh
less menší men-shee
letter (mail) dopis ⓜ do-pis
lettuce hlávkový salát ⓜ
    hlaf-ko-vee suh-lat
liar lhář ⓜ lharzh
librarian knihovník/knihovnice ⓜ/ⓕ
    knyi-hov-nyeek/knyi-hov-nyi-tse
library knihovna ⓕ knyi-hov-nuh
lice veš ⓕ vesh
licence povolení ⓝ po-vo-le-nyee
license plate number tabulka se státní
    poznávací značkou ⓕ tuh-bul-kuh se
    stat-nyee poz-na-vuh-tsee znuch-koh
lie (not stand) v ležet le-zhet
lie (not tell the truth) v lhát lhat
life život ⓜ zhi-vot
life jacket plovací vesta ⓕ
    plo-vuh-tsee ves-tuh
lift (elevator) výtah ⓜ vee-tah
light světlo ⓝ svyet-lo
light (colour) světlý svyet-lee
light (weight) lehký leh-kee
light bulb žárovka ⓕ zha-rof-kuh
lighter (cigarette) zapalovač ⓜ
    zuh-puh-lo-vuhch
light meter expozimetr ⓜ eks-po-zi-me-tr
like v mít rád meet rad
lime limeta ⓕ li-me-tuh
linen (material) lněná tkanina ⓕ
    lnye-na tkuh-nyi-nuh
linen (sheets) ložní prádlo ⓝ pl
    lozh-nyee prad-lo
linguist lingvista ⓜ ling-vis-tuh
lip balm pomáda na rty ⓕ
    po-ma-duh nuh rti
lips rty ⓕ pl rti
lipstick rtěnka ⓕ rtyen-kuh
listen poslouchat po-sloh-khuht
little (quantity) málo ⓝ ma-lo
little (size) a malý muh-lee
live (life) žít zheet
live (somewhere) bydlet bid-let
liver játra ⓕ ya-truh
lizard ještěrka ⓕ yesh-tyer-kuh
local a místní meest-nyee
lock zámek ⓜ za-mek
lock v zamknout zuhm-knoht
locked zamknutý zuhm-knu-tee
lollies lízátka ⓝ pl lee-zat-kuh
long dlouhý dloh-hee

look v dívat se dyee-vuht se
look after starat se stuh-ruht se
look for hledat hle-duht
lookout vyhlídka ⓕ vih-leed-kuh
loose volný vol-nee
loose change drobné ⓝ pl drob-nair
lose ztratit ztruh-tyit
lost ztracený ztruh-tse-nee
lost-property office ztráty a nálezy ⓕ
    ztra-ti uh na-le-zi
(a) lot hodně hod-nye
loud hlasitý hluh-si-tee
love láska ⓕ las-kuh
love v milovat mi-lo-vuht
lover milenec/milenka ⓜ/ⓕ
    mi-le-nets/mi-len-kuh
low nízký nyeez-kee
lubricant mazivo ⓝ muh-zi-vo
luck štěstí ⓝ shtyes-tyee
lucky šťastný shtyast-nee
luggage zavazadlo ⓝ zuh-vuh-zuhd-lo
luggage locker zavazadlová schránka ⓕ
    zuh-vuh-zuhd-lo-va skhran-kuh
luggage tag zavazadlový lístek ⓜ
    zuh-vuh-zuhd-lo-vee lees-tek
lump boule ⓕ boh-le
lunch oběd ⓜ o-byed
lung plíce ⓕ plee-tse
luxurious přepychový przhe-pi-kho-vee

M

machine stroj ⓜ stroy
magazine časopis ⓜ chuh-so-pis
mail (letters/postal system) pošta ⓕ
    posh-tuh
mail v odeslat o-des-luht
mailbox poštovní schránka ⓕ
    posh-tov-nyee skhran-kuh
main a hlavní hluhv-nyee
main road hlavní silnice ⓕ
    hluhv-nyee sil-nyi-tse
make v dělat dye-luht
make-up líčidlo ⓝ lee-chid-lo
mammogram mamogram ⓜ
    muh-mo-gruhm
man muž ⓜ muzh
manager (business) ředitel(ka) ⓜ/ⓕ
    rzhe-dyi-tel(-kuh)
manager (sport) manažer(ka) ⓜ/ⓕ
    muh-nuh-zher(-kuh)
mandarin mandarinka ⓕ
    muhn-duh-rin-kuh

mango *mango* ⓝ muhn-go
manual worker ⓜ *dělník* dyel-nyeek
many *mnohý* mno-hee
map (of country) *mapa* ⓕ muh-puh
map (of town) *plán* ⓜ plan
March *březen* ⓜ brzhe-zen
margarine *margarín* ⓕ muhr-guh-reen
marijuana *marihuana* ⓕ muh-ri-hu-uh-nuh
marital status *rodinný stav* ⓜ
ro-dyi-nee stuhf
market *trh* ⓜ trh
marriage *manželství* ⓝ muhn-zhels-tvee
married (man) *ženatý* zhe-nuh-tee
married (woman) *vdaná* f-duh-na
marry (man) *oženit se* o-zhe-nyit se
marry (woman) *vdát se* f-dat se
martial arts *bojová umění* ⓝ pl
bo-yo-va u-mye-nyee
mass (Catholic) *mše* ⓕ mshe
massage *masáž* ⓕ muh-sazh
masseur *masér* ⓜ muh-ser
masseuse *masérka* ⓕ muh-ser-kuh
mat *rohožka* ⓕ ro-hozh-kuh
match (sports) *zápas* ⓜ za-puhs
matches (for lighting) *zápalky* ⓕ pl
za-puhl-ki
mattress *matrace* ⓕ muh-truh-tse
May *květen* ⓜ kvye-ten
maybe *možná* mozh-na
mayonnaise *majonéza* ⓕ muh-yo-nair-zuh
mayor *starosta/starostka* ⓜ/ⓕ
stuh-ros-tuh/stuh-rost-kuh
me *mě* mye
meal *jídlo* ⓝ yeed-lo
measles *spalničky* ⓕ pl spuhl-nyich-ki
meat *maso* ⓝ muh-so
mechanic *mechanik* ⓜ me-khuh-nik
media *média* ⓝ pl mair-di-yuh
medicine (medication) *lék* ⓜ lairk
medicine (profession) *lékařství* ⓝ
lair-kuhrzh-stvee
medicine (study) *medicína* ⓕ
me-di-tsee-nuh
meditation *meditace* ⓕ me-di-tuh-tse
meet (first time) v *potkat* pot-kuht
meet (get together) v *sejít se* se-yeet se
melon *meloun* ⓜ me-lohn
member *člen/členka* ⓜ/ⓕ
chlen/chlen-kuh
memory card *paměťová karta* ⓕ
puh-mye-to-va kuhr-tuh
menstruation *menstruace* ⓕ
men-stru-uh-tse

menu *jídelní lístek* ⓜ yee-del-nyee lees-tek
message *zpráva* ⓕ zpra-vuh
metal *kov* ⓜ kov
metre *metr* ⓜ me-tr
metro (train) *metro* ⓝ met-ro
metro station *stanice metra* ⓕ
stuh-nyi-tse met-ruh
microwave oven *mikrovlná trouba* ⓕ
mi-kro-vl-na troh-buh
midday *poledne* ⓝ po-led-ne
midnight *půlnoc* ⓕ pool-nots
migraine *migréna* ⓕ mi-grair-nuh
military *branná moc* ⓕ bruh-na mots
military service *vojenská služba* ⓕ
vo-yens-ka sluzh-buh
milk *mléko* ⓝ mlair-ko
millimetre *milimetr* ⓜ mi-li-me-tr
million *milion* ⓜ mi-li-yon
mince meat *mleté maso* ⓝ mle-tair muh-so
mineral water *minerálka* ⓕ mi-ne-ral-kuh
minute *minuta* ⓕ mi-nu-tuh
mirror *zrcadlo* ⓝ zr-tsuhd-lo
miscarriage *samovolný potrat* ⓜ
suh-mo-vol-nee po-truht
Miss *slečna* ⓕ slech-nuh
miss (feel absence of) *postrádat*
pos-tra-duht
miss (not catch train etc) *zmeškat*
zmesh-kuht
mistake *chyba* ⓕ khi-buh
mix v *míchat* mee-khuht
mobile phone *mobil* ⓜ mo-bil
modem *modem* ⓜ mo-dem
modern *moderní* mo-der-nyee
moisturiser *hydratační krém* ⓜ
hi-druh-tuhch-nyee krairm
monastery *klášter* ⓜ klash-ter
Monday *pondělí* ⓝ pon-dye-lee
money *peníze* ⓝ pl pe-nyee-ze
monk *mnich* ⓜ mnyikh
month *měsíc* ⓜ mye-seets
monument *pomník* ⓜ pom-nyeek
moon *měsíc* ⓜ mye-seets
more *více* vee-tse
morning *ráno* ⓝ ra-no
morning sickness *ranní nevolnost* ⓕ
ruh-nyee ne-vol-nost
mosque *mešita* ⓕ me-shi-tuh
mosquito *komár* ⓜ ko-mar
mosquito net *moskitiéra* ⓕ
mos-ki-ti-yair-ruh
motel *motel* ⓜ mo-tel
mother *matka* ⓕ muht-kuh

mother-in-law *tchýně* ① *tkhee*-nye
motorbike *motorka* ① *mo*-tor-kuh
motorboat *motorový člun* ⑩
  mo-to-ro-vee chlun
motorway (tollway) *dálnice* ① *dal*-nyi-tse
mountain *hora* ① *ho*-ruh
mountain bike *horské kolo* ⑩
  hors-kair ko-lo
mountaineering *horolezectví* ⑩
  ho-ro-le-zets-tvee
mountain path *horská stezka* ①
  hors-ka stez-kuh
mountain range *pohoří* ⑩ po-ho-rzhee
mouse *myš* ① mish
mouth *ústa* ① *oos*-tuh
movie *film* ⑩ film
Mr *pan* ⑩ puhn
Mrs *paní* ① *puh*-nyee
Ms *slečna* ① *slech*-nuh
mud *bahno* ⑩ *buh*-no
muesli *muesli* ① *mis*-li
mum *máma* ① *ma*-muh
mumps *příušnice* ① pl *przhi*-ush-nyi-tse
murder *vražda* ① *vruzh*-duh
murder v *vraždit* *vruzh*-dyit
muscle *sval* ⑩ svuhl
museum *muzeum* ⑩ *mu*-ze-um
mushroom *houba* ① *hoh*-buh
music *hudba* ① *hud*-buh
musician *hudebník/hudebnice* ⑩/①
  hu-deb-nyeek/hu-deb-nyi-tse
music shop *obchod s hudebninami* ⑩
  op-khod s hu-deb-nyi-nuh-mi
Muslim *muslim(ka)* ⑩/① *mus*-lim(-kuh)
mussel *slávka jedlá* ① *slaf*-kuh yed-la
mustard *hořčice* ① *horzh*-chi-tse
mute a *němý* *nye*-mee
my *můj* mooy

N

nail clippers *kleštičky na nehty* ① pl
  klesh-tyich-ki nuh nekh-ti
name *jméno* ① *ymair*-no
napkin *ubrousek* ① *u*-broh-sek
nappy *plenka* ① *plen*-kuh
nappy rash *vyrážka* ① *vi*-razh-kuh
nationality *národnost* ① *na*-rod-nost
national park *národní park* ⑩
  na-rod-nyee puhrk
nature *příroda* ① *przhe*-ro-duh
naturopathy *přírodní medicína* ①
  przhe-rod-nyee me-di-tsee-nuh

nausea *nevolnost* ① *ne*-vol-nost
near prep *blízko* *bleez*-ko
nearby *nedaleko* ne-duh-le-ko
nearest *nejbližší* *ney*-blizh-shee
necessary *nutný* *nut*-nee
neck *krk* ⑩ krk
necklace *náhrdelník* ⑩ *na*-hr-del-nyeek
nectarine *nektarínka* ① *nek*-tuh-reen-kuh
need v *potřebovat* pot-rzhe-bo-vuht
needle (sewing/syringe) *jehla* ① *yeh*-luh
negative a *záporný* *za*-por-nee
negatives (photos) *negativy* ⑩ pl
  ne-guh-ti-vi
neither adv *také ne* tuh-kair ne
net *síť* ① seet'
Netherlands *Nizozemí* ① *nyi*-zo-ze-mee
network (phone) *síť* ① seet'
never *nikdy* nyik-di
new *nový* no-vee
news *zprávy* ① pl *zpra*-vi
newsagency *tisková agentura* ①
  tyis-ko-va *uh*-gen-tu-ruh
newspaper *noviny* ① pl no-vi-ni
newsstand *novinový stánek* ⑩
  no-vi-no-vee sta-nek
New Year's Day *Nový rok* ⑩ no-vee rok
New Year's Eve *Silvestr* ⑩ *sil*-ves-tr
New Zealand *Nový Zéland* ⑩
  no-vee zair-luhnd
next (following) *následující*
  nas-le-du-yee-tsee
next to *vedle* ved-le
nice *příjemný* przhe-yem-nee
nickname *přezdívka* ① *przhez*-dyeef-kuh
night *noc* ① nots
nightclub *noční klub* ⑩ *noch*-nyee klub
night out (party) *večírek/mejdan* ⑩
  ve-chee-rek/*mey*-duhn
no *ne* ne
noisy *hlučný* *hluch*-nee
none *žádný* *zhad*-nee
nonsmoking *nekuřácký* ne-ku-rzhats-kee
noodles *nudle* ① *nud*-le
noon *poledne* ① po-led-ne
north *sever* ⑩ *se*-ver
Norway *Norsko* ① *nors*-ko
nose *nos* ⑩ nos
not *ne* ne
notebook *zápisník* ⑩ *za*-pis-nyeek
nothing *nic* ⑩ nyits
no vacancy *obsazeno* op-*suh*-ze-no
November *listopad* ⑩ *lis*-to-puhd
now *teď* ted'

nuclear energy *jaderná energie* ①
  yuh·der·na e·ner·gi·ye
nuclear testing *atomové pokusy* ⑩ pl
  uh·to·mo·vair po·ku·si
nuclear waste *atomový odpad* ⑩
  uh·to·mo·vee od·puhd
number *číslo* ⑪ chees·lo
numberplate *poznávací značka* ①
  poz·na·vuh·tsee znuch·kuh
nun *jeptiška* ① yep·tyish·kuh
nurse *zdravotní sestra* ①
  zdruh·vot·nyee ses·truh
nut (food) *ořech* ⑩ o·rzhekh

O

oats *oves* ① o·ves
ocean *oceán* ⑩ o·tse·an
October *říjen* ⑩ rzhee·yen
off (power) *zhasnuto* zhuhs·nu·to
off (spoilt) *zkažený* zkuh·zhe·nee
office *kancelář* ① kuhn·tse·larzh
office worker *administrativní
  pracovník/pracovnice* ⑩/①
  uhd·mi·ni·struh·tiv·nyee
  pruh·tsov·nyeek/pruh·tsov·nyi·tse
often *často* chuhs·to
oil (cooking) *stolní olej* ⑩ stol·nyee o·ley
oil (petrol) *benzín* ⑩ ben·zeen
old *starý* stuh·ree
olive *oliva* ① o·li·vuh
olive oil *olivový olej* ⑩ o·li·vo·vee o·ley
Olympic Games *olympijské hry* ① pl
  o·lim·piy·skair hri
omelette *omeleta* ① o·me·le·tuh
on *na* nuh
on (power) *zapnuto* zuhp·nu·to
once *jednou* yed·noh
one *jeden* ye·den
one-way ticket *jednoduchá jízdenka* ①
  yed·no·du·kha yeez·den·kuh
onion *cibule* ① tsi·bu·le
only *jen* yen
on time *včas* fchuhs
open (business) a *otevřený* o·tev·rzhe·nee
open v *otevřít* o·tev·rzheet
opening hours *otevírací hodiny* ① pl
  o·te·vee·ruh·tsee ho·dyi·ni
opera *opera* ① o·pe·ruh
opera house *opera* ① o·pe·ruh
operation (medical) *operace* ①
  o·pe·ruh·tse

operator (telephone) *operátor* ⑩
  o·pe·ra·tor
opinion *názor* ⑩ na·zor
opposite prep *proti* pro·tyi
optometrist *oční lékař* ⑩
  och·nye lair·kuhrzh
or *nebo* ne·bo
orange (fruit) *pomeranč* ⑩ po·me·ruhnch
orange (colour) *oranžový* o·ruhn·zho·vee
orange juice *pomerančový džus* ⑩
  po·me·ruhn·cho·vee dzhus
orchestra *orchestr* ⑩ or·khes·tr
order *pořadí* ① po·rzha·dyee
order v *objednat* ob·yed·nuht
ordinary *obyčejný* o·bi·chey·nee
orgasm *orgasmus* ⑩ or·guhs·mus
original a *původní* poo·vod·nyee
other *další* duh·shee
our *náš* nash
out of order *nefunguje* ne·fun·gu·ye
outside adv *venku* ven·ku
ovarian cyst *vaječníková cysta* ①
  vuh·yech·nyee·ko·va tsis·tuh
ovaries *vaječník* ⑩ vuh·yech·nyeek
oven *trouba* ① troh·buh
overcoat *svrchník* ⑩ svrkh·nyeek
overdose *nadměrná dávka* ①
  nuhd·myer·na daf·kuh
overnight adv *přes noc* przhes nots
overseas *v zámoří* v za·mo·rzhee
owe *dlužit* dlu·zhit
owner *majitel(ka)* ⑩/① muh·yi·tel(·kuh)
oxygen *kyslík* ⑩ kis·leek
oyster *ústřice* ① oost·rzhi·tse
ozone layer *ozónová vrstva* ①
  o·zaw·no·va vrst·vuh

P

pacemaker *kardiostimulátor* ⑩
  kuhr·di·o·sti·mu·la·tor
pacifier (dummy) *dudlík* ⑩ dud·leek
package *balík* ⑩ buh·leek
packet (general) *balíček* ⑩ buh·lee·chek
padlock *visací zámek* ⑩ vi·suh·tsee za·mek
page *strana* ① struh·nuh
pain *bolest* ① bo·lest
painful *bolestivý* bo·les·tyi·vee
painkiller *lék proti bolestem* ⑩
  lairk pro·tyi bo·les·tem
painter (artist) *malíř(ka)* ⑩/①
  muh·leerzh(·kuh)

painter (tradesperson) *malíř pokojů* m
  muh-leerzh po-ko-yoo
painting (a work) *natírání* n
  nuh-tyee-ra-nyee
painting (the art) *malování* n
  muh-lo-va-nyee
pair (couple) *pár* m *par*
palace *palác* m *puh-lats*
pan *pánev* f *pa-nef*
pants (trousers) *kalhoty* f pl *kuhl-ho-ti*
pantyhose *punčochové kalhoty* f pl
  pun-cho-kho-vair kuhl-ho-ti
panty liner *podšívkovina* f
  pod-sheef-ko-vi-nuh
paper *papír* m *puh-peer*
paperwork *doklady* m pl *do-kluh-di*
pap smear *stěr hrdla* m *styer hrd-luh*
paraplegic *paraplegik* m *puh-ruh-ple-gik*
parcel *balíček* m *buh-lee-chek*
parents *rodiče* m pl *ro-dyi-che*
park *park* m *puhrk*
park (a car) v *parkovat* *puhr-ko-vuht*
parliament *parlament* m *puhr-luh-ment*
part (component) *část* f *chast*
part-time *na zkrácený úvazek*
  nuh zkra-tse-nee oo-vuh-zek
party (night out) *večírek/mejdan* m
  ve-chee-rek/mey-duhn
party (politics) *strana* f *struh-nuh*
pass (go by) v *projet* *pro-yet*
pass (kick/throw) v *přihrát* *przhi-hrat*
passenger *cestující* m&f *tses-tu-yee-tsee*
passionfruit *pasiflora* f *puh-si-flo-ruh*
passport *pas* m *puhs*
passport number *číslo pasu* n
  chees-lo puh-su
past *minulost* f *mi-nu-lost*
pasta *těstovina* f *tyes-to-vi-nuh*
path *stezka* f *stez-kuh*
pay v *platit* *pluh-tyit*
payment *placení* n *pluh-tse-nyee*
pea *hrách* m *hrakh*
peace *mír* m *meer*
peach *broskev* f *bros-kef*
peak (mountain) *vrchol* m *vr-khol*
peanut *arašíd* m *uh-ruh-sheed*
pear *hruška* f *hrush-kuh*
pedal *pedál* m *pe-dal*
pedestrian *chodec/chodkyně* m/f
  kho-dets/khod-ki-nye
pen (ballpoint) *propiska* f *pro-pis-kuh*
pencil *tužka* f *tuzh-kuh*
penis *penis* m *pe-nis*

penknife *kapesní nůž* m
  kuh-pes-nyee noozh
pensioner *důchodce/důchodkyně* m/f
  doo-khod-tse/doo-khod-ki-nye
people *lid* m pl *lid*
pepper *pepř* m *pe-przh*
pepper (bell) *paprika* f *puh-pri-kuh*
per (day) *na* *nuh*
per cent *procento* n *pro-tsen-to*
perfect a *dokonalý* *do-ko-nuh-lee*
performance *představení* n
  przhed-stuh-ve-nyee
perfume *parfém* m *puhr-fairm*
period pain *menstruační bolest* f
  men-stru-uhch-nyee bo-lest
permission *dovolení* n *do-vo-le-nyee*
permit *povolení* n *po-vo-le-nyee*
person *osoba* f *o-so-buh*
petition *petice* f *pe-ti-tse*
petrol *benzín* m *ben-zeen*
petrol station *benzínová pumpa* f
  ben-zee-no-va pum-puh
pharmacist *lékárník* m *lair-kar-nyeek*
pharmacy *lékárna* f *lair-kar-nuh*
phone book *telefonní seznam* m
  te-le-fo-nyee sez-nuhm
phone box *telefonní budka* f
  te-le-fo-nyee bud-kuh
phonecard *telefonní karta* f
  te-le-fo-nyee kuhr-tuh
photo *fotka* f *fot-kuh*
photograph v *fotografovat*
  fo-to-gruh-fo-vuht
photographer *fotograf* m *fo-to-gruhf*
photography *fotografie* f *fo-to-gruh-fi-ye*
phrasebook *konverzační příručka* f
  kon-ver-zuhch-nyee przhee-ruch-kuh
piano *klavír* m *kluh-veer*
pickaxe *krumpáč* m *krum-pach*
pickles *nakládaná zelenina* f
  nuh-kla-duh-na ze-le-nyi-nuh
picnic *piknik* m *pik-nik*
piece *kus* m *kus*
pig *prase* n *pruh-se*
pill *pilulka* f *pi-lul-kuh*
(the) pill *antikoncepční pilulka* f
  uhn-ti-kon-tsep-chnyee pi-lul-kuh
pillow *polštář* m *polsh-tarzh*
pillowcase *povlak na polštář* m
  po-vluhk nuh polsh-tarzh
pineapple *ananas* m *uh-nuh-nuhs*
pink *růžový* *roo-zho-vee*
pistachio *pistácie* f *pis-ta-tsi-ye*

place *místo* ⓝ mees·to
place of birth *místo narození* ⓝ
  mees·to nuh·ro·ze·nyee
plane *letadlo* ⓝ le·tuhd·lo
planet *planeta* ⓕ pluh·ne·tuh
plant *rostlina* ⓕ rost·li·nuh
plastic a *plastický* pluhs·tits·kee
plate *talíř* ⓜ tuh·leerzh
plateau *náhorní plošina* ⓕ
  na·hor·nyee plo·shi·nuh
platform *nástupiště* ⓝ nas·tu·pish·tye
play (cards) v *hrát* hrat
play (guitar) v *hrát na* hrat nuh
play (theatre) *hra* ⓕ hruh
plug (bath) *zátka* ⓕ zat·kuh
plug (electricity) *zástrčka* ⓕ zas·trch·kuh
plum *švestka* ⓕ shvest·kuh
plumber *instalatér* ⓜ ins·tuh·luh·ter
poached (egg) *vařit ve skle*
  vuh·rzhit ve skle
pocket *kapsa* ⓕ kuhp·suh
pocket knife *kapesní nůž* ⓜ
  kuh·pes·nyee noozh
poetry *poezie* ⓕ po·e·zi·ye
point v *ukazovat* u·kuh·zo·vuht
poisonous *jedovatý* ye·do·vuh·tee
Poland *Polsko* ⓝ pols·ko
police *policie* ⓕ po·li·tsi·ye
police officer (in city) *městský policista* ⓜ
  myest·skee po·li·tsis·tuh
police officer (in country) *policista* ⓜ
  po·li·tsis·tuh
police station *policejní stanice* ⓕ
  po·li·tsey·nyee stuh·nyi·tse
policy *politická linie* ⓕ po·li·tits·ka *li·ni·ye*
politician *politik/politička* ⓜ/ⓕ
  po·li·tik/po·li·tich·kuh
politics *politika* ⓕ po·li·ti·kuh
pollen *pyl* ⓜ pil
pollution *znečištění* ⓝ zne·chis·tye·nyee
pool (game) *kulečník* ⓜ ku·lech·nyeek
pool (swimming) *bazén* ⓜ buh·zairn
poor (wealth) *chudý* khu·dee
popular *populární* po·pu·lar·nyee
porcelain *porcelán* ⓜ por·tse·lan
pork *vepřové maso* ⓝ
  vep·rzho·vair muh·so
pork sausage *vuřt* ⓜ vurzht
port (river/sea) *přístav* ⓜ przhees·tuhf
positive a *kladný* kluhd·nee
possible *možný* mozh·nee
post (mail) *pošta* ⓜ posh·tuh
post v *odeslat* o·des·luht

postage *poštovné* ⓝ posh·tov·nair
postcard *pohled* ⓜ po·hled
postcode *poštovní směrovací číslo* ⓝ
  posh·tov·nyee smye·ro·vuh·tsee chee·slo
poster *plakát* ⓜ pluh·kat
post office *pošta* ⓕ posh·tuh
pot (ceramics) *nádoba* ⓕ na·do·buh
pot (cooking) *hrnec* ⓜ hr·nets
potato *brambor* ⓜ bruhm·bor
pottery *keramika* ⓕ ke·ruh·mi·kuh
pound (money) *libra šterlinků* ⓕ
  lib·ruh shter·lin·koo
pound (weight) *libra* ⓕ lib·ruh
poverty *chudoba* ⓕ khu·do·buh
powder *prášek* ⓜ pra·shek
power *síla* ⓕ see·luh
Prague *Praha* ⓕ pruh·huh
prawn *kreveta* ⓕ kre·ve·tuh
prayer *modlitba* ⓕ mod·lit·buh
prayer book *modlitební knížka* ⓕ
  mod·li·teb·nyee knyezh·kuh
prefer *dávat přednost* da·vuht przhed·nost
pregnancy test kit *těhotenský test* ⓜ
  tye·ho·ten·skee test
pregnant *těhotná* tye·hot·na
premenstrual tension *premenstruální
  tenze* ⓕ pre·mens·tru·al·nyee ten·ze
prepare *připravit* przhi·pruh·vit
prescription *lékařský předpis* ⓜ
  lair·kuhrzh·skee przhed·pis
present (gift) *dárek* ⓜ da·rek
present (time) *přítomnost* ⓕ
  przhee·tom·nost
president *president(ka)* ⓜ/ⓕ
  pre·zi·dent(·kuh)
pressure (tyre) *tlak* ⓜ tluhk
pretty *hezký* hez·kee
price *cena* ⓕ tse·nuh
priest *kněz* ⓜ knyez
prime minister *premiér(ka)* ⓜ/ⓕ
  pre·mi·yer(·kuh)
printer (computer) *tiskárna* ⓕ tyis·kar·nuh
prison *vězení* ⓝ vye·ze·nyee
prisoner *vězeň(kyně)* ⓜ/ⓕ
  vye·zen'(·ki·nye)
private *soukromý* soh·kro·mee
produce v *vyrobit* vi·ro·bit
profit *zisk* ⓜ zisk
program *program* ⓜ pro·gruhm
projector *projektor* ⓜ pro·yek·tor
promise v *slíbit* slee·bit
prostitute *prostitut(ka)* ⓜ/ⓕ
  pros·ti·tut(·kuh)
protect v *chránit* khra·nyit

protected *chráněný* khra·nye·nee
protest *protest* ⓜ pro·test
protest v *protestovat* pro·tes·to·vuht
provisions *potraviny* ① pl po·truh·vi·ni
pub (bar) *hospoda* ① hos·po·duh
public gardens *veřejné zahrady* ① pl
    ve·rzhey·nair zuh·hruh·di
public phone *veřejná telefonní budka* ①
    ve·rzhey·na te·le·fo·nyee bud·kuh
public relations *styk s veřejností* ⓜ pl
    stik s ve·rzhey·nos·tyee
public toilet *veřejné toalety* ① pl
    ve·rzhey·nair to·uh·le·ti
pull v *táhnout* tah·noht
pump *hustilka* ① hus·tyil·kuh
pumpkin *dýně* ① dee·nye
puncture *defekt* ⓜ de·fekt
puppet *loutka* ① loht·kuh
puppet show *loutkové představení* ①
    loht·ko·vair przhed·stuh·ve·nyee
puppet theatre *loutkové divadlo* ①
    loht·ko·vair dyi·vuhd·lo
pure *čistý* chis·tee
purple *fialový* fi·yuh·lo·vee
purse *peněženka* ① pe·nye·zhen·kuh
push v *tlačit* tluh·chit
put *dát* dat

Q

quadriplegic *kvadruplegik* ⓜ
    kvuh·drup·le·gik
qualifications *vzdělání* ⓝ pl vzdye·la·nyee
quality *kvalita* ① kvuh·li·tuh
quarantine *karanténa* ①
    kuh·ruhn·tair·nuh
quarter *čtvrtina* ① chtvr·tyi·nuh
queen *královna* ① kra·lov·nuh
question *otázka* ① o·taz·kuh
queue *fronta* ① fron·tuh
quick *rychlý* rikh·lee
quiet *tichý* tyi·khee
quit *nechat* ne·khuht

R

rabbit *králík* ⓜ kra·leek
rabies *vzteklina* ① vztek·li·nuh
race (sport) *závod* ⓜ za·vod
racetrack *dostihová dráha* ①
    dos·tyi·ho·va dra·huh

racing bike *závodní kolo* ⓝ
    za·vod·nyee ko·lo
racism *rasismus* ⓜ ruh·sis·mus
racquet *raketa* ① ruh·ke·tuh
radiator *chladič* ⓜ khlu·dyich
radio *rádio* ⓝ ra·di·yo
radish *ředkvička* ① rzhed·kvich·kuh
railway station *železniční nádraží* ⓝ
    zhe·lez·nyich·nyee na·druh·zhee
rain *déšť* ⓜ dairshť
raincoat *pláštěnka* ① plash·tyen·kuh
raisin *hrozinka* ① hro·zin·kuh
rally (protest) *manifestace* ①
    muh·ni·fes·tuh·tse
rape *znásilnění* ⓝ zna·sil·nye·nyee
rape v *znásilnit* zna·sil·nyit
rare (steak) *krvavý* krva·vee
rare (uncommon) *vzácný* vzats·nee
rash *vyrážka* ① vi·razh·kuh
raspberry *malina* ① muh·li·nuh
rat *krysa* ① kri·suh
rave (party) *techno party* ① tekh·no par·ti
raw *syrový* si·ro·vee
razor *břitva* ① brzhit·vuh
razor blade *žiletka* ① zhi·let·kuh
read v *číst* cheest
reading *čtení* ⓝ chte·nyee
ready a *připravený* przhi·pruh·ve·nee
real estate agent *realitní kancelář* ①
    re·uh·lit·nyee kuhn·tse·larzh
realistic *realistický* re·uh·lis·tits·kee
rear (location) a *zadní* zuhd·nyee
reason *důvod* ⓜ doo·vod
receipt *stvrzenka* ① stvr·zen·kuh
recently *nedávno* ne·dav·no
recommend *doporučit* do·po·ru·chit
record v *zaznamenat* zuhz·nuh·me·nuht
recording *nahrávka* ① nuh·hraf·kuh
recyclable *recyklovatelný*
    re·tsi·klo·vuh·tel·nee
recycle *recyklovat* re·tsi·klo·vuht
red *červený* cher·ve·nee
red wine *červené víno* ⓝ cher·ve·nair
    vee·no
referee *rozhodčí* ⓜ roz·hod·chee
reference *zmínka* ① zmeen·kuh
reflexology *reflexní terapie* ①
    re·fleks·nee te·ruh·pi·ye
refrigerator *lednička* ① led·nyich·kuh
refugee *uprchlík/uprchlice* ⓜ/①
    u·pr·khleek/u·pr·khli·tse
refund *vrácení peněz* ⓝ
    vruh·tse·nyee pe·nyez

refuse v odmítnout *od·meet·noht*
regional a oblastní *o·blust·nyee*
registered mail doporučená zásilka ⓕ *do·po·ru·che·na za·sil·kuh*
rehydration salts iontový nápoj ⓜ *yon·to·vee na·poy*
reiki reiki ⓝ *rey·ki*
relationship vztah ⓜ vztah
relax uvolnit se *u·vol·nyit se*
relic relikvie ⓕ *re·lik·vi·ye*
religion náboženství ⓝ *na·bo·zhens·tvee*
religious a náboženský *na·bo·zhens·kee*
remote a vzdálený *vzda·le·nee*
remote control dálkový ovládač ⓜ *dal·ko·vee ov·la·duch*
rent činže ⓕ *chin·zhe*
rent v pronajmout *pro·nai·moht*
repair v opravit *o·pruh·vit*
republic republika ⓕ *re·pu·bli·kuh*
reservation (booking) rezervace ⓕ *re·zer·vuh·tse*
rest v odpočinout si *od·po·chi·noht si*
restaurant restaurace ⓕ *res·tow·ruh·tse*
résumé (CV) životopis ⓜ *zhi·vo·to·pis*
retired důchodový *doo·kho·do·vee*
return v vrátit se *vra·tyit se*
return ticket zpáteční jízdenka ⓕ *zpa·tech·nyee yeez·den·kuh*
review kritika ⓕ *kri·ti·kuh*
rhythm rytmus ⓜ *rit·mus*
rib (body) žebro ⓝ *zheb·ro*
rice rýže ⓕ *ree·zhe*
rich (wealthy) bohatý *bo·huh·tee*
ride jízda ⓕ *yeez·duh*
ride (bike, horse) v jezdit na *yez·dyit nuh*
right (correct) správný *sprav·nee*
right (direction) pravý *pruh·vee*
right-wing pravicový *pruh·vi·tso·vee*
ring (jewellery) prsten ⓜ *prs·ten*
ring (phone) v zvonit *zvo·nyit*
rip-off zloděina ⓕ *zlo·dyey·nuh*
risk riziko ⓝ *ri·zi·ko*
river řeka ⓕ *rzhe·kuh*
road silnice ⓕ *sil·nyi·tse*
road map automapa ⓕ *ow·to·muh·puh*
rob okrást *o·krast*
rock skála ⓕ *ska·luh*
rock (music) bigbít ⓜ *big·beet*
rock climbing horolezectví ⓝ *ho·ro·le·zets·tvee*
rock group rocková skupina ⓕ *ro·ko·va sku·pi·nuh*
rockmelon kantalup ⓜ *kuhn·tuh·lup*

rollerblading jízda na kolečkových bruslích ⓕ *yeez·duh nuh ko·lech·ko·veekh brus·leekh*
romantic a romantický *ro·muhn·tits·kee*
room pokoj ⓜ *po·koy*
room number číslo pokoje ⓝ *chees·lo po·ko·ye*
rope provaz ⓜ *pro·vuhz*
round (drinks) runda ⓕ *run·duh*
round a kulatý *ku·luh·tee*
roundabout kruhový objezd ⓜ *kru·ho·vee ob·yezd*
route trasa ⓕ *truh·suh*
rowing veslování ⓝ *ves·lo·va·nyee*
rubbish odpad ⓜ *od·puhd*
rubella zarděnky ⓕ pl *zuhr·dyen·ki*
rug koberáček ⓜ *ko·be·re·chek*
rugby ragby ⓝ *ruhg·bi*
ruins zřícenina ⓕ *zrzhee·tse·nyi·nuh*
rule pravidlo ⓝ *pruh·vid·lo*
rum rum ⓜ rum
run v běžet *bye·zhet*
running běh ⓜ byeh
runny nose rýma ⓕ *ree·muh*

S

sad smutný *smut·nee*
saddle sedlo ⓝ *sed·lo*
safe trezor ⓜ *tre·zor*
safe a bezpečný *bez·pech·nee*
safe sex bezpečný sex ⓜ *bez·pech·nee seks*
sailboarding surfing ⓝ *sur·fing*
saint svatý *svuh·tee*
salad salát ⓜ *suh·lat*
salami salám ⓜ *suh·lam*
salary plat ⓜ *pluht*
sale prodej ⓜ *pro·dey*
sales assistant prodavač(ka) ⓜ/ⓕ *pro·duh·vuhch(·kuh)*
sales tax daň z obratu ⓕ *duhn' z o·bruh·tu*
salmon losos ⓜ *lo·sos*
salt sůl ⓕ *sool*
same stejný *stey·nee*
sand písek ⓜ *pee·sek*
sandals sandále ⓜ pl *suhn·da·le*
sandwich sendvič ⓜ *send·vich*
sandwich shop lahůdky ⓕ pl *luh·hood·ki*
sanitary napkins dámské vložky ⓕ pl *dams·kair vlozh·ki*
sardine sardinka ⓕ *suhr·din·kuh*
Saturday sobota ⓕ *so·bo·tuh*
sauce omáčka ⓕ *o·mach·kuh*

saucepan *kastrol* ⓜ *kuhs*·trol

sauna *sauna* ⓕ *sow*·nuh

saxophone *saxofon* ⓜ *suhk*·so·fon

say v *říci* rzhee·tsi

scalp *kůže na hlavě* ⓕ
koo·zhe nuh *hluh*·vye

scarf *šála* ⓕ *sha*·luh

school *škola* ⓕ *shko*·luh

science *věda* ⓕ *vye*·duh

scientist *vědec/vědkyně* ⓜ/ⓕ
vye·dets/*vyed*·ki·nye

scissors *nůžky* ⓕ pl *noozh*·ki

score v *bodovat* bo·do·vuht

scoreboard *ukazatel skóre* ⓜ
u·kuh·zuh·tel *skaw*·re

Scotland *Skotsko* ⓝ *skots*·ko

scrambled *míchaný* *mee*·khuh·nee

sculpture *socha* ⓕ *so*·khuh

sea *moře* ⓝ *mo*·rzhe

seaside *pobřeží* ⓝ *pob*·rzhe·zhee

season *roční období* ⓝ
roch·nye ob·do·bee

seat (place) *místo* ⓝ *mees*·to

seatbelt *bezpečnostní pás* ⓜ
bez·pech·nost·nyee pas

second *vteřina* ⓕ *fte*·rzhi·nuh

second a *druhý* dru·hee

second class *druhá třída* ⓕ
dru·ha trzhee·duh

secondhand *použití* po·u·zhi·tee

secondhand shop *bazar* ⓜ *buh*·zuhr

secretary *sekretář(ka)* ⓜ/ⓕ
se·kre·tarzh(·kuh)

see v *vidět* vi·dyet

self-employed *samostatně výdělečně
činný* suh·mos·tuht·nye
vee·dye·lech·nye *chí*·nee

selfish *sobecký* so·bets·kee

self-service a *samoobslužný*
suh·mo·ob·sluzh·nee

sell v *prodávat* pro·da·vuht

send v *poslat* pos·luht

sensible *rozumný* ro·zum·nee

sensual *senzuální* sen·zu·al·nyee

separate a *oddělený* od·dye·le·nee

September *září* ⓝ *za*·rzhee

serious *vážný* vazh·nee

service *služba* ⓕ *sluzh*·buh

service charge *přirážka za obsluhu* ⓕ
przhi·razh·kuh zuh op·slu·hu

service station *benzínová pumpa* ⓕ
ben·zee·no·va *pum*·puh

serviette *ubrousek* ⓜ u·broh·sek

several *několik* nye·ko·lik

sew *šít* sheet

sex *pohlaví* ⓝ po·hluh·vee

sexism *sexismus* ⓜ *sek*·sis·mus

sexy *erotický* e·ro·tits·kee

shade *odstín* ⓜ od·styeen

shadow *stín* ⓜ styeen

shampoo *šampon* ⓜ *shuhm*·pon

shape *tvar* ⓜ tvuhr

share (accommodation) v *spoluobývat*
spo·lu·o·bee·vuht

share (with) v *bydlet spolu* bid·let spo·lu

shave v *holit* ho·lit

shaving cream *pěna na holení* ⓕ
pye·nuh nuh ho·le·nyee

she *ona* o·nuh

sheep *ovce* ⓕ of·tse

sheet (bed) *prostěradlo* ⓝ *pros*·tye·ruhd·lo

shelf *police* ⓕ po·li·tse

shiatsu *shiatsu* ⓝ *shi*·uh·tsu

shingles (illness) *pásový opar* ⓜ
pa·so·vee o·puhr

ship *loď* ⓕ lod'

shirt *košile* ⓕ *ko*·shi·le

shoe *bota* ⓕ bo·tuh

shoelace *tkanička* ⓕ *tkuh*·nyich·kuh

shoes *boty* ⓕ pl bo·ti

shoe shop *obchod s obuví* ⓜ
op·khod s o·bu·vee

shoot v *střelit* strzhe·lit

shop *obchod* ⓜ *op*·khod

shop v *nakupovat* nuh·ku·po·vuht

shopping *nakupování* ⓝ
nuh·ku·po·va·nyee

shopping centre *nákupní centrum* ⓝ
na·kup·nyee tsen·trum

short (height) *malý* muh·lee

short (length) *krátký* krat·kee

shortage *nedostatek* ⓜ *ne*·dos·tuh·tek

shorts *šortky* ⓕ pl short·ki

shoulder *rameno* ⓝ *ruh*·me·no

shout v *křičet* krzhi·chet

show *představení* ⓝ *przhed*·stuh·ve·nyee

show v *ukázat* u·ka·zuht

shower *sprcha* ⓕ *spr*·khuh

shrine *svatyně* ⓕ *svuh*·ti·nye

shut a *zavřený* zuhv·rzhe·nee

shy *stydlivý* stid·li·vee

sick *nemocný* ne·mots·nee

side *strana* ⓕ *struh*·nuh

sign *nápis* ⓜ *na*·pis

sign v *podepsat* po·dep·suht

signature *podpis* ⓜ *pod*·pis

silk *hedvábí* ⓝ hed·va·bee
silver *stříbro* ⓝ strzee·bro
SIM card *SIM karta* ⓕ sim kuhr·tuh
similar *podobný* po·dob·nee
simple *jednoduchý* yed·no·du·khee
since (time) *od* od
sing ⓥ *zpívat* zpee·vuht
singer *zpěvák/zpěvačka* ⓜ/ⓕ
  spye·vak/spye·vuhch·kuh
single (person) *svobodný* svo·bod·nee
single room *jednolůžkový pokoj* ⓜ
  yed·no·loozh·ko·vee po·koy
singlet *nátělník* ⓜ na·tyel·nyeek
sister *sestra* ⓕ ses·truh
sit ⓥ *posadit* po·suh·dyit
size (general) *velikost* ⓕ ve·li·kost
skate ⓥ *bruslit* brus·lit
skateboarding *skateboarding* ⓜ
  skeyt·bor·ding
ski *lyže* ⓕ li·zhe
ski ⓥ *lyžovat* li·zho·vuht
skiing *lyžování* ⓝ li·zho·va·nyee
skim milk *odstředěné mléko* ⓝ
  od·strzhe·dye·nair mlair·ko
skin *kůže* ⓕ koo·zhe
skirt *sukně* ⓕ suk·nye
skull *lebka* ⓕ leb·kuh
sky *nebe* ⓝ ne·be
sleep *spánek* ⓜ spa·nek
sleep ⓥ *spát* spat
sleeping bag *spací pytel* ⓜ spuh·tsee pi·tel
sleeping berth *lehátko* ⓝ le·hat·ko
sleeping car *spací vůz* ⓜ spuh·tsee vooz
sleeping pills *prášek na spaní* ⓜ
  pra·shek nuh spuh·nyee
sleepy *ospalý* os·puh·lee
slice *krajíc* ⓜ kruh·yeets
slide *diapozitivní film* ⓜ
  di·uh·po·zi·tiv·nyee film
Slovakia *Slovensko* ⓝ slo·ven·sko
slow a *pomalý* po·muh·lee
slowly *pomalu* po·muh·lu
small *malý* muh·lee
smaller *menší* men·shee
smallest *nejmenší* ney·men·shee
smell *pach* ⓜ puhkh
smile ⓥ *usmát se* us·mat se
smoke ⓥ *kouřit* koh·rzhit
snack *svačina* ⓕ svuh·chi·nuh
snail *šnek* ⓜ shnek
snake *had* ⓜ huhd
snorkelling *šnorchlování* ⓝ
  shnor·khlo·va·nyee

snow *sníh* ⓜ snyeeh
snowboarding *snowboarding* ⓝ
  snoh·bor·ding
snow pea *cisařský lusk* ⓜ
  tsee·suhrzh·skee lusk
soap *mýdlo* ⓝ meed·lo
soap opera *telenovela* ⓕ te·le·no·ve·luh
soccer *fotbal* ⓜ fot·buhl
socialist *socialista/socialistka* ⓜ/ⓕ
  so·tsi·uh·lis·tuh/so·tsi·uh·list·kuh
social welfare *sociální péče* ⓕ
  so·tsi·al·nyee pair·che
socks *ponožky* ⓕ pl po·nozh·ki
soft-boiled *na měkko* nuh mye·ko
soft drink *nealkoholický nápoj* ⓜ
  ne·uhl·ko·ho·lits·kee na·poy
soldier *voják* ⓜ vo·yak
some *několik* nye·ko·lik
someone *někdo* nyek·do
something *něco* nye·tso
sometimes *někdy* nyek·di
son *syn* ⓜ sin
song *píseň* ⓕ pee·sen'
soon *brzy* br·zi
sore a *bolestivý* bo·les·tyi·vee
soup *polévka* ⓕ po·lairf·kuh
sour cream *kyselá smetana* ⓕ
  ki·se·la sme·tuh·nuh
south *jih* ⓜ yih
souvenir *suvenýr* ⓜ su·ve·neer
souvenir shop *obchod se suvenýry* ⓜ
  op·khod se su·ve·nee·ri
soy milk *sójové mléko* ⓝ
  saw·yo·vair mlair·ko
soy sauce *sójová omáčka* ⓕ
  saw·yo·va o·mach·kuh
space (room) *prostor* ⓜ pros·tor
Spain *Španělsko* ⓝ shpuh·nyels·ko
sparkling wine *šumivé víno* ⓝ
  shu·mi·vair vee·no
speak *říci* rzhee·tsi
special a *mimořádný* mi·mo·rzhad·nee
specialist *odborník* ⓜ od·bor·nyeek
speed (drug) *amfetamin* ⓜ
  uhm·fe·tuh·min
speed (travel) *rychlost* ⓕ rikh·lost
speed limit *omezend rychlost* ⓕ
  o·me·ze·na rikh·lost
speedometer *tachometr* ⓜ tuh·kho·me·tr
spider *pavouk* ⓜ puh·vohk
spinach *špenát* ⓜ shpe·nat
spoilt (food) *zkažený* skuh·zhe·nee
spoke *říkal* ⓜ rzhee·kuhl

spoon *lžíce* ① *lzhee·tse*
sport *sport* ⑩ *sport*
sportsperson *sportovec/sportovkyně* ⑩/① *spor·to·vets/spor·tof·ki·nye*
sports store *obchod se sportovními potřebami* ⑩ *op·khod se spor·tov·nyee·mi pot·rzhe·buh·mi*
sprain *výron* ⑩ *vee·ron*
spring (coil) *spirálová pružina* ① *spi·ra·lo·va pru·zhi·nuh*
spring (season) *jaro* ⑩ *yuh·ro*
square (town) *náměstí* ⑩ *na·myes·tyee*
stadium *stadion* ⑩ *stuh·di·yon*
stairway *schodiště* ⑩ *skho·dyish·tye*
stale *okoralý* *o·ko·ruh·lee*
stamp (postage) *známka* ① *znam·kuh*
star *hvězda* ① *hvyez·duh*
(four-)star *(čtyř) hvězdičkový* *(chtirzh) hvyez·dyich·ko·vee*
start *začátek* ⑩ *zuh·cha·tek*
start v *začít* *zuh·cheet*
station *nádraží* ⑩ *na·druh·zhee*
stationer *papírnictví* ⑩ *puh·peer·nits·tvee*
statue *socha* ① *so·khuh*
stay (at a hotel) v *bydlet* *bid·let*
stay (in one place) v *zůstat* *zoos·tuht*
steak (beef) *biftek* ⑩ *bif·tek*
steal v *ukrást* *u·krast*
steep *strmý* *str·mee*
step *krok* ⑩ *krok*
stereo *stereo* ⑩ *ste·re·o*
still water *neperlivá voda* ① *ne·per·li·va vo·duh*
stock (food) *zásoba* ① *za·so·buh*
stockings *punčochy* ① pl *pun·cho·khi*
stolen *kradený* *kruh·de·nee*
stomach *žaludek* ⑩ *zhuh·lu·dek*
stomachache *bolesti žaludku* ① pl *bo·les·tyi zhuh·lud·ku*
stone *kámen* ⑩ *ka·men*
stoned (drugged) *zhulený* *zhu·le·nee*
stop (bus, tram) *zastávka* ① *zuhs·taf·kuh*
stop (cease) v *zastavit* *zuhs·tuh·vit*
stop (prevent) v *zabránit* *zuh·bruh·nyit*
storm *bouře* ① *boh·rzhe*
story *příběh* ⑩ *przhee·byeh*
stove *kamna* ① *kuhm·nuh*
straight *rovný* *rov·nee*
strange *cizí* *tsi·zee*
stranger *neznámý/á* ⑩/① *nez·na·mee/a*
strawberry *jahoda* ① *yuh·ho·duh*
stream *potok* ⑩ *po·tok*
street *ulice* ① *u·li·tse*

street market *pouliční trh* ⑩ *po·u·lich·nyee trh*
strike *stávka* ① *staf·kuh*
string *provázek* ⑩ *pro·va·zek*
stroke (health) *mrtvice* ① *mrt·vi·tse*
stroller *sportovní skládací kočárek* ⑩ *spor·tov·nyee skla·da·tsee ko·cha·rek*
strong *silný* *sil·nee*
stubborn *tvrdohlavý* *tvr·do·hluh·vee*
student *student(ka)* ⑩/① *stu·dent(·kuh)*
studio *ateliér* ⑩ *uh·te·li·yer*
stupid *hloupý* *hloh·pee*
style *styl* ⑩ *stil*
subtitles *titulky* ① pl *ti·tul·ki*
suburb (town) *čtvrť* ① *chtvrť*
subway (train) *metro* ⑩ *me·tro*
sugar *cukr* ⑩ *tsu·kr*
suitcase *kufr* ⑩ *ku·fr*
sultana *rozinka* ① *ro·zin·kuh*
summer *léto* ⑩ *lair·to*
sun *slunce* ① *slun·tse*
sunblock *opalovací krém* ⑩ *o·puh·lo·vuh·tsee krairm*
sunburn *spálený sluncem* ⑩ *spa·le·nee slun·tsem*
Sunday *neděle* ① *ne·dye·le*
sunglasses *sluneční brýle* ① pl *slu·nech·nyee bree·le*
sunny *slunečný* *slu·nech·nee*
sunrise *východ slunce* ⑩ *vee·khod slun·tse*
sunset *západ slunce* ⑩ *za·puhd slun·tse*
sunstroke *úžeh* ⑩ *oo·zheh*
supermarket *samoobsluha* ① *suh·mo·ob·slu·huh*
superstition *pověra* ① *po·vye·ruh*
supporter (politics) *stoupenec* ⑩ *stoh·pe·nets*
supporter (sport) *fanoušek* ⑩ *fuh·noh·shek*
surf (sport) *surfing* ⑩ *sur·fing*
surf (wave) *vlny* ① *vl·ni*
surf v *surfovat* *sur·fo·vuht*
surface mail (land) *obyčejná pošta* ① *o·bi·chey·na posh·tuh*
surface mail (sea) *obyčejná pošta lodí* ① *o·bi·chey·na posh·tuh lo·dyee*
surfboard *surfovací prkno* ⑩ *sur·fo·vuh·tsee prk·no*
surfing *surfing* ⑩ *sur·fing*
surname *příjmení* ⑩ *przhee·me·nyee*
surprise *překvapení* ⑩ *przhek·vuh·pe·nyee*
sweater *svetr* ⑩ *sve·tr*
Sweden *Švédsko* ⑩ *shvaird·sko*

sweet a *sladký sluhd*·kee
sweets *cukroví* ⑩ pl *tsu*·kro·vee
swelling *otok* ⑩ o·tok
swim v *plavat pluh*·vuht
swimming *plavání* ⑩ *pluh*·va·nyee
swimming pool *bazén* ⑩ *buh*·zairn
swimsuit *plavky* ① pl *pluhf*·ki
Switzerland *Švýcarsko* ⑩ *shvee*·tsuhr·sko
synagogue *synagoga* ① *si*·nuh·go·guh
synthetic a *syntetický sin*·te·tits·kee
syringe *stříkačka* ① *strzhee*·kuhch·kuh

T

table *stůl* ⑩ stool
tablecloth *ubrus* ⑩ *ub*·rus
table tennis *stolní tenis* ⑩ *stol*·nyee *te*·nis
tail *ocas* ⑩ o·tsuhs
tailor *krejčí/krejčová* ⑩/① *krey*·chee/*krey*·cho·va
take v *vzít* vzeet
take a photo *vyfotit ví*·fo·tyit
talk v *mluvit mlu*·vit
tall *vysoký vi*·so·kee
tampon *tampon* ⑩ *tuhm*·pon
tanning lotion *opalovací mléko* ⑩ o·puh·lo·vuh·tsee *mlair*·ko
tap *kohoutek* ⑩ *ko*·hoh·tek
tap water *voda z kohoutku* ① *vo*·duh s *ko*·hoht·ku
tasty *chutný khut*·nee
tax *daň* ① duhn'
taxi *taxík* ⑩ *tuhk*·seek
taxi stand *taxi stanoviště* ⑩ *tuhk*·si *stuh*·no·vish·tye
tea *čaj* ⑩ chai
teacher *učitel(ka)* ⑩/① *u*·chi·tel(·kuh)
team *mužstvo* ⑩ *muzh*·stvo
teaspoon *lžička* ① *lzhich*·kuh
technique *metoda* ① *me*·to·duh
teeth *zuby* ⑩ pl *zu*·bi
telegram *telegram* ⑩ *te*·le·gruhm
telephone *telefon* ⑩ *te*·le·fon
telephone v *telefonovat te*·le·fo·no·vuht
telephone centre *telefonní centrum* ⑩ *te*·le·fo·nyee *tsen*·trum
telescope *dalekohled* ⑩ *duh*·le·ko·hled
television *televize* ① *te*·le·vi·ze
tell *povědět po*·vye·dyet
temperature (fever) *horečka* ① *ho*·rech·kuh
temperature (weather) *teplota* ① *te*·plo·tuh

temple (body) *spánek* ⑩ *spa*·nek
temple (building) *chrám* ⑩ khram
tennis *tenis* ⑩ *te*·nis
tennis court *tenisový kurt* ⑩ *te*·ni·so·vee kurt
tent *stan* ⑩ stuhn
tent peg *stanový kolík* ⑩ *stuh*·no·vee ko·leek
terrible *hrozný hroz*·nee
terrorism *terorismus* ⑩ *te*·ro·ris·mus
test *zkouška* ① *skohsh*·kuh
thank *poděkovat po*·dye·ko·vuht
that a *ten* ten
that (one) pron *tamten tuhm*·ten
theatre *divadlo* ⑩ *dyi*·vuhd·lo
their *jejich ye*·yikh
there *tam* tuhm
they *oni* o·nyi
thick *silný sil*·nee
thief *zloděj* ⑩ *zlo*·dyey
thin *tenký ten*·kee
think *myslet mis*·let
third a *třetí trzhe*·tyee
thirsty *žíznivý zheez*·nyi·vee
this a *tento ten*·to
this (one) pron *tenhle ten*·hle
thread *nit* ① nyit
throat *hrdlo* ⑩ *hrd*·lo
thrush (health) *mykóza* ① *mi*·kaw·zuh
thunderstorm *bouře* ① *boh*·rzhe
Thursday *čtvrtek* ⑩ *chtvr*·tek
ticket *vstupenka* ① *fstu*·pen·kuh
ticket collector *výběrčí lístků* ⑩ *vee*·byer·chee *leest*·koo
ticket machine *automat na lístky* ⑩ *ow*·to·muht nuh *leest*·ki
ticket office *pokladna* ① *po*·kluhd·nuh
tide (high) *příliv* ⑩ *przhee*·lif
tide (low) *odliv* ⑩ *od*·lif
tight *těsný tyes*·nee
time *čas* ⑩ chuhs
time difference *časový rozdíl* ⑩ *chuh*·so·vee roz·dyeel
timetable *jízdní řád* ⑩ *yeezd*·nyee rzhad
tin (can) *plechovka* ① *ple*·khof·kuh
tin opener *otvírač konzerv* ⑩ *ot*·vee·ruhch kon·zerf
tiny *maličký muh*·lich·kee
tip (gratuity) *spropitné* ⑩ *spro*·pit·nair
tire *pneumatika* ① *pne*·u·muh·ti·kuh
tired *unavený u*·nuh·ve·nee
tissues *kosmetické kapesníčky* ⑩ pl *kos*·me·tits·kair kuh·pes·neech·ki

to *do/na* do/nuh
toast (food) *toast* ⓜ tohst
toaster *toastovač* ⓜ tohs-to-vuhch
tobacco *tabák* ⓜ tuh-bak
tobacconist *trafikant* ⓜ truh-fi-kuhnt
tobogganing *sáňkování* ⓝ san'ko-va-nye
today *dnes* dnes
toe *prst u nohy* prst u no-hi
tofu *sójový tvaroh* ⓜ saw-yo-vee tvuh-rawh
together *spolu* spo-lu
toilet *toaleta* ⓕ to-uh-le-tuh
toilet paper *toaletní papír* ⓜ
  to-uh-let-nyee puh-peer
tomato *rajské jablko* ⓝ rais-kair yuh-bl-ko
tomato sauce *rajská omáčka* ⓕ
  rais-ka o-mach-kuh
tomorrow *zítra* zeet-ruh
tomorrow afternoon *zítra odpoledne*
  zeet-ruh od-po-led-ne
tomorrow evening *zítra večer*
  zeet-ruh ve-cher
tomorrow morning *zítra ráno*
  zeet-ruh ra-no
tonight *dnes večer* dnes ve-cher
too (also) *také* tuh-kair
too (much) *příliš mnoho*
  przhee-lish mno-ho
tooth *zub* ⓜ zub
toothache *bolení zubu* ⓝ bo-le-nyee zu-bu
toothbrush *zubní kartáček* ⓜ
  zub-nyee kuhr-ta-chek
toothpaste *zubní pasta* ⓕ
  zub-nyee puhs-tuh
toothpick *párátko* ⓝ pa-rat-ko
torch (flashlight) *baterka* ⓕ buh-ter-kuh
touch v *dotknout se* dot-knoht se
tour *okružní jízda* ⓕ o-kruzh-nyee yeez-duh
tourist *turista* ⓜ tu-ris-tuh
tourist office *turistická informační
  kancelář* ⓕ tu-ris-tits-ka
  in-for-muhch-nyee kuhn-tse-larzh
towards *směrem k* smye-rem k
towel *ručník* ⓜ ruch-nyeek
tower *věž* ⓕ vyezh
toxic waste *toxický odpad* ⓜ
  tok-sits-kee od-puhd
toy shop *hračkářství* ⓝ hruhch-karzh-stvee
track (path) *stezka* ⓕ stez-kuh
track (sport) *dráha* ⓕ dra-huh
trade *obchod* ⓜ op-khod
tradesperson *řemeslník/řemeslnice* ⓜ/ⓕ
  rzhe-me-sl-nyeek/rzhe-me-sl-nyi-tse
traffic *doprava* ⓕ do-pruh-vuh

traffic lights *semafor* ⓜ se-muh-for
trail *stezka* ⓕ stez-kuh
train *vlak* ⓜ vluhk
train station *nádraží* ⓝ na-druh-zhee
tram *tramvaj* ⓕ truhm-vai
transit lounge *tranzitní salónek* ⓜ
  truhn-zit-nyee suh-law-nek
translate *přeložit* przhe-lo-zhit
translator *překladatel(ka)* ⓜ/ⓕ
  przhe-kluh-duh-tel(-kuh)
transport *přeprava* ⓕ przhe-pruh-vuh
travel v *cestovat* tses-to-vuht
travel agency *cestovní kancelář* ⓕ
  tses-tov-nyee kuhn-tse-larzh
travellers cheque *cestovní šek* ⓜ
  tses-tov-nyee shek
travel sickness *nevolnost při cestování* ⓕ
  ne-vol-nost przhi tses-to-va-nyee
tree *strom* ⓜ strom
trip (journey) *výlet* ⓜ vee-let
trolley *vozík* ⓜ vo-zeek
trolleybus *trolejbus* ⓜ tro-ley-bus
trousers *kalhoty* ⓕ pl kuhl-ho-ti
truck *nákladní auto* ⓝ
  na-kluhd-nyee ow-to
trumpet *trumpeta* ⓕ trum-pe-tuh
trust v *důvěřovat* doo-vye-rzho-vuht
try (attempt) v *zkusit* sku-sit
T-shirt *tričko* ⓝ trich-ko
tube (tyre) *duše* ⓕ du-she
Tuesday *úterý* ⓜ oo-te-ree
tumour *nádor* ⓜ na-dor
tuna *tuňák* ⓜ tu-nyak
tune *melodie* ⓕ me-lo-di-ye
turkey *krůta* ⓕ kroo-tuh
turn v *zahnout* zuh-hnoht
TV *televize* ⓕ te-le-vi-ze
tweezers *pinzeta* ⓕ pin-ze-tuh
twice *dvakrát* dvuh-krat
twin beds *dvoupostel* ⓕ dvoh-pos-tel
twins *dvojčata* ⓝ pl dvoy-chuh-tuh
two *dva* dvuh
type *druh* ⓜ drooh
typical *typický* ti-pits-kee
tyre *pneumatika* ⓕ pne-u-muh-ti-kuh

U

ultrasound *ultrazvuk* ⓜ ul-truh-zvuk
umbrella *deštník* ⓕ desht-nyeek
uncomfortable *nepohodlný*
  ne-po-ho-dl-nee
understand *rozumět* ro-zu-myet

underwear *spodní prádlo* ⓝ
spod-nyee prad-lo
unemployed *nezaměstnaný*
ne-zuh-myest-nuh-nee
unfair *nespravedlivý* ne-spruh-ved-li-vee
uniform *uniforma* ⓕ u-ni-for-muh
universe *vesmír* ⓜ ves-meer
university *univerzita* ⓕ u-ni-ver-zi-tuh
unleaded petrol *natural* ⓜ nuh-tu-ruhl
unsafe *nebezpečný* ne-bez-pech-nee
until *až do* uhzh do
unusual *neobvyklý* ne-ob-vik-lee
up *nahoru* nuh-ho-ru
uphill *do kopce* do kop-tse
urgent *naléhavý* nuh-lair-huh-vee
urinary infection *infekce močových cest*
ⓕ in-fek-tse mo-cho-veech tsest
USA *Spojené státy americké*
spo-ye-nair sta-ti uh-me-rits-kair
useful *užitečný* u-zhi-tech-nee

V

vacancy *volno* ⓝ vol-no
vacant *volný* vol-nee
vacation (from school) *prázdniny* ⓕ
prazd-nyi-ni
vacation (from work) *dovolená* ⓕ
do-vo-le-na
vaccination *očkování* ⓝ och-ko-va-nyee
vagina *vagina* ⓕ vuh-gi-nuh
validate *označit* oz-nuh-chit
valley *údolí* ⓝ oo-do-lee
valuable *cenný* tse-nee
value (price) *cena* ⓕ tse-nuh
van *dodávka* ⓕ do-daf-kuh
veal *telecí* ⓝ te-le-tsee
vegetable *zelenina* ⓕ ze-le-nyi-nuh
vegetarian *vegetarián(ka)* ⓜ/ⓕ
ve-ge-tuh-ri-yan(-kuh)
vegetarian a *vegetariánský*
ve-ge-tuh-ri-yans-kee
vein *žíla* ⓕ zhee-luh
venereal disease *pohlavní nemoc* ⓕ
po-hlav-nyee ne-mots
venue *zábavný podnik* ⓜ
za-buhv-nee pod-nik
very *velmi* vel-mi
video camera *videokamera* ⓕ
vi-de-o-kuh-me-ruh
video recorder *videonahrávač* ⓜ
vi-de-o-nuh-hra-vuhch
video tape *videopásek* ⓜ vi-de-o-pa-sek

Vienna *Vídeň* ⓕ vee-den'
view *pohled* ⓜ po-hled
village *vesnice* ⓕ ves-nyi-tse
vine *vinná réva* ⓕ vi-na rair-vuh
vinegar *ocet* ⓜ o-tset
vineyard *vinice* ⓕ vi-nyi-tse
violin *housle* ⓕ pl hoh-sle
virus *vir* ⓜ vir
visa *vízum* ⓝ vee-zum
visit v *navštívit* nuhf-shtye-vit
visually impaired *slabozraký*
sluh-bo-zruh-kee
vitamins *vitaminy* ⓜ pl vi-tuh-mi-ni
vodka *vodka* ⓕ vod-kuh
voice *hlas* ⓜ hluhs
volleyball *odbíjená* ⓕ od-bee-ye-na
volume (sound) *hlasitost* ⓕ hluh-si-tost
vote v *hlasování* hluh-so-va-nyee

W

wage *mzda* ⓕ mzduh
wait *čekat* che-kuht
waiter *číšník/číšnice* ⓜ/ⓕ
cheesh-nyeek/cheesh-nyi-tse
waiting room *čekárna* ⓕ che-kar-nuh
wake (someone) up *probudit* pro-bu-dyit
walk v *jít* yeet
wall *zeď* ⓕ zed'
want v *chtít* khtyeet
war *válka* ⓕ val-kuh
wardrobe *skříň* ⓕ skrzheen'
warm a *teplý* tep-lee
warn *varovat* vuh-ro-vuht
Warsaw *Varšava* ⓕ vuhr-shuh-vuh
wash (oneself) v *mýt se* meet se
wash (something) v *umýt* u-meet
wash cloth (flannel) *utěrka* ⓕ u-tyer-kuh
washing machine *pračka* ⓕ pruhch-kuh
wasp *vosa* ⓕ vo-suh
watch *hodinky* ⓕ pl ho-dyin-ki
watch v *dívat se* dyee-vuht se
water *voda* ⓕ vo-duh
water bottle *láhev na vodu* ⓕ
la-hef nuh vo-du
waterfall *vodopád* ⓜ vo-do-pad
watermelon *meloun* ⓜ me-lohn
waterproof *nepromokavý*
ne-pro-mo-kuh-vee
water-skiing *vodní lyžování* ⓝ
vod-nyee li-zho-va-nyee
wave (beach) *vlna* ⓕ vl-nuh
way *cesta* ⓕ tses-tuh

we *my* mi
weak *slabý* sluh·bee
wealthy *bohatý* bo·huh·tee
wear *nosit* no·sit
weather *počasí* ① po·chuh·see
wedding *svatba* ① svuht·buh
wedding cake *svatební dort* ⑩
    svuh·teb·nyee dort
wedding present *svatební dar* ⑩
    svuh·teb·nyee duhr
Wednesday *středa* ① strzhe·duh
week *týden* ⑩ tee·den
weekend *víkend* ⑩ vee·kend
weigh *vážit* va·zhit
weight *váha* ① va·huh
weights *činky* ① pl chin·ki
welcome v *uvítat* u·vee·tuht
welfare *sociální péče* ①
    so·tsi·al·nyee pair·che
well adv *dobře* dob·rzhe
west *západ* ⑩ za·puhd
wet a *mokrý* mok·ree
what *co* tso
wheel *kolo* ⑩ ko·lo
wheelchair *invalidní vozík* ⑩
    in·vuh·lid·nyee vo·zeek
when *kdy* gdi
where *kde* gde
which *který* kte·ree
whisky *whisky* ① vis·ki
white *bílý* bee·lee
white wine *bílé víno* ⑩ bee·lair vee·no
who *kdo* gdo
wholemeal bread *celozrný chléb* ⑩
    tse·lo·zr·nee khlairb
why *proč* proch
wide *široký* shi·ro·kee
wife *manželka* ① muhn·zhel·kuh
win v *vyhrát* vih·rat
wind *vítr* ⑩ vee·tr
window *okno* ⑩ ok·no
windscreen *přední sklo* ⑩
    przhed·nyee sklo
wine *víno* ⑩ vee·no
wings *křídla* ① pl krzheed·luh
winner *vítěz* ⑩ vee·tyez
winter *zima* ① zi·muh
wire *drát* ⑩ drat
wish v *přát* przhat
with *s* s
within (time) *do* do
without *bez* bez
wok *wok* ⑩ wok

woman *žena* ① zhe·nuh
wonderful *báječný* ba·yech·nee
wood *dřevo* ⑩ drzhe·vo
wool *vlna* ① vl·nuh
word *slovo* ⑩ slo·vo
work *práce* ① pra·tse
work v *pracovat* pruh·tso·vuht
work experience *praxe* ① pruhk·se
work permit *pracovní povolení* ⑩
    pruh·tsov·nyee po·vo·le·nyee
workout *cvičení* ⑩ tsvi·che·nyee
workshop *dílna* ① dyeel·nuh
world *svět* ⑩ svyet
World Cup *světový pohár* ⑩
    svye·to·vee po·har
worms (intestinal) *cizopasník* ⑩
    tsi·zo·puhs·nyeek
worried *ustaraný* us·tuh·ruh·nee
worship v *uctívat* uts·tyee·vuht
wrist *zápěstí* ⑩ za·pyes·tee
write *psát* p·sat
writer *spisovatel(ka)* ⑩/①
    spi·so·vuh·tel(·kuh)
wrong a *nesprávný* nes·prav·nee

Y

year *rok* ⑩ rok
yellow *žlutý* zhlu·tee
yes *ano* uh·no
yesterday *včera* fche·ruh
yet *ještě* yesh·tye
yoga *jóga* ① yaw·guh
yogurt *jogurt* ⑩ yo·gurt
you sg inf *ty* ti
you sg pol&pl *vy* vi
young a *mladý* mluh·dee
your sg inf *tvůj* tvooy
your sg pol&pl *váš* vash
youth hostel *mládežnická ubytovna* ①
    mla·dezh·nyits·ka u·bi·tov·nuh

Z

zip/zipper *zdrhovadlo* ⑩ zdr·ho·vuhd·lo
zodiac *zvěrokruh* ⑩ zvye·ro·krooh
zoo *zoo* ① zo·o
zoom lens *zůmový objektiv* ⑩
    zoo·mo·vee ob·yek·tif
zucchini *cuketa* ① tsu·ke·tuh

This dictionary is arranged according to the Czech alphabetical order (shown below). Czech nouns in the **dictionary** have their gender indicated by ⓜ (masculine), ① (feminine) or ⑩ (neuter). If it's a plural noun, you'll also see pl. When a word that could be either a noun or a verb has no gender indicated, it's a verb. For added clarity, certain words are marked as adjectives a or verbs v. Adjectives, however, are given in the masculine form only. Both nouns and adjectives are provided in the nominative case only. For information on case and gender, refer to the **phrasebuilder**. For any food terms, refer to the **menu decoder**.

alphabet

Aa	Áá	Bb	Cc	Čč	Dd	Ďď	Ee	Éé	Ěě	Ff	Gg	Hh	Ch ch
Ii	Íí	Jj	Kk	Ll	Mm	Nn	Ňň	Oo	Óó	Pp	Qq	Rr	Řř
Ss	Šš	Tt	Ťť	Uu	Úú	Ůů	Vv	Ww	Xx	Yy	Ýý	Zz	Žž

A

a uh *and*
adresa ① uh·dre·suh *address*
advokát(ka) ⓜ/① uhd·vo·kat(·kuh) *lawyer*
aerolinie ① uh·e·ro·li·ni·ye *airline*
aktovka ① uh·tof·kuh *briefcase*
ale uh·le *but*
alergie ① uh·ler·gi·ye *allergy*
alkoholický nápoj ⓜ uhl·ko·ho·lits·kee na·poy *alcoholic drink*
angličan(ka) ⓜ/① uhn·gli·chuhn(·kuh) *English (nationality)*
angličtina ① uhn·glich·tyi·nuh *English (language)*
Anglie ① uhn·gli·ye *England*
ano uh·no *yes*
antický uhn·tits·kee *classical*
auto ⑩ ow·to *car*
autobus ⓜ ow·to·bus *bus*
autobusová zastávka ① ow·to·bu·so·va zuhs·taf·kuh *bus stop*
autobusové nádraží ⑩ ow·to·bu·so·vair nad·ruh·zhee *bus station*
autokar ⓜ ow·to·kuhr *bus • coach*

automat na lístky ⓜ ow·to·muht nuh leest·ki *ticket machine*
autosedačka ⑩ ow·to·se·duhch·kuh *child seat*
až do uhzh do *until*

B

babička ① buh·bich·kuh *grandmother*
báječný ba·yech·nee *great (wonderful)*
balíček ⓜ buh·lee·chek *packet • parcel*
banka ① buhn·kuh *bank*
bankomat ⓜ buhn·ko·muht *ATM*
bankovka ① buhn·kof·kuh *banknote*
bankovní účet ⓜ buhn·kov·nyee oo·chet *bank account*
barva ① buhr·vuh *colour*
baterie ① buh·te·ri·ye *battery*
baterka ① buh·ter·kuh *flashlight (torch)*
batoh ⓜ buh·tawh *backpack*
bavlna ① buh·vl·nuh *cotton*
bazén ⓜ buh·zairn *swimming pool*
benzín ⓜ ben·zeen *gas (petrol)*
benzínová pumpa ① ben·zee·no·va pum·puh *petrol station*
bez bez *without*
bez cla bez tsluh *duty-free*

bezpečnostní pás ⓜ
bez·pech·nost·nyee pas seatbelt
bezpečný *bez·pech·nee safe* a
bezplatný *bez·pluht·nee*
complimentary (free)
bigbít ⓜ *big·beet rock music*
bílý *bee·lee white*
blahopřání *bluh·ho·przha·nyee*
congratulations
bleší trh ⓜ *ble·shee trh fleamarket*
blízko *bleez·ko near* prep
blízký *bleez·kee close* a
bolení hlavy ⓣ *bo·le·nyee hluh·vi headache*
bolení zubu *bo·le·nyee zu·bu toothache*
bolest ⓣ *bo·lest pain*
bolesti žaludku ⓣ pl
bo·les·tyi zhuh·lud·ku stomachache
bolestivý *bo·les·tyi·vee painful*
bota ⓣ *bo·tuh boot • shoe*
boty ⓣ pl *bo·ti shoes*
bratr ⓜ *bruh·tr brother*
brožura ⓣ *bro·zhu·rah brochure*
brýle ⓣ pl *bree·le glasses (spectacles)*
brzdy ⓣ pl *brz·di brakes*
brzy *br·zi soon*
břitva ⓣ *brzhit·vuh razor*
budík ⓜ *bu·dyeek alarm clock*
budova ⓣ *bu·do·vuh building*
business třída ⓣ *biz·nis trzhee·duh business class*
bydlet spolu *bid·let spo·lu share (with)* v
byt ⓜ *bit apartment*
být *beet be*

C

celnice ⓣ *tsel·ni·tse customs*
cena ⓣ *tse·nuh cost (price)*
cenný *tse·nee valuable*
centrum ⓜ *tsen·trum city centre*
cesta ⓣ *tses·tuh journey*
cestovní kancelář ⓣ *tses·tov·nyee kuhn·tse·larzh travel agency*
cestovní šek ⓜ *tses·tov·nyee shek travellers cheque*
cestující ⓜ&ⓣ *tses·tu·yee·tsee passenger*
chráněný *khra·nye·nee protected*
cigareta ⓣ *tsi·guh·re·tuh cigarette*
cíl cesty ⓜ *tseel tses·ti destination*
cit ⓜ *tsit feeling (physical)*
citlivost ⓣ *tsi·tli·vost film speed*
cizí *tsi·zee foreign*

co ⓝ *tso what*
cukrárna ⓣ *tsu·krar·nuh cake shop*
cukrovka ⓣ *tsu·krof·kuh diabetes*

Č

čas ⓜ *chuhs time*
časně *chuhs·nye early* adv
časový rozdíl ⓜ *chuh·so·vee roz·dyeel time difference*
často *chuhs·to often*
Čech/Češka ⓜ/ⓣ *chekh/chesh·kuh Czech (nationality)*
čekárna ⓣ *che·kar·nuh waiting room*
čekat *che·kuht wait*
čepice ⓣ *che·pi·tse soft hat*
černobílý *cher·no·bee·lee B&W (film)*
černý *cher·nee black • dark (night)*
čerstvý *cherst·vee fresh*
červený *cher·ve·nee red*
Česká republika ⓣ *ches·ka re·pu·bli·kuh Czech Republic*
český *ches·kee Czech* a
čeština ⓣ *chesh·tyi·nuh Czech (language)*
činže ⓣ *chin·zhe rent*
číslo ⓝ *chees·lo number*
číslo pasu ⓝ *chees·lo puh·su passport number*
číslo pokoje ⓝ *chees·lo po·ko·ye room number*
čistit *chis·tyit clean* v
čistý *chis·tee clean* a
číšník/číšnice ⓜ/ⓣ *cheesh·nyeek/cheesh·nyi·tse waiter*
člun ⓜ *chlun boat*

D

daleko *duh·le·ko far*
dálkový ovládač ⓜ *dal·ko·vee o·vla·duhch remote control*
dálnice ⓣ *dal·nyi·tse highway • motorway (tollway)*
další *duhl·shee another • other*
dámské vložky ⓣ pl *dams·kair vlozh·ki sanitary napkin*
daň ⓣ *duhn' tax*
dar ⓜ *duhr gift*
dárek ⓜ *da·rek present (gift)*
datum ⓝ *duh·tum date (day)*
datum narození ⓝ *duh·tum nuh·ro·ze·nyee date of birth*

dcera ① *dtse-ruh* daughter
dědeček ⓜ *dye-de-chek* grandfather
deka ① *de-kuh* blanket
den ⓜ den day
denně *de-nye* daily adv
denník ⓜ *de-nyeek* diary
dentální nit ① *den-tal-nyee nyit* dental floss
déšť ⓜ *dairsht'* rain
deštník ⓜ *desht-nyeek* umbrella
děti ① pl *dye-tyi* children
dětská výživa ① *dyets-ka vee-zhi-vuh* baby food
diapozitivní film ⓜ *di-uh-po-zi-tiv-nyee film* slide film
disketa ① *dis-ke-tuh* floppy disk
dítě ⓝ *dyee-tye* child
divadlo ⓝ *dyi-vuhd-lo* theatre
dívka ① *dyeef-kuh* girl
dlouhý *dloh-hee* long
dnes dnes today
dnes večer dnes *ve-cher* tonight
dno ⓝ dno bottom (position)
dobře *dob-rzhe* well adv
dobrý *do-bree* good
doklad o vlastnictví auta ⓝ *dok-luhd o vluhst-nyits-tvee ow-tuh* car owner's title
doklad totožnosti ⓜ *dok-luhd to-tozh-nos-tyi* identification card (ID)
doklady ⓜ pl *do-kluh-di* paperwork
doktor(ka) ⓜ/① *dok-tor(-kuh)* doctor
dolů *do-loo* down
domov ⓜ *do-mof* home
dopis ⓜ *do-pis* letter (mail)
doporučená zásilka ① *do-po-ru-che-na za-sil-kuh* registered mail
doporučit *do-po-ru-chit* recommend
dort ⓜ dort cake
dost dost enough
dotknout se *dot-knoht se* touch v
doutník ⓜ *doht-nyeek* cigar
dovézt *do-vairzt* deliver
dovolená ① *do-vo-le-na* holidays • vacation (from work)
drahý *druh-hee* expensive
drobné ⓝ *drob-nair* change (coins)
drogy ① pl *dro-gi* drugs (illicit)
druhá třída ① *dru-ha trzhee-duh* second class
dudlík ⓜ *dud-leek* dummy (pacifier)

důchodce/důchodkyně ⓜ/① *doo-khod-tse/doo-khod-ki-nye* pensioner
důležitý *doo-le-zhi-tee* important
dům ⓜ doom house
dva dvuh two
dveře ① pl *dve-rzhe* door
dvojitý *dvo-yi-tee* double a
dvoulůžkový pokoj ⓜ *dvoh-loozh-ko-vee po-koy* double room
dvoupostel ① *dvoh-pos-tel* twin beds
džíny ① pl *dzhee-ni* jeans

E

elektrický proud ⓜ *e-lek-trits-kee prohd* current (electricity)
elektro obchod ⓜ *e-lek-tro op-khod* electrical store
elektřina ① *e-lek-trzhi-nuh* electricity
Evropa ① *e-vro-puh* Europe
Evropská unie ① *e-vrops-ka u-ni-ye* European Union
expozimetr ⓜ *eks-po-zi-me-tr* light meter
expresní zásilka ①
  eks-pres-nyee za-sil-kuh express mail

F

fialový *fi-yuh-lo-vee* purple
fotka ① *fot-kuh* photo
fotoaparát ⓜ *fo-to-uh-puh-rat* camera
fotograf ⓜ *fo-to-gruhf* photographer
fotografie ① *fo-to-gruh-fi-ye* photography
fronta ① *fron-tuh* queue

G

galerie ① *guh-le-ri-ye* art gallery
golfové hřiště ⓝ *gol-fo-vair hrzhish-tye* golf course
granát ⓜ *gruh-nat* garnet

H

hedvábí ⓝ *hed-va-bee* silk
herec/herečka ⓜ/① *he-rets/he-rech-kuh* actor
hezký *hez-kee* handsome • pretty
historický *his-to-rits-kee* historical

hladový *hluh-do-vee* hungry
hlasitý *hluh-si-tee* loud
hlava ① *hluh-vuh* head
hlavní silnice ① *hluhv-nyee sil-nyi-tse* main road
hlučný *hluch-nee* noisy
hnědý *hnye-dee* brown
hňup ⓜ *hnyup* dope (drugs)
hodina ① *ho-dyi-nuh* hour
hodinky ① pl *ho-dyin-ki* watch
hodně *hod-nye* (a) lot
holič ⓜ *ho-lich* hairdresser for men
holit *ho-lit* shave v
hora ① *ho-ruh* mountain
horko ⓝ *hor-ko* heat
horký *hor-kee* hot
hořký *horzh-kee* bitter
hospoda ① *hos-po-duh* pub (bar)
hotovost ① *ho-to-vost* cash
hovor na účet volaného ⓝ *ho-vor nuh oo-chet vo-luh-nair-ho* collect call
hra ① *hruh* game (general) • play (theatre)
hrad ⓜ *hruhd* castle
hranice ① *hruh-nyi-tse* border
hrdlo ⓝ *hrd-lo* throat
hrnec ⓜ *hr-nets* pot (cooking)
hrozný *hroz-nee* awful
hruď ① *hrud'* chest (body)
hřbitov ⓜ *hrzh-bi-tov* cemetery
hřeben ⓜ *hrzhe-ben* comb
hudebník/hudebnice ⓜ/①
hu-deb-nyeek/hu-deb-nyi-tse musician
hudba ① *hud-buh* music

Ch

chladný *khluhd-nee* cold a
chlapec ⓜ *khluh-pets* boy
chléb ⓜ *khlairb* bread
chodidlo ⓝ *kho-dyid-lo* foot (body)
chodník ⓜ *khod-nyeek* footpath
chřipka ① *khrzhip-kuh* flu • influenza
chutný *khut-nee* tasty
chůva ① *khoo-vuh* babysitter
chyba ① *khi-buh* mistake

I

infekce ① *in-fek-tse* infection
informace ① *in-for-muh-tse* information
injekce ① *in-yek-tse* injection

inkasovat šek *in-kuh-so-vuht shek* cash a cheque v
internetová kavárna ① *in-ter-ne-to-va kuh-var-nuh* Internet café
invalidní *in-vuh-lid-nyee* disabled
invalidní vozík ⓜ *in-vuh-lid-nyee vo-zeek* wheelchair
inženýr(ka) ⓜ/① *in-zhe-neer(-kuh)* engineer
itinerář ⓜ *i-ti-ne-rarzh* itinerary

J

já *ya* I
jak *yuhk* how
jaro ⓝ *yuh-ro* spring (season)
jazyk ⓜ *yuh-zik* language
jeden *ye-den* one
jednoduchá jízdenka ① *yed-no-du-kha yeez-den-kuh* one-way ticket
jednolůžkový pokoj ⓝ *yed-no-loozh-ko-vee po-koy* single room
jedovatý *ye-do-vuh-tee* poisonous
jehla ① *yeh-luh* needle (sewing/syringe)
jeho *ye-ho* his
její *ye-yee* her (possessive)
jejich *ye-yikh* their
jen *yen* only
jezero ⓝ *ye-ze-ro* lake
jídelna ① *yee-del-nuh* cafeteria
jídelní lístek ⓜ *yee-del-nyee lees-tek* menu
jídelní vůz ⓜ *yee-del-nyee vooz* dining car
jídlo ⓝ *yeed-lo* food • meal
jih ⓜ *yih* south
jíst *yeest* eat v
jít *yeet* go • walk v
jít na nákupy *yeet nuh na-ku-pi* go shopping
jízda na koni ① *yeez-duh nuh ko-nyi* horse riding
jízdné ⓝ *yeezd-nair* fare
jízdní řád ⓜ *yeezd-nyee rzhad* timetable
jméno ⓝ *ymair-no* name

K

kabát ⓜ *kuh-bat* coat
kabelka ① *kuh-bel-kuh* handbag
kadeřník ⓜ *kuh-derzh-nyeek* hairdresser for women
kajakování ⓝ *kuh-yuh-ko-va-nyee* kayaking

kalhoty ① pl *kuhl*-ho-ti *pants (trousers)*
kalkulačka ① *kuhl*-ku-luhch-kuh *calculator*
kancelář ① *kuhn*-tse-larzh *office*
kanoistika ① *kuh*-no-is-ti-kuh *canoeing*
kapesní nůž ⑩ *kuh*-pes-nyee noozh *penknife*
kapesník ⑩ *kuh*-pes-nyeek *handkerchief*
kartáč ⑩ *kuhr*-tach *brush*
kašlat *kuhsh*-luht *cough* v
káva ① *ka*-vuh *coffee*
kavárna ① *kuh*-var-nuh *café*
kazeta ① *kuh*-ze-tuh *cassette*
každý *kuhzh*-dee *each • every* a
kde gde *where*
kdo gdo *who*
kdy gdi *when*
kino ⑩ *ki*-no *cinema*
klíč ⑩ kleech *key (door etc)*
klimatizovaný *kli*-muh-ti-zo-vuh-nee *air-conditioned*
klobouk ⑩ *klo*-bohk *hard hat*
kniha ① *knyi*-huh *book*
knihkupectví ⑩ *knikh*-ku-pets-tvee *book shop*
knihovna ① *knyi*-hov-nuh *library*
knoflík ⑩ *knof*-leek *button*
kohoutek ⑩ *ko*-hoh-tek *faucet (tap)*
kolega/kolegyně ⑩/① *ko*-le-guh/*ko*-le-gi-nye *colleague*
koleno ⑩ *ko*-le-no *knee*
kolik *ko*-lik *how much*
kolo ⑩ *ko*-lo *bicycle*
konec ⑩ *ko*-nets *finish*
kontaktní čočky ① pl *kon*-tuhkt-nyee *choch*-ki *contact lenses*
konverzační příručka ① *kon*-ver-zuhch-nyee *przhee*-ruch-kuh *phrasebook*
konzum ⑩ *kon*-zum *grocery store*
kopec ⑩ *ko*-pets *hill*
kosmetické kapesníčky ① pl *kos*-me-tits-kair *kuh*-pes-neech-ki *tissues*
kosmetické polštářky ⑩ pl *kos*-me-tits-kair *polsh*-tarzh-ki *cotton balls*
kosmetický salón ⑩ *kos*-me-tits-kee *suh*-lawn *beauty salon*
kost ① kost *bone*
kostel ⑩ *kos*-tel *church*
košile ① *ko*-shi-le *shirt*
kotník ⑩ *kot*-nyeek *ankle*
kotviště ⑩ *kot*-vish-tye *berth*
koupel ① *koh*-pel *bath*

koupelna ① *koh*-pel-nuh *bathroom*
koupit *koh*-pit *buy* v
kouřit *koh*-rzhit *smoke* v
krabice ① *kruh*-bi-tse *box*
kradený *kruh*-de-nee *stolen*
krajíc ⑩ *kruh*-yeets *slice*
krásný *kras*-nee *beautiful*
krátký *krat*-kee *short (length)*
kreditní karta ① *kre*-dit-nyee *kuhr*-tuh *credit card*
krejčí/krejčová ⑩/① *krey*-chee/*krey*-cho-va *tailor*
krev ① kref *blood*
krevní skupina ① *krev*-nyee *sku*-pi-nuh *blood group*
krk ⑩ krk *neck*
křehký *krzheh*-kee *fragile*
křestní jméno ⑩ *krzhest*-nyee *ymair*-no *first name*
který *kte*-ree *which*
kufr ⑩ *ku*-fr *suitcase*
kuchař(ka) ⑩/① *ku*-kharzh(-kuh) *cook*
kuchyň ① *ku*-khin' *kitchen*
kurt ⑩ kurt *tennis court*
kůže ① *koo*-zhe *leather*
květinář ⑩ *kvye*-tyi-narzh *florist*
kyselý déšť ⑩ *ki*-se-lee desht' *acid rain*
kytara ① *ki*-tuh-ruh *guitar*

L

láhev ① *la*-hef *bottle*
lahůdky ① pl *luh*-hood-ki *delicatessen • sandwich shop*
láska ① *las*-kuh *love*
laskavý *luhs*-kuh-vee *kind (nice)*
látka ① *lat*-kuh *fabric*
led ⑩ led *ice*
lednička ① *led*-nyich-kuh *refrigerator*
lední hokej ⑩ *led*-nyee ho-key *ice hockey*
legrační *le*-gruhch-nyee *funny*
lehátko ⑩ *le*-hat-ko *couchette • sleeping berth*
lehký *leh*-kee *light (weight)*
lék ⑩ lairk *drug (medication)*
lék proti bolestem ⑩ lairk *pro*-tyi bo-les-tem *painkiller*
lék proti kašli ⑩ lairk *pro*-tyi *kuhsh*-li *cough medicine*
lékárna ① *lair*-kar-nuh *pharmacy*
lékárnička ① *le*-kar-nyich-kuh *first-aid kit*
lékárník ⑩ *lair*-kar-nyeek *pharmacist*

lékařský předpis ⓜ
 lair·kuhrzh·skee *przhed·*pis *prescription*
lékařství ⓝ lair·kuhrzh·stvee
 medicine (profession)
lepší lep·shee *better*
les ⓜ les *forest*
lesbička ⓕ les·bich·kuh *lesbian*
let ⓜ let *flight*
letadlo ⓝ le·tuhd·lo *airplane*
létat lair·tuht *fly* v
letecká pošta ⓕ le·tets·ka posh·tuh
 airmail
letiště ⓝ le·tyish·tye *airport*
letištní poplatek ⓜ
 le·tyisht·nyee po·pluh·tek *airport tax*
léto ⓝ lair·to *summer*
leukoplast ⓜ leu·ko·pluhst *Band-Aid*
levný lev·nee *cheap*
levý le·vee *left (direction)*
libra šterlinků ⓕ lib·ruh shter·lin·koo
 pound (money)
líčidlo ⓝ lee·chid·lo *make-up*
lid ⓜ pl lid *people*
lněná tkanina ⓕ lnye·na tkuh·nyi·nuh
 linen (material)
loutka ⓕ loht·kuh *puppet*
loutkové divadlo ⓝ
 loht·ko·vair dyi·vuh·dlo *puppet theatre*
loutkové představení ⓝ loht·ko·vair
 przhed·stuh·ve·nyee *puppet show*
ložní prádlo ⓝ lozh·nyee prad·lo
 bed linen (sheets)
ložnice ⓕ lozh·nyi·tse *bedroom*
lyže ⓕ li·zhe *ski*
lyžování ⓝ li·zho·va·nyee *skiing*
lžíce ⓕ lzhee·tse *spoon*
lžička ⓕ lzhich·kuh *teaspoon*

M

majitel(ka) ⓜ/ⓕ muh·yi·tel(·kuh) *owner*
malíř(ka) ⓜ/ⓕ muh·leerzh(·kuh)
 painter (artist)
málo ma·lo *few • little (quantity)*
malý muh·lee *short (height) • small*
manžel ⓜ muhn·zhel *husband*
manželka ⓕ muhn·zhel·kuh *wife*
manželská postel ⓕ
 muhn·zhels·ka pos·tel *double bed*
mapa ⓕ muh·puh *map of country*
masér ⓜ muh·ser *masseur*
masérka ⓕ muh·ser·kuh *masseuse*
maso ⓝ muh·so *meat*

matka ⓕ muht·kuh *mother*
matrace ⓕ muh·truh·tse *mattress*
mazivo ⓝ muh·zi·vo *lubricant*
mě mye *me*
medicína ⓕ me·di·tsee·nuh
 medicine (study)
mejdan ⓜ mey·duhn *party (entertainment)*
menší men·shee *less • smaller*
měsíc ⓜ mye·seets *month*
město ⓝ myes·to *city*
městský policista ⓜ
 myest·skee po·li·tsis·tuh *city police officer*
metr ⓜ me·tr *metre*
metro ⓝ me·tro *subway (train)*
mezi me·zi *between*
mikrovlná trouba ⓕ
 mi·kro·vl·na troh·buh *microwave oven*
milovat mi·lo·vuht *love* v
mimořádný mi·mo·rzhad·nee *special* a
mince ⓕ min·tse *coins*
minerálka ⓕ mi·ne·ral·kuh *mineral water*
minuta ⓕ mi·nu·tuh *minute*
miska ⓝ mis·kuh *bowl (plate)*
místní meest·nyee *local* a
místo ⓝ mees·to *seat*
místo narození ⓝ
 mees·to nuh·ro·ze·nyee *place of birth*
mít meet *have*
mít rád meet rad *like* v
mládežnická ubytovna ⓕ
 mla·dezh·nyits·ka u·bi·tov·nuh
 youth hostel
mladý mluh·dee *young* a
mléko ⓝ mlair·ko *milk*
mnohý mno·hee *many*
mobil ⓜ mo·bil *mobile phone*
móda ⓕ maw·duh *fashion*
moderní mo·der·nyee *modern*
modrý mod·ree *blue*
mokrý mok·ree *wet* a
moře ⓝ mo·rzhe *sea*
most ⓜ most *bridge (structure)*
motor ⓜ mo·tor *engine*
moučník ⓜ mohch·nyeek *dessert*
možná mozh·na *maybe*
možný mozh·nee *possible*
můj mooy *my*
muzeum ⓝ mu·ze·um *museum*
muž ⓜ muzh *man*
my mi *we*
mýdlo ⓝ meed·lo *soap*

DICTIONARY

N

na nuh *at • on • per • to*
náboženství ⓝ na·bo·zhens·tvee *religion*
nad nuhd *above*
na palubě nuh puh·lu·bye *aboard*
na shledanou nuh·skhle·duh·noh *goodbye*
nábytek ⓜ na·bi·tek *furniture*
nacpaný nuhts·puh·nee *crowded*
nadměrné zavazadlo ⓝ nuhd·myer·nair zuh·vuh·zuhd·lo *excess baggage*
nádraží ⓝ na·druh·zhee *station*
nahoru nuh·ho·ru *up*
náhrdelník ⓜ na·hr·del·nyeek *necklace*
nachlazení ⓝ nuh·khluh·ze·nyee *cold (illness)*
nákupní centrum ⓝ na·kup·nyee tsen·trum *shopping centre*
nakupovat nuh·ku·po·vuht *shop* v
naléhavý nuh·lair·huh·vee *urgent*
náměstí ⓝ na·myes·tyee *town square*
nápoj ⓜ na·poy *drink*
národnost ⓕ na·rod·nost *nationality*
narozeniny ⓝ pl nuh·ro·ze·nyi·ni *birthday*
následující nas·le·du·yee·tsee *next (following)*
nastoupit nuhs·toh·pit *board (plane, ship)* v
nástupiště ⓝ nas·tu·pish·tye *platform*
náš nash *our*
náušnice ⓕ na·ush·nyi·tse *earrings*
ne ne *no*
nebe ⓝ ne·be *sky*
nebezpečný ne·bez·pech·nee *dangerous*
nedaleko ne·duh·le·ko *nearby*
nefunguje ne·fun·gu·ye *out of order*
nehoda ⓕ ne·ho·duh *accident*
nejbližší ney·blizh·shee *nearest*
nejlepší ney·lep·shee *best*
nejmenší ney·men·shee *smallest*
největší ney·vyet·shee *biggest*
někdy nyek·di *sometimes*
několik nye·ko·lik *several • some*
nekuřácký ne·ku·rzhats·kee *nonsmoking*
nemluvně ⓝ nem·luv·nye *baby*
nemocnice ⓕ ne·mots·nyi·tse *hospital*
nemocný ne·mots·nee *ill • sick*
nemožný ne·mozh·nee *impossible*
nepohodlný ne·po·ho·dl·nee *uncomfortable*
nesprávný nes·prav·nee *wrong* a

nevolnost ⓕ ne·vol·nost *nausea*
nevolnost při cestování ⓕ ne·vol·nost przhi tses·to·va·nyee *travel sickness*
nic ⓝ nyits *nothing*
nikdy nyik·di *never*
nízký nyeez·kee *low*
noc ⓕ nots *night*
noční klub ⓜ noch·nyee klub *nightclub*
noha ⓕ no·huh *leg (body)*
nos ⓜ nos *nose*
novinář(ka) ⓜ/ⓕ no·vi·narzh(·kuh) *journalist*
noviny ⓝ pl no·vi·ni *newspaper*
nový no·vee *new*
nudný nud·nee *boring*
nůž ⓜ noozh *knife*
nůžky ⓝ pl noozh·ki *scissors*

O

o o *about*
oba o·buh *both*
obálka ⓕ o·bal·kuh *envelope*
oběd ⓜ o·byed *lunch*
obchod ⓜ op·khod *business • shop*
obchod s hudebninami ⓜ op·khod s hu·deb·nyi·nuh·mi *music shop*
obchod s oblečením ⓜ op·khod s o·ble·che·nyeem *clothing store*
obchod s obuví ⓜ op·khod s o·bu·vee *shoe shop*
obchod s rybami ⓜ op·khod s ri·buh·mi *fish shop*
obchod se sportovními potřebami ⓜ op·khod se spor·tov·nyee·mi po·trzhe·buh·mi *sports store*
obchod se suvenýry ⓜ op·khod se su·ve·nee·ri *souvenir shop*
obchodní dům ⓜ op·khod·nyee doom *department store*
objednat ob·yed·nuht *order* v
objektiv ⓜ ob·yek·tif *lens (camera)*
obličej ⓜ o·bli·chey *face*
obsazeno op·suh·ze·no *booked out*
obvaz ⓜ ob·vuhz *bandage*
obyčejná pošta ⓕ o·bi·chey·na posh·tuh *surface mail (land)*
obyčejná pošta lodí ⓕ o·bi·chey·na posh·tuh lo·dyee *surface mail (sea)*
očkování ⓝ och·ko·va·nyee *vaccination*
od od *since (time)*
oddělený od·dye·le·nee *separate* a
odjet od·yet *depart*

odjezd ⓜ *od*·yezd *departure*
odlišný *od*·lish·nee *different*
odpoledne *ot*·po·led·ne *afternoon*
odpověď ⓕ *ot*·po·vyed' *answer*
oheň ⓜ *o*·hen' *fire*
ohřívací láhev ⓕ o·hrzhee·vuh·tsee *la*·hef
  hot water bottle
ohřívač ⓜ o·hrzhee·vuhch *heater*
okno ⓝ *ok*·no *window*
oko ⓝ *o*·ko *eye*
okoralý *o*·ko·ruh·lee *stale*
okružní jízda ⓕ *o*·kruzh·nyee *yeez*·duh
  tour
omezená rychlost ⓕ *o*·me·ze·na *rikh*·lost
  speed limit
on on *he*
ona *o*·nuh *she*
oni *o*·nyi *they*
opalovací krém ⓜ
  o·puh·lo·vuh·tsee krairm *sunblock*
opalovací mléko ⓝ
  o·puh·lo·vuh·tsee *mlair*·ko *tanning lotion*
opěradlo ⓝ *o*·pye·ruhd·lo *back (position)*
opilý *o*·pi·leee *drunk*
opravit o·pruh·vit *repair* v
oranžový *o*·ruhn·zho·vee *orange (colour)*
osoba ⓕ *o*·so·buh *person*
osobní doklad ⓕ *o*·sob·nyee *dok*·luhd
  identification
ostrov ⓜ *os*·trov *island*
ostříhání vlasů ⓝ
  os·trzhee·ha·nyee vluh·soo *haircut*
osvědčení o registraci ⓝ
  o·svyed·che·nyee o re·gis·truh·tsi
  car registration
otázka ⓕ *o*·taz·kuh *question*
otec ⓜ *o*·tets *father*
otřes mozku ⓜ *o*·trzhes *moz*·ku
  concussion
otvírací hodiny ⓕ pl *ot*·vee·ruh·tsee
  ho·dyi·ni *opening hours*
otvírák na konzervy ⓜ *ot*·vee·rak nuh
  kon·zer·vi *can (tin) opener*
otvírák na láhve ⓜ *ot*·vee·rak nuh *lah*·ve
  bottle opener
ovoce ⓝ *o*·vo·tse *fruit*
ovocný bar ⓜ *o*·vots·nee buhr
  ice-cream parlour
označit *oz*·nuh·chit *validate*
oznamovací tón ⓜ *oz*·nuh·mo·vuh·tsee
  tawn *dial tone*

P

pach ⓜ pukh *smell*
palác ⓜ *puh*·lats *palace*
palubní vstupenka ⓕ *puh*·lub·nyee
  fstu·pen·kuh *boarding pass*
pan ⓜ puhn *Mr*
panenka ⓕ *puh*·nen·kuh *doll*
pánev ⓕ *pa*·nef *frying pan*
paní ⓕ *puh*·nyee *Mrs*
papír ⓜ *puh*·peer *paper*
papírnictví ⓝ *puh*·peer·nits·tvee
  stationer
parfém ⓜ *puhr*·fairm *perfume*
parkovat *puhr*·ko·vuht *park a car* v
pas ⓜ puhs *passport*
pásmová nemoc ⓕ *pas*·mo·va *ne*·mots
  jet lag
paže ⓕ *puh*·zhe *arm (body)*
pekárna ⓕ *pe*·kar·nuh *bakery*
pěna na holení ⓕ
  pye·nuh nuh *ho*·le·nyee *shaving cream*
peněženka ⓕ *pe*·nye·zhen·kuh *purse*
peníze ⓜ pl *pe*·nye·ze *money*
penzion ⓜ *pen*·zi·on
  boarding house • guesthouse
pes ⓜ pes *dog*
pilulka ⓕ *pi*·lul·kuh *pill*
pinzeta ⓕ *pin*·ze·tuh *tweezers*
pít peet *drink* v
pivo ⓝ *pi*·vo *beer*
placení ⓝ *pluh*·tse·nyee *payment*
plán ⓜ plan *map of town*
plastický *pluhs*·tits·kee *plastic*
pláštěnka ⓕ *plash*·tyen·kuh *raincoat*
platit *pluh*·tyit *pay* v
plavat *pluh*·vuht *swim* v
plechovka ⓕ *ple*·khof·kuh *tin (can)*
plenka ⓕ *plen*·kuh *nappy (diaper)*
plný *pl*·nee *full*
plovací vesta ⓕ *plo*·vuh·tsee *ves*·tuh
  life jacket
pneumatika ⓕ *pne*·u·muh·ti·kuh *tire (tyre)*
po po *after*
počasí ⓝ *po*·chuh·see *weather*
počítač ⓜ *po*·chee·tuhch *computer*
pod pod *below*
podepsat *po*·dep·suht *sign* v
podobný *po*·dob·nee *similar*
podprsenka ⓕ *pod*·pr·sen·kuh *bra*
podrobnosti ⓕ *po*·drob·nos·tyi *details*
pohlaví ⓝ *po*·hluh·vee *sex*
pohled ⓜ *poh*·led *postcard • view*

pohodlný po·ho·dl·nee comfortable
pohotovost ① po·ho·to·vost emergency
pojištění ① po·yish·tye·nyee insurance
pokladna ① po·kluhd·nuh
cash register • ticket office
pokladník ⓜ po·kluhd·nyeek cashier
pokoj ⓜ po·koy room
pokrm ⓜ po·krm dish
pokuta ① po·ku·tuh fine
poledne ① po·led·ne noon
policejní stanice ①
po·li·tsey·nyee stuh·nyi·tse police station
policie ① po·li·tsi·ye police
policista ⓜ po·li·tsis·tuh
police officer in country
polovina ① po·lo·vi·nuh half
polštář ⓜ polsh·tarzh pillow
pomalu po·muh·lu slowly
pomník ⓜ pom·nyeek monument
pomoc ① po·mots help
pomoci po·mo·tsi help v
ponožky ① pl po·nozh·ki socks
popelnice ① po·pel·nyi·tse garbage can
popelník ⓜ po·pel·nyeek ashtray
populární po·pu·lar·nyee popular
porada ① po·ruh·duh small conference
porcelán ⓜ por·tse·lan porcelain
poschodí ① pos·kho·dyee floor (storey)
poslední pos·led·nyee last (final)
poslouchat po·sloh·khuht listen
postel ① pos·tel bed
pošta ⓜ posh·tuh post office
poštovní schránka ①
posh·tov·nyee skhran·kuh mailbox
poštovní směrovací číslo ①
posh·tov·nyee smye·ro·vuh·tsee
chee·slo postcode
potravina ① pot·ruh·vi·nuh grocery
potvrdit po·tvr·dyit confirm (a booking)
pouliční trh ⓜ po·u·lich·nyee trh
street market
použitý po·u·zhi·tee secondhand
povlak na polštář ⓜ
po·vluhk nuh polsh·tarzh pillowcase
povolená váha zavazadel ①
po·vo·le·na va·huh zuh·vuh·zuh·del
baggage allowance
povolení ① po·vo·le·nyee permit
pozdě poz·dye late adv
později poz·dye·yi later
pozítří ① po·zee·trzhee
day after tomorrow
práce ① pra·tse work

pračka ① pruch·kuh washing machine
prádelna ① pra·del·nuh laundry (place)
(samoobslužná) pradlenka ①
(suh·mo·ob·sluzh·na) pruhd·len·kuh
launderette
prádlo ⓜ prad·lo laundry (clothes)
Praha ① pruh·huh Prague
právo ① pra·vo law (study/profession)
pravý pruh·vee right (direction)
prázdniny ① prazd·nyi·ni
vacation (from school)
prázdný prazd·nee empty a
překvapení ⓜ przhe·kvuh·pe·nyee surprise
přes przhez across
prezervativ ⓜ pre·zer·vuh·tif condom
probudit pro·bu·dyit wake (someone) up
proč proch why
prodej ⓜ pro·dey sale
projímadlo ⓜ pro·yee·muhd·lo laxative
pronajmout pro·nai·moht rent v
propiska ① pro·pis·kuh ballpoint pen
prostěradlo ⓜ pros·tye·ruhd·lo sheet (bed)
proti pro·tyi opposite prep
prso ① pr·so breast (body)
prst ⓜ prst finger
prst u nohy prst u no·hi toe
prsten ⓜ prs·ten ring (jewellery)
průjem ⓜ proo·yem diarrhoea
průvodce ⓜ proo·vod·tse
guide (person) • guidebook
první třída ① prv·nyee trzhee·duh
first class
před przhed before • in front of
předešlý przhe·desh·lee last (previous)
předevčírem ⓜ przhe·def·chee·rem
day before yesterday
představení ⓜ przhed·stuh·ve·nyee
show
přehled kulturních pořadů ⓜ
przhe·hled kul·tur·nyeekh po·rzha·doo
entertainment guide
přeložit przhe·lo·zhit translate
přepychový przhe·pi·kho·vee luxurious
přes noc przhes nots overnight adv
přesně przhes·nye exactly
přestávka ① przhe·staf·kuh intermission
příbory ① pl przhee·bo·ri cutlery
příjemný przhee·yem·nee nice
příjezd ⓜ przhee·yezd arrivals
příjmení ⓜ przheey·me·nyee
family name (surname)
příliš mnoho przhee·lish mno·ho
too (much)

přímé volání ⓝ *przhee·mair vo·la·nyee* direct-dial
přímý *przhee·mee* direct a
připravený *przhi·pruh·ve·nee* ready a
přirážka za obsluhu ① *przhi·razh·kuh zuh op·slu·hu* service charge
příroda ① *przhee·ro·duh* nature
přítel ⓜ *przhee·tel* boyfriend • friend
přítelkyně ① *przhee·tel·ki·nye* girlfriend
psát *p·sat* write
puchýř ⓜ *pu·kheerzh* blister
půjčovna aut ① *pooy·chov·nuh owt* car hire
půlnoc ① *pool·nots* midnight
punčochy ⓝ pl *pun·cho·khi* stockings
původní *poo·vod·nyee* original a

R

rada ① *ruh·duh* advice
rameno ⓝ *ruh·me·no* shoulder
ráno ① *ra·no* morning
realitní kancelář ① *re·uh·lit·nyee kuhn·tse·larzh* estate agency
recepce ① *re·tsep·tse* check-in (desk)
reflektor ⓜ *re·flek·tor* headlights
restaurace ① *res·tow·ruh·tse* restaurant
rezervace ① *re·zer·vuh·tse* reservation (booking)
riziko ⓝ *ri·zi·ko* risk
rocková skupina ① *ro·ko·va sku·pi·nuh* rock group
roční období ⓝ *roch·nyee ob·do·bee* season
rodiče ⓜ pl *ro·dyi·che* parents
rodina ① *ro·dyi·nuh* family
roh ⓜ *rokh* corner
rok ⓜ *rok* year
romantický *ro·muhn·tits·kee* romantic a
rovný *rov·nee* straight
rozbitý *roz·bi·tee* broken down
rozhněvaný *roz·hnye·vuh·nee* angry
rozpočet ⓜ *roz·po·chet* budget
rozumět *ro·zu·myet* understand
rozvedený *roz·ve·de·nee* divorced a
rtěnka ① *rtyen·kuh* lipstick
ručně vyrobeno *ruch·nye vi·ro·be·no* handmade
ručník ⓜ *ruch·nyeek* towel
ruka ① *ru·kuh* hand
rukavice ① pl *ru·kuh·vi·tse* gloves (clothing)
růžový *roo·zho·vee* pink

rybolov ⓜ *ri·bo·lov* fishing
rychlostní skříň ①
  ri·khlost·nyee skrzheen' gearbox
rychlý *rikh·lee* fast a

Ř

ředitel(ka) ⓜ/① *rzhe·dyi·tel(·kuh)* manager (business)
řeka ① *rzhe·kuh* river
řeznictví ⓝ *rzhez·nyits·tvee* butcher's shop
říci *rzhee·tsi* speak
řidičský průkaz ⓜ
  rzhi·dyich·skee proo·kuhz drivers licence
řídit *rzhee·dyit* drive v
říznout *rzheez·noht* cut (with knife) v

S

s *s* with
sáhnout *sah·noht* feel (touch) v
sako ⓝ *suh·ko* jacket
sám *sam* alone
samoobsluha ① *suh·mo·ob·slu·huh* supermarket
samoobslužný *suh·mo·ob·sluzh·nee* self-service a
sedačka ① *se·duhch·kuh* chairlift (skiing)
semafor ⓜ *se·muh·for* traffic lights
sen ⓜ *sen* dream
senná rýma ① *se·na ree·muh* hay fever
sestra ① *ses·truh* sister
sever ⓜ *se·ver* north
schodiště ⓝ *skho·dyish·tye* stairway
schůzka ① *skhooz·kuh* appointment
silnice ① *sil·nyi·tse* road
silný *sil·nee* strong • thick
skleněné zboží ① *skle·nye·nair zbo·zhee* glassware
sklenička ① *skle·nyich·kuh* glass (drinking)
skupina ① *sku·pi·nuh* band (music)
sladký *sluhd·kee* sweet a
slečna ① *slech·nuh* Miss • Ms
sleva ① *sle·vuh* discount
Slovensko ⓝ *slo·ven·sko* Slovakia
slovník ⓜ *slov·nyeek* dictionary
slovo ⓝ *slo·vo* word
slunce ⓝ *slun·tse* sun
sluneční brýle ⓝ pl *slu·nech·nyee bree·le* sunglasses
slunečný *slu·nech·nee* sunny
služba ① *sluzh·buh* service

služba pro hlídání dětí ① *sluzh-buh pro hlee-da-nyee dye-tyee* child-minding service

služební cesta ① *slu-zheb-nyee tses-tuh* business trip

smažit *smuh-zhit fry* v

směnárna ① *smye-nar-nuh* currency exchange

směnný kurs *smye-nee kurz* exchange rate

směr ⓜ *smyer* direction

smutný *smut-nee* sad

snídaně ① *snee-duh-nye* breakfast

sníh ⓜ *snyeeh* snow

snoubenec ⓜ *snoh-be-nets* fiancé

snoubenka ① *snoh-ben-kuh* fiancée

socha ① *so-khuh* sculpture

soukromý *soh-kro-mee* private

spací pytel ⓜ *spuh-tsee pi-tel* sleeping bag

spací vůz ⓜ *spuh-tsee vooz* sleeping car

spálenina ① *spa-le-nyi-nuh* burn

spálený sluncem *spa-le-nee slun-tsem* sunburn

spát *spat sleep* v

spěšně *spyesh-nye* in a hurry

spisovatel(ka) ⓜ/① *spi-so-vuh-tel(-kuh)* writer

spodní prádlo ⓝ *spod-nyee prad-lo* underwear

spojení ⓝ *spo-ye-nyee* connection (transport)

společník/společnice ⓜ/① *spo-lech-nyeek/spo-lech-nyi-tse* companion

společnost ⓜ *spo-lech-nost* company (firm)

spolu *spo-lu* together

spolubývat *spo-lu-o-bee-vuht* share (accommodation) v

sportovní skládací kočárek ⓜ *spor-tov-nyee skla-da-tsee ko-cha-rek* stroller

správný *sprav-nee* right (correct)

sprcha ① *spr-khuh* shower

spropitné ⓝ *spro-pit-nair* tip (gratuity)

srdce ⓝ *srd-tse* heart

srdeční porucha ① *sr-dech-nyee po-ru-khuh* heart condition

stan ⓜ *stuhn* tent

stánek ⓜ *sta-nek* kiosk

stanice metra ① *stuh-nyi-tse met-ruh* metro station

stanový tábor ⓜ *stuh-no-vee ta-bor* camping ground

starožitnost ① *stuh-ro-zhit-nost* antique

starý *stuh-ree* old

stát *stat cost* v

stávka ① *staf-kuh* strike

stejný *stey-nee* same

stezka ① *stez-kuh* path

stín ⓜ *styeen* shade

stížnost ① *styeezh-nost* complaint

stolní olej ⓜ *stol-nyee o-ley* oil (cooking)

stopovat *sto-po-vuht* hitchhike

strana ① *struh-nuh* side

strojírenství ⓝ *stro-yee-rens-tvee* engineering

střed ⓜ *strzhed* centre

střed města ⓜ/ⓝ *strzhed myes-tuh* city centre

stříbro ⓝ *strzee-bro* silver

stříhat *strzhee-hut* cut (with scissors) v

stupeň ⓜ *stu-pen'* degrees (temperature)

stůl ⓜ *stool* table

stvrzenka ① *stvr-zen-kuh* receipt

stydlivý *stid-li-vee* shy

styl ⓜ *stil* style

suchý *su-khee* dry a

sukně ① *suk-nye* skirt

sušit *su-shit* dry (clothes) v

svačina ① *svuh-chi-nuh* snack

svatební cesta ① *svuh-teb-nyee tses-tuh* honeymoon

svědění ⓝ *svye-dye-nyee* itch

světlo ⓝ *svyet-lo* light

světlý *svyet-lee* light (colour)

svetr ⓜ *sve-tr* jumper (sweater)

svítání ⓝ *svee-ta-nyee* dawn

svobodný *svo-bod-nee* single (person)

syn ⓜ *sin* son

Š

šála ① *sha-luh* scarf

šálek ⓜ *sha-lek* cup

šampaňské ⓝ *shuhm-puhn'-skair* champagne

šatna ① *shuht-nuh* changing room · cloakroom

šaty ⓜ pl *shuh-ti* clothing · dress

šedivý *she-dyi-vee* grey

šéfkuchař(ka) ⓜ/① *shairf-ku-khuhrzh(-kuh)* chef

šek ⓜ *shek* check (banking)

šortky ① pl *short-ki* shorts

T

špatný *shpuht·nee* bad
šperky ⓝ pl *shper·ki* jewellery
špinavý *shpi·nuh·vee* dirty
šťastný *shtyast·nee* happy

T

tady *tuh·di* here
také *tuh·kair* also
talíř ⓜ *tuh·leerzh* plate
tam *tuhm* there
tam ten *tuhm ten* that (one) pron
tancovat *tuhn·tso·vuht* dance v
tanec ⓜ *tuh·nets* dance · dancing
taška ① *tuhsh·kuh* bag
taxi stanoviště ⓝ *tuhk·si stuh·no·vish·tye*
    taxi stand
teď *ted'* now
těhotná *tye·hot·na* pregnant
telefonní budka ① *te·le·fo·nyee bud·kuh*
    phone box
telefonní karta ① *te·le·fo·nyee kuhr·tuh*
    phonecard
telefonní seznam ⓜ
    te·le·fo·nyee sez·nuhm phone book
telefonovat *te·le·fo·no·vuht* telephone v
televize ① *te·le·vi·ze* television
tělo ⓝ *tye·lo* body
tělocvična ① *tye·lots·vich·nuh* gym (place)
ten *ten* that a
tenhle *ten·hle* this (one) pron
tenisový kurt *te·ni·so·vee kurt*
    tennis court
tenký *ten·kee* thin
tento *ten·to* this a
teplota ① *te·plo·tuh*
    temperature (weather)
teplý *tep·lee* warm a
teta ① *te·tuh* aunt
těžký *tyezh·kee* heavy (weight)
tchán ⓜ *tkhan* father-in-law
tchýně ① *tkhee·nye* mother-in-law
tichý *tyi·khee* quiet
tiskárna ① *tyis·kar·nuh* printer (computer)
tisková agentúra ①
    tyis·ko·va uh·gen·too·ruh newsagency
titulky ⓝ pl *ti·tul·ki* subtitles
tlumočník/tlumočnice ⓜ/①
    tlu·moch·nyeek/tlu·moch·nyi·tse
    interpreter
tlustý *tlus·tee* fat a
tmavý *tmuh·vee* dark (colour)
to *to* it

toaleta ① *to·uh·le·tuh* toilet
toaletní papír ⓜ *to·uh·let·nyee puh·peer*
    toilet paper
toastovač ⓜ *tohs·to·vuhch* toaster
topení ⓝ *to·pe·nyee* heating
trajekt ⓜ *truh·yekt* ferry
trampovat *truhm·po·vuht* hike v
tramvaj ① *truhm·vai* tram
tranzitní salónek ⓜ
    truhn·zit·nyee suh·law·nek transit lounge
trh ⓜ *trh* market
tričko ⓝ *trich·ko* T-shirt
turistická informační kancelář ①
    *tu·ri·stits·ka in·for·muhch·nyee
    kuhn·tse·larzh* tourist office
turistická třída ① *tu·ris·tits·ka trzhee·duh*
    economy class
turistika ① *tu·ris·ti·kuh* hiking
tužka ① *tuzh·kuh* pencil
tvrdý *tvr·dee* hard (not soft)
tvůj *tvooy* your inf sg
ty *ti* you inf sg
týden ⓜ *tee·den* week
typický *ti·pits·kee* typical

U

ubytování ⓝ *u·bi·to·va·nyee*
    accommodation
ucpaný *uts·puh·nee* blocked
účet ⓜ *oo·chet* account · bill · check
učitel(ka) ⓜ/① *u·chi·tel·(kuh)* teacher
ucho ⓝ *u·kho* ear
ukázat *u·ka·zuht* show v
ukazovat *u·kuh·zo·vuht* point v
úklid ⓜ *oo·klid* cleaning
ulice ① *u·li·tse* street
ulička ① *u·lich·kuh* aisle (on plane)
umělec/umělkyně ⓜ/①
    u·mye·lets/u·myel·ki·nye artist
umělecká řemesla ⓝ pl
    u·mye·lets·ka rzhe·mes·luh crafts
umělecké řemeslo ⓝ
    u·mye·lets·kair rzhe·mes·lo handicraft
umění ⓝ *u·mye·nyee* art
umýt *u·meet* wash (something) v
unavený *u·nuh·ve·nee* tired
úschovna zavazadel ① *oos·khov·nuh
    zuh·vuh·zuh·del* left-luggage office
ústa ① *oos·tuh* mouth
ustaraný *us·tuh·ruh·nee* worried
úvěr ⓜ *oo·vyer* credit
užitečný *u·zhi·tech·nee* useful

V

v v *in*
vadný vuhd-nee *faulty*
vaření ① vuh-rzhe-nye *cooking*
vařit vuh-rzhit *cook* v
váš vash *your* sg pol&pl
včas fchuhs *on time*
včera fche-ruh *yesterday*
včetně fchet-nye *included*
vdaná f-duh-nuh *married (woman)*
vděčný vdyech-nee *grateful*
večer ⓜ ve-cher *evening*
večerka ① ve-cher-kuh *milk bar*
večeře ① ve-che-rzhe *dinner*
večírek ⓜ ve-chee-rek *night out • party*
věda ① vye-duh *science*
vědec/vědkyně ⓜ/①
    vye-dets/vyed-ki-nye *scientist*
vedle ved-le *next to*
vegetariánský ve-ge-tuh-ri-yans-kee
    vegetarian a
věk ⓜ vyek *age*
velikost ① ve-li-kost *size (general)*
velký vel-kee *big*
velvyslanectví ⓝ vel-vi-sluh-nets-tvee
    embassy
venkov ⓜ ven-kof *countryside*
venku ven-ku *outside* adv
veřejná telefonní budka ① ve-rzhey-na
    te-le-fo-nyee bud-kuh *public phone*
veřejné toalety ① pl
    ve-rzhey-nair to-uh-le-ti *public toilet*
vesnice ① ves-nyi-tse *village*
větrák ⓜ vye-trak *fan (machine)*
větší vyet-shee *bigger*
více vee-tse *more*
videonahrávač ⓜ/① vi-de-o-nuh-hra-vuhch
    video recorder
videopásek ⓜ vi-de-o-pa-sek *video tape*
vidlička ① vid-lich-kuh *fork*
víno ⓝ vee-no *wine*
visací zámek ⓜ vi-suh-tsee za-mek
    padlock
vítr ⓜ vee-tr *wind*
vízum ⓝ vee-zum *visa*
vklad ⓜ fkluhd *deposit*
vlak ⓜ vluhk *train*
vlasy ⓜ pl vluh-si *hair*
vlna ① vl-nuh *wool*
vnitřní vnyi-trzh-nyee *inside* adv
vnuk/vnučka ⓜ/① vnuk/vnuch-kuh
    grandchild

voda ① vo-duh *water*
voda po holení ① vo-duh po ho-le-nyee
    aftershave
volno ⓝ vol-no *vacancy*
volný vol-nee *free (available)* a • *vacant*
vozík ⓜ vo-zeek *trolley*
vrácení peněz ⓝ vruh-tse-nyee pe-nyez
    refund
vrátit se vra-tyit se *return* v
vstoupit vstoh-pit *enter*
vstup ⓜ vstup *entry*
vstupenka ① fstu-pen-kuh *ticket*
vstupné ⓝ fstup-nair
    admission (price) • *cover charge*
všechno ⓝ vshekh-no *everything*
všichni vshikh-nyi *all* • *everyone*
vy vi *you* sg pol&pl
výdej zavazadel ⓝ
    vee-dey zuh-vuh-zuh-del *baggage
    claim*
vyfotit vi-fo-tyit *take a photo*
východ ⓜ vee-khod *east* • *exit*
východ slunce ⓜ vee-khod slun-tse
    sunrise
vyjít vi-yeet *go out*
výlet ⓜ vee-let *trip (journey)*
výměna ① vee-mye-nuh *exchange*
vyměnit vi-mye-nyit
    change (money) v • *exchange* v
vynikající vi-nyi-kuh-yee-tsee *fine* a
vypůjčit vi-pooy-chit *hire* v
výron ⓜ vee-ron *sprain*
vysoký vi-so-kee *high (tall)*
výstava ① vees-tuh-vuh *exhibition*
vystoupit vis-toh-pit *get off (bus, train)*
výtah ⓜ vee-tah *lift (elevator)*
vytápěný vi-ta-pye-nee *heated*
vývozní povolení ⓝ
    vee-voz-nyee po-vo-le-nyee *export permit*
vývrtka ① vee-vrt-kuh *corkscrew*
vzácný vzats-nee *rare (uncommon)*
vzduch ⓜ vzdukh *air*
vzteklina ① vztek-li-nuh *rabies*
vždy vzhdi *always*

Z

z z *from*
za zuh *behind*
zabít zuh-beet *kill* v
zácpa ① zats-puh *constipation*
začátek ⓜ zuh-cha-tek *start*
záda ⓝ za-duh *back (body)*

zadek ⓜ *zuh*-dek *bottom (body)*
zadní *zuhd*-nyee *rear (location)* a
zahrada ⓕ *zuh*-hruh-duh *garden*
zajímavý *zuh*-yee-muh-vee *interesting*
zakázka ⓕ *zuh*-kaz-kuh *commission*
zákazník/zákaznice ⓜ/ⓕ
   za-kuhz-nyeek/*za*-kuhz-nyi-tse *client*
zákon ⓜ *za*-kon *law (legislation)*
zámek ⓜ *za*-mek *castle*
zaměstnání ⓝ *zuh*-myest-na-nyee *job*
zamknout *zuhm*-knoht *lock* v
zamknutý *zuhm*-knu-tee *locked*
zámoří ⓝ *za*-mo-rzhee *overseas*
zaneprázdněný *zuh*-ne-prazd-nye-nee *busy*
západ ⓜ *za*-puhd *west*
západ slunce ⓜ *za*-puhd slun-tse *sunset*
zápalky ⓕ pl *za*-puhl-ki
   matches (for lighting)
zapalovač ⓜ *zuh*-puh-lo-vuhch
   cigarette lighter
zápas ⓜ *za*-puhs *match (sport)*
zápisník ⓜ *za*-pis-nyeek *notebook*
záruka ⓕ *za*-ru-kuh *guarantee*
zasnoubení ⓝ *zuh*-snoh-be-nyee
   engagement (to marry)
zasnoubený *zuh*-snoh-be-nee
   engaged (to be married)
zásoby potravin ⓕ pl
   za-so-bi po-truh-vin *food supplies*
zástrčka ⓕ *zas*-trch-kuh *plug (electricity)*
zataženo *zuh*-tuh-zhe-no *cloudy*
zátka ⓕ *zat*-kuh *plug (bath)*
zavazadlo ⓝ *zuh*-vuh-zuhd-lo
   baggage (luggage)
zavazadlová schránka ⓕ
   zuh-vuh-zuhd-lo-va skhran-kuh
   luggage locker
zavírat *zuh*-vee-ruht *close* v
zavřený *zuh*-vrzhe-nee *closed · shut* a
zdraví ⓝ *zdra*-vee *health*
zdravotní sestra ⓕ
   zdruh-vot-nyee ses-truh *nurse*
zdrhovadlo ⓝ *zdr*-ho-vuhd-lo *zip (zipper)*
zelenina ⓕ *ze*-le-nyi-nuh *vegetable*
zelený *ze*-le-nee *green*
země ⓕ *ze*-mye *country*
zima ⓕ *zi*-muh *winter*
zítra *zeet*-ruh *tomorrow*
zkažený *zkuh*-zhe-nee *off (spoilt)*

zkusit *sku*-sit *try (attempt)* v
zloděJna ⓕ *zlo*-dyey-nuh *rip-off*
zlato ⓝ *zluh*-to *gold*
zlomený *zlo*-me-nee *broken*
změna ⓕ *zmye*-nuh *change*
zmeškat *zmesh*-kuht
   miss (not catch train etc)
zmrzlina ⓕ *zmrz*-li-nuh *ice cream*
zmrzlý *zmrz*-lee *frozen*
známka ⓕ *znam*-kuh *stamp (postage)*
znovu *zno*-vu *again*
zpáteční jízdenka ⓕ
   zpa-tech-nyee yeez-den-kuh *return ticket*
zpěvák/zpěvačka ⓜ/ⓕ
   spye-vak/*spye*-vuhch-kuh *singer*
zpoždění ⓝ *zpozh*-dye-nyee *delay*
zpráva ⓕ *zpra*-vuh *message*
zprávy ⓕ pl *zpra*-vi *news*
zranění ⓝ *zruh*-nye-nyee *injury*
zraněný *zruh*-nye-nee *injured*
zrcadlo ⓝ *zr*-tsuhd-lo *mirror*
zrušit *zru*-shit *cancel*
zříceniny ⓕ pl *zrzhee*-tse-nyi-ni *ruins*
ztracený *ztruh*-tse-nee *lost*
ztráty a nálezy ⓕ *ztra*-ti uh *na*-le-zi
   lost-property office
zub ⓜ zub *tooth*
zubař(ka) ⓜ/ⓕ *zu*-buhrzh(-kuh) *dentist*
zubní kartáček ⓜ *zub*-nyee kuhr-ta-chek
   toothbrush
zubní pasta ⓕ *zub*-nyee puhs-tuh
   toothpaste
zvyk ⓜ zvik *custom*

Ž

žádný *zhad*-nee *none*
žaludek ⓜ *zhuh*-lu-dek *stomach*
žehlička ⓕ *zheh*-lich-kuh *iron (for clothes)*
železniční nádraží ⓝ *zhe*-lez-nyich-nyee
   na-druh-zhee *railway station*
žena ⓕ *zhe*-nuh *woman*
ženatý *zhe*-nuh-tee *married (man)*
ženský *zhens*-kee *female* a
židle ⓕ *zhid*-le *chair*
žiletka ⓕ *zhi*-let-kuh *razor blade*
život ⓜ *zhi*-vot *life*
žíznivý *zheez*-nyi-vee *thirsty*
žlutý *zhlu*-tee *yellow*

The topics covered in this book are listed below in Czech. If you're having trouble understanding Czech, show this page to whoever you're talking to so they can look up the relevant section.

KEY PATTERNS

When's (the next bus)?	V kolik jede (příští autobus)?	f ko·lik ye·de (przhee·shtyee ow·to·bus)
Where's (the station)?	Kde je (nádraží)?	gde ye (na·dra·zhee)
Where can I (buy a ticket)?	Kde (koupím jízdenku)?	gde (koh·peem yeez·den·ku)
How much is (a room)?	Kolik stojí (pokoj)?	ko·lik sto·yee (po·koy)
I have (a reservation).	Mám (rezervaci).	mam (re·zer·vuh·tsi)
Is there (a toilet)?	Je tam (toaleta)?	ye tuhm (to·uh·le·tuh)
Do you have (a map)?	Máte (mapu)?	ma·te (muh·pu)
I need (a can opener).	Potřebuji (otvírák na konzervy).	po·trzhe·bu·yi (ot·vee·rak nuh kon·zer·vi)
I'd like (the menu).	Chtěl/Chtěla bych (jídelníček). m/f	khtyel/khtye·luh bikh (yee·del·nye·chek)
I'd like (to hire a car).	Chtěl/Chtěla bych (si půjčit auto). m/f	khtyel/khtye·luh bikh (si pooy·chit ow·to)
Can I (camp here)?	Mohu (zde stanovat)?	mo·hu (zde stuh·no·vuht)
Could you please (help me)?	Můžete prosím (pomoci)?	moo·zhe·te pro·seem (po·mo·tsi)